Mass Media, Politics, and Society in the Middle East

The Hampton Press Communication Series
Political Communication
David L. Paletz, Editor

Eastern European Journalism
> Jerome Aumente, Peter Gross, Ray Hiebert, Owen Johnson,
> and Dean Mills

The In/Outsiders: The Mass Media in Israel
> Dan Caspi and Yehiel Limor

Islam and the West in the Mass Media
> Kai Hafez (ed.)

Eden Online: Re-inventing Humanity in a Technological Universe
> Lisa St. Clair Harvey

Civic Dialogue in the 1996 Presidential Campaign
> Lynda Lee Kaid, Mitchell S. McKinney, and John C. Tedesco

Media Entrepreneurs and the Media Enterprise in the United States
> Congress: Influencing Policy in the Washington Community
> Karen M. Kedrowski

Mediated Women: Representations in Popular Culture
> Marian Meyers (ed.)

Political Communication in Action: States, Institutions,
> Movements, Audiences
> David L. Paletz (ed.)

Glasnost and After: Media and Change in Central and Eastern Europe
> David L. Paletz, Karol Jakubowicz, and Pavao Novosel (eds.)

Germany's "Unity Election": Voters and the Media
> Holli A. Semetko and Klaus Schoenbach

Gender, Politics and Communication
> Annabelle Sreberny and Liesbet van Zoonen (eds.)

Strategic Failures in the Modern Presidency
> Mary E. Stuckey

War in the Media Age
> A. Trevor Thrall

forthcoming

Business as Usual: Continuity and Change in Central and
> Eastern European Media
> David L. Paletz and Karol Jakubowicz (eds.)

Mass Media, Politics, and Society in the Middle East

edited by

Kai Hafez

**German Institute for Middle East Studies, Hamburg
and Institute for Political Science, University of
Hamburg**

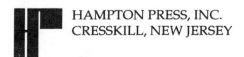

HAMPTON PRESS, INC.
CRESSKILL, NEW JERSEY

Printed in the United States of America

Library of Congress Cataloging-in-Publication Data

Mass media, politics, and society in the Middle East / edited by Kai Hafez
      p. cm. -- (The Hampton Press communication series)
      Includes bibliographical references and index.
    Contents: Mass media in Arab states between diversification and stagnation / Hussein Amin--Saudi Arabia's international media strategy / Douglas A. Boyd--Restructuring television in Egypt / Tourya Guaaybess--Freedom of the press in Jordanian press laws, 1927-1998 / Orayb Aref Najjar--The changing face of Arab communications / Muhammad I. Ayish--Internet in the Arab world / Henner Kirchner--Distribution of ideas ; book production and publishing in Egypt, Lebanon, and the Middle East / Stefan Winkler--Interaction between traditional communication and modern media : implications for social change in Iran and Pakistan / Shir Mohammad Rawan--"Coming close to God" through the media : a phenomenology of the media practices of Islamist women in Egypt / Karin Werner--The global flow of information : a critical appraisal from the perspective of Arab-Islamic information sciences / Dagmar Glass.
    ISBN 1-57273-303-9 -- ISBN 1-57273-304-7 (pbk.)
   1. Mass media--Middle East I. Hafez, Kai, 1964- II. Series

P92.M5 M374 2000
302.23'0956--dc21

                            00-053557

Cover photo © Norbert Mattes, Dahlmannstr. 31, 10629 Berlin, Germany

Hampton Press, Inc.
23 Broadway
Cresskill, NJ 07626

Contents

Acknowledgments

As in the case of the book *Islam and the West in the Mass Media* (Hampton Press 2000), the editor is indebted to Mary Ann Kenny for her meticulous, untiring, and informed assistance with the language editing. She studied German literature and philosophy at the University of Tübingen, Germany, and is currently employed as Lecturer in German at the Institute of Technology, Blanchardstown, Dublin, Ireland.

I would also like to thank the series editor Professor David Paletz of Duke University and Mrs. Barbara Bernstein, the President of Hampton Press, for supporting research in the field of mass media, the Middle East, and Islam.

About the Contributors

Amin, Prof. Hussein, Associate Professor and a Senior Fellow at the Adham Center for Television Journalism, American University in Cairo.

Ayish, Dr. Mohammed I., Chairman of the Department of Communication, College of Arts and Sciences, University of Sharjah, UAE.

Boyd, Prof. Douglas A., Professor and Dean of the College of Communications and Information Studies, University of Kentucky, Lexington.

Glass, Dr. Dagmar, Assistant Professor at the Oriental Institute of the University of Leipzig, Germany.

Guaaybess, Tourya, Ph.D. candidate at the University of Lyon, France, and Research Fellow of the Groupe de Recherches et d'Études sur la Méditerranée et le Moyen-Orient (GREMMO) in Lyon and at the Centre d'Études et de Documentation Économique, Juridique et Sociale (CEDEJ), Cairo, Egypt.

Kirchner, Henner, M.A., a writer and analyst who has published several articles in German dealing with the issue of Internet in the Arab world.

Najjar, Prof. Orayb Aref, Associate Professor at the Department of Communication, Northern Illinois University, DeKalb, Illinois.

Rawan, Dr. Shir Mohammed, Assistant Professor at the Institute for Communication and Media Science, University of Leipzig, Germany.

Werner, Dr. Karin, Associate Researcher and Lecturer of the Faculty of Sociology of the University of Bielefeld, Germany.

Winkler, Stefan, M.A., Lecturer of the German Academic Exchange Service (DAAD), University of Aleppo, Syria.

Introduction
Mass Media in the Middle East:
Patterns of Political and
Societal Change

Kai Hafez

The mass media in the Arab world and the Middle East have undergone profound changes since the beginning of the 1990s. The introduction and spread of new technologies such as satellite television and the Internet have extended media spaces beyond the local, national, and regional realm. Transborder flows of communication have enabled some consumers—those with access to the new technologies—to interact with a global discourse and bypass the limits of authoritarian information control. Since the Gulf war in 1991, when people in the Middle East tuned into CNN to receive fresh (albeit U.S. censored) news from the Gulf, media development in the area has been determined by both indigenous and external factors. An effective closure of national media spaces against the forces of globalization is less likely today than it ever was before.

The question remains, however, whether new access to external media and the widening of media horizons is sufficient to generate political and social changes in the Arab world and the Middle East. To suggest that access to foreign media alone could revolutionize Middle

1

Eastern societies, wipe away authoritarian rule, or modernize tradition-alist lifestyles would be rather simplistic. Western satellite TV, to take one example, is no substitute for domestically produced television; it is not even particularly competitive in many countries. Technical or finan-cial hurdles and, more importantly, cultural and language barriers mean that extensive exposure to foreign programs has been limited to elites while the vast majority of TV audiences continues to consume indige-nous programs. The size and composition of the audiences varies from country to country. Due to the different styles of French and British colo-nialism, the understanding of French programs in the francophone Maghreb (Algeria, Libya, Morocco, Tunisia) poses less of a problem than the consumption of English programs in the Middle East. Even in the Maghreb, however, French channels like TV 5 or France 2 are primarily consumed by members of the educated and well-off upper and upper-middle classes. The lower-middle or lower classes have less aptitude in French and often feel a greater cultural gap between their own lifestyles and those represented in French programs (Mostefaoui 1997: 430 f.). Larbi Chouikha has spoken of a "cut" (coupure) between the audiences of external satellite programs and those who are more oriented towards the indigenous media (Chouikha 1992: 44). One of the greatest limits to the effect of external TV and radio is the fact that the lower-middle class-es (students, teachers, state officials, military, etc.), who through their membership in nationalist and, more recently, Islamist movements have had a considerable influence on the history of the area, are still primarily consumers of the indigenous media.

Another problem is that even if the consumption of foreign (Western) media can be considered a mass phenomenon, the content and quality of the programs leaves doubts as to whether they can have any real impact on the development of the Middle East. Western media rarely cover the Middle East, with the exception of, for example, certain crisis periods and special aspects such as Muslim fundamentalism (Hafez 2000). Although Western and international programs are often welcomed as alternative sources of information, there is also consider-able skepticism regarding the quality of Western foreign reports and the image of Asians and of Islam they depict (Mostefaoui 1997: 448-450). Muhammad Ayish argues that even the vernacular external media, such as BBC Arabic Service, which deal on an ongoing basis with the affairs of the Arab world and the Middle East and have gained a large audience among Arab populations, cannot substitute for the indigenous media's principal task of creating public opinion and successful communication between state and society. He therefore proposes to look at the external programs primarily in terms of a challenge, but not an alternative to the development of the domestic media of the Middle East:

From a political perspective, the BBC's "stealing" of national radio
listeners is likely to disrupt communications between ruling elites
and masses in the Arab World via radio and other media. Turning to
BBC en masse, particularly in crisis times, seems to widen the gap
between the rulers and the ruled. (...) [A]udiences lost to foreign
media may be regained only through development of national good
quality programme output capable of surmounting the temptations
of outside broadcasters. In the light of the current mass media situation in the Arab World, this challenge does not seem to be seriously
considered by Arab broadcasters. (Ayish 1991: 383)

In terms of its *direct* effects, the media from outside the Middle East are
not as appealing to the consumers and societies of the Middle East or as
socially mobilizing as one might suppose. There have been a number of
indirect effects, however. The new globalized media spaces have begun
to change the fabric of the mass media in the Middle East, whether state-
owned or in private ownership. Whereas Ayish's doubts as to whether
the indigenous media would be able to cope with the global challenges
were justified in 1991, analyses in the mid-1990s sound more optimistic.
John Sinclair, Elizabeth Jacka, and Stuart Cunningham argued in 1996:

Although evidence from Europe and elsewhere indicates that satellite services originating outside national borders do not usually
attract levels of audience that would really threaten traditional
national viewing patterns, the ability of satellite delivery to transgress borders has been enough to encourage generally otherwise
reluctant governments to allow greater internal commercialization
and competition. (Sinclair et al. 1996: 2)

The following graph lists some of the direct and indirect effects of media
globalization on the mass media in the Arab world and the Middle East
(Table 0.1). Besides the effects mentioned by Sinclair, Jacka, and
Cunningham—commercialization and competition—one of the most
outstanding changes to affect the Middle East is the increase in the number of media. This is largely due to the influx of external media and the
establishment if indigenous satellite TV and radio networks like the
Saudi-owned private Middle East Broadcasting System (MBC) with a
large audience throughout the Arabic-speaking world. Those networks
are really the indirect result of external media penetration because the
Middle Eastern states felt the competition of external programs and
slowly started to deregulate their media monopolies by inviting private
investors to establish national alternatives to foreign satellite TV and
radio. Most new channels are much more professional than the often
monotonous and dull state-owned competitors.

Table 01: Effects of External Media on the Middle East.

Effects of External Mass Media on Middle East Consumers	Effects of External Mass Media on Middle East Media
1. Opening up of censored national media spaces	1. Competition between external and indigenous media
2. Differentiation between national (or traditional) and international or Western) oriented consumption styles	2. Increase in the number of indigenous media
3. Changes of indigenous media sector	3. Professionalization of indigenous media
	4. Deregulation of state monopolies and privatization of indigenous media

One of the most important questions relating to prospects of political and societal change in the Middle East is whether the old and new mass media of the Middle East will be politically and culturally liberalizing in the age of globalized media spaces. Although some positive aspects of this development are already visible, countertrends are also apparent. It is rather doubtful whether the new indigenous media allow for greater freedom of speech than the state media. The use of the media for participatory development and modernization is less important in current media debates than it was in previous decades. Instead, there is an inherent danger that the discourse on communication and mass media will become an integral part of new ideological debates about a supposed cultural gap between "the West" and "Islam."

INFORMATION CONTROL AND OWNERSHIP

Comparative analyses of global media development consider the Middle Eastern media system the most closed and controlled in the world (Sinclair et al. 1996: 4). Without doubt, information control and censorship are severe in the Middle East. At the same time Wolfgang Slim Freund has maintained that the diversity of the media often counteracts its negative reputation and that the Arab press, for example, is more critical and open in some countries than in others (Freund 1992). To maintain that the Middle Eastern media is the most controlled in the world is to presuppose that there is some definite and ultimate criterion for comparison with China, for example, or large parts of south Asia or the Far East which are not famous for defending freedom of speech. Before resorting to vague generalizations, it seems useful to look at some significant contemporary patterns of media development in the Arab world and the Middle East concerning freedom of speech and media ownership.

Media Freedom and Control

In 1979 William Rugh distinguished between three different types of Arab press: (1) the "mobilized press," which is characterized by the almost total subordination of the media system to the political system and is controlled by revolutionary governments (Algeria, Egypt, Iraq, Libya, Syria, [South] Yemen, and Sudan); (2) the "loyalist press," which is privately owned and sometimes not even exposed to state censorship, but continues to support the regimes, especially as those regimes can still control their resources (like paper) and persecute journalists through the legal systems (Bahrain, Jordan, Qatar, Saudi Arabia, Tunisia, United Arab Emirates); and (3) the "diverse press," where the press is free (Morocco, Lebanon, and Kuwait, although Kuwait and Morocco also revealed loyalist features) (Rugh 1979: XVII).[1]

Rugh's basic typology is, by and large, still in use and can be extended to other media beyond the print media. However, his analysis of freedom of speech and media freedom in individual countries no longer applies in some cases. The categorization of some countries has to be revised, and others bear traits of more than one category.[2] Kuwait has partially restricted its formerly lauded freedom of the press through state censorship since 1986, the year when the national constitution was suspended, and the Gulf War of 1991 has favored a trend towards loyalist self-censorship among journalists (Kazan 1994: 157; see also Alqudsi-Ghabra 1995). Egypt in the era of Sadat and Mubarak has diversified its private press, and even state-owned papers like *Ruz Al-Yussuf* often criticize the government. The result, however, is that journalists are often persecuted and publications that "insult" the state or interfere with national security and public order are banned (Ezzeldin 1997). Even after the revocation of Law 93 (of 1995) in 1996, journalists remain vulnerable to such charges. The print media in Jordan before 1993 and in Algeria around the early 1990s was quite diverse. However, in the course of the decade both countries reintroduced heavy information control (for Jordan see Chapter 4 of this book: see also Najjar 1998; Campagna 1998; for Algeria see Mouffok 1997; Ibrahimi 1997). Insecurity over the political and economic situation and growing opposition led to a reversal of press liberalization. In Jordan, King Hussein was afraid of internal (Palestinian) criticism of the peace process with Israel; in Algeria, the regime became increasingly sensitive about critical voices against its treatment of the Islamists. The same is true of Algeria's neighbors, Morocco and, even more so, Tunisia, which "has become among the most restricted in the Arab world," according to the Committee to Protect Journalists (CPJ).[3] Even in Lebanon, which Rugh classified as an open system allowing press freedom in 1979, the government—under the influence of Syrian and Israeli military occupation—restricts licenses for oppositional sectarian papers like those controlled by *Hizbollah*, the Phalange, or the Communists. Israel, without doubt the country with the most diverse media system in the Middle East, applies heavy military censorship to its own and to the Palestinian and southern Lebanese press (Lahav 1993; Shahak 1997: 13-27). Somewhat like Turkey, where pro-Kurdish political commentary is effectively banned and journalists are prohibited from freewheeling in the country's southeast, Israel has given up democratic principles for the sake of national goals. Iran is the country with a contradictory media development. Mohammed Chatami, who was elected as President in 1997, called for the end to censorship, and this has led to an easing of information control. In 1998—for the first time since 1989—criticism of Iran's line in the Rushdie affair was even published (Behbahani 1998). In 1999, however, Chalami's conservative opponents around Ajatollah Khamenei started to roll back many of the liberalization efforts.

There are some states in the Arab world and the Middle East such as Saudi Arabia and the Arab Gulf states, Iraq, Syria, Libya, Pakistan, or Afghanistan where such fluctuations in press freedom do not occur. In Pakistan, for example, there have been few positive developments, despite the promises of Benazir Bhutto in the early 1990s (Napoli 1991). Freedom of speech is restricted in almost all Arab and Middle Eastern countries, but except for very strict countries the execution of restrictions, whether legalist or purely arbitrary in nature, fluctuates depending on regime requirements. The limits on freedom of speech are therefore hard to define. The degree of press freedom corresponds to the nature of the respective political system in the sense that systems that are semiauthoritarian and patrimonial (Egypt, Morocco, Jordan, etc.) have allowed for more diversity than totalitarian and technocratic (military) systems (Iraq, Syria, etc.). But because the character of many or most systems has changed gradually with successive regimes— the increase of political liberalism from Nasser to Mubarak in Egypt is one example—and because each regime has varied its policies on freedom of speech, the typology of media systems is always in flux.

In 1979, when Rugh analyzed the Middle East press, TV and radio broadcasting were owned and controlled by the state in all countries.

Today this picture has changed. Satellite TV and radio have transgressed country borders from outside the area and have induced a number of states to encourage the domestic private sector to face this foreign competition. The Middle East Broadcasting Center (MBC) and Arab Radio and Television (ART) are owned by wealthy Saudi businessmen (see below). Most private TV networks, like most big private newspapers in the region, are "loyalist" in the sense that, despite their professional, often Westernized news policies, their programs include critical reports and commentary only insofar as they do not concern the national government or the governments of befriended states. For example, MBC has broadcast criticism of the Oslo peace process between Israel and the Palestinians, but no mention of state repression, torture, or similar issues in the Arab world is ever made. The only TV channel that deserves to be called "diverse" is Al-Jazeera (Qatar), a popular channel in the whole Arabic speaking world due to its treatment of "hot issues" like corruption and Islamic polygamy. In the final analysis, Rugh's typology of "mobilized," "loyalist," and "diverse" press systems can be transferred to the broadcasting systems in the area. State-owned national "mobilized" programs coexist with private "loyalist," and, in the case of Al-Jazeera, "diverse" programs.

Rugh's typology, however helpful and correct, seems insufficient for the classification of modern media systems in the area of freedom of speech. With the spread of fax machines, xerox machines, computers, video recorders, and all sorts of hardware necessary for media reproduction, the definition of what "mass media" really is is becoming increasingly problematic. If we use the very vague and tentative definition of a mass medium as a means to communicate texts or programs on a regular basis to large audiences, then there is another important sector of the mass media that is often ignored or underestimated: the "alternative-independent" media. Formally, the term describes the low-budget media sector, such as magazines with a print run of only a few thousand. A second criterion for describing media as alternative is their ability to uphold different positions from the official or loyalist media. Using this definition, we become aware that even countries with a "loyalist" press system—Iran, for example—can have a very "diverse" alternative media sector. The Iranian government, to stick with this example, applies censorship to newspapers and to books, but it excludes magazines and allows public opinion greater freedom in this publication segment.

However, in the final analysis the above record of media freedom with regard to the press and TV/radio shows that the growing reception of external, foreign, mostly Western satellite channels in many countries of the Middle East has not been accompanied by a definite and clearly identifiable move by the indigenous mass media towards liberalization. On the contrary, even gradual liberal developments in the print and electronic media are often countered by a rollback in the national policies of information control and the tightening up of media laws. At the same time, the sheer growth in the number of media in many countries will make it increasingly difficult for authoritarian governments to control public opinion.

From the point of view of comparative democratization theory the only way to "erode" authoritarian rule is to establish firm programmatic and institutional alternatives. This can be achieved primarily by those who oppose the authoritarian status quo—which in the case of the mass media is quite naturally the journalists. The resistance of Egyptian journalists to Law 93 finally forced the Mubarak government to make concessions. The Arab Journalism Federation (AJF) has also protested repeatedly against all sorts of repression by Arab governments.[4] Future research must address the question whether Arab journalists consider themselves an avant-garde of democratization or whether they, in fact, collaborate with the rulers and exercise self-censorship (see below).

Media Ownership

Another trend is becoming increasingly obvious: the alteration of the structures of media ownership. Three main factors have motivated some states, such as Egypt, to gradually let go of their TV and radio monopolies. Firstly, as already mentioned, the competition of global, mostly Western satellite programs has made it necessary for Middle Eastern states to fill the professionalization and information gap between the old national state-owned and the foreign programs. To this end, private capital has been allowed into the game, financing satellite TV networks, film production, or advertising activities. Secondly, external competition has spurred the ambitions of some countries in the Middle East to broaden their influence in the region and make their new programs attractive to larger audiences beyond their national confines. This in turn has heightened regional competition. Saudi Arabia has built up a whole media empire for the Arab world with a growing number of satellite programs. Thirdly, pressure from the World Bank and the International Monetary Fund (IMF) has increased the willingness of Middle Eastern governments to include the media sector in their economic adjustment and privatization programs (Napoli et al. 1995).

Regional competition has contributed greatly to the alteration of ownership and the privatization of indigenous media in the Arab world and the Middle East. The Saudi TV empire adds to the influence already exerted by Saudi Arabia through other media: it owns or partly owns media in many Arab countries as well as a large share of the Arab press published outside the Arab world (especially in London). It is also the most important customer of the Arab and especially Egyptian TV film industry, which is almost entirely dependent on the Saudi dominated market and therefore often hesitates to touch upon matters sensitive to the Saudi state and its traditional-puritan Islamic value system (Atwan/Khazen 1997; Gerlach 1997). In Saudi-financed projects, "drinks" or kisses may not be shown, unless the couple is actually married in real life. Critics have identified an inner-regional brain drain from the media industries of many Arab countries to those of their rich cousins of the Arab peninsula. Nabil Abd al-Fattah of the Centre for Political and Strategic Studies/Al-Ahram Foundation in Cairo even refers to the "beduinization of Arab culture" (El-Gawhary 1995). Although the Saudi state felt threatened by radio broadcasts from Arab socialist Egypt in the 1960s, Saudi Arabia now seems to have found an effective means of turning the tables and exerting a very authoritarian and conservative influence on the media systems of the Middle East, which used to be a lot more diverse.

With the concentration of private capital, especially Saudi capital, there is an inherent danger that the Arab states' broadcasting monopolies will merely be replaced by private oligopolies. If this is the case, even privatization is no guarantee for liberalization and diversity. Moreover, privatization is sometimes a form of continued, but disguised state control, as in the case of Saudi satellite TV where the private owners of the new media are in fact relatives of the ruling Saud family and the Saudi King. In other countries the borderline between state and private capital becomes blurred because private owners are part of a "neopatrimonial" power framework in which private and state interests are inseparably intertwined. In cases like these, the private media are inclined to be loyal to the state and the government and to resist liberalization and the diversification of programs.

In the final analysis, private ownership does not necessarily lead to liberalization in the same way as state ownership is not equivalent to censorship and information control, as the European experience of the BBC, for example, has shown. In the Arab world and the Middle East, however, where most if not all governments and regimes resist the democratization of society, privatization of media ownership seems to be a *prerequisite* for media freedom.

MASS MEDIA AND DEVELOPMENT

"Participatory development," a phrase used by Muhammad Ayish, is based on the idea that mass communication is a central means to include the people in political, societal, and cultural developments. In the classical works of modernization theory, mass communication is seen as a precondition for socioeconomic change, as knowledge can be exchanged, reproduced, or enriched by large-scale social interaction. Many theorists have looked at the mass media as a development instrument for the Third World, and according to Ithiel de Sola Pool, mass communication can create a process of global knowledge accumulation whereby the electronic media in particular represent important "floodgates of discourse" (Pool 1983: 251).

The contribution of the Arab and Middle Eastern mass media to participatory development is certainly limited. Many of the media do not, in fact, transfer "knowledge" and information but act as a government-controlled apparatus to create and distribute pseudo-facts and disguise information about the most important political, social, and cultural developments in the country concerned. Such control over information, which means that it cannot be properly exchanged, reproduced, or enriched, is the opposite of participatory development through mass communication, however.

At the same time, development and modernization are not the responsibility of the state alone. The question is how Arab and Middle Eastern societies as a whole articulate themselves through the mass media.

One important segment of the media for knowledge generation is books. In many respects, book publishers are really the "gatekeepers of ideas" and the gatekeepers of the abovementioned "floodgates of discourse." Whereas Middle Eastern book production and consumption is still impressive in terms of quantity, the banning of books is very widespread in the area, as in the case of the book *Muhammad* by the highly renowned French Orientalist Maxime Rodinson. The American University in Cairo (AUC) removed the book from its shelves and library database after a columnist in the Al-Ahram newspaper (May 13, 1998) had called the book an insult to Islam. By doing this, the university, which certainly deserves credit for being among the most open and critical institutions in the region, went beyond the Higher Education Ministry's request to remove the book from a teaching course.[5] The incident shows that the banning of books is not limited to state intervention. On the contrary, governments often react to what they perceive to be the dominant public mood. As in the case of Rodinson's work and the American University, neoconservative self-censorship and the restriction of participatory development through mass communication have many social agents.

The Internet is another development issue. The medium has raised high hopes for participatory development. These hopes have not yet been fulfilled, however. In many Arab states the system is used for chat lines or, at best, commercial advertising. However, despite the growth of cyber cafés in cities like Cairo, access to the Internet is almost confined to a Western-oriented, English-trained and commercially successful upper or upper-middle class (Möller 1997). The lower and lower-middle classes, who are important for participatory development, are much less involved here than in the abovementioned case of satellite TV. Hopes for a top-to-bottom-effect of information diffusion and pessimistic visions of an ever-growing "information gap" between the users and nonusers of the Internet are firmly rooted in the old but still vivid competition between mainstream modernization and dependency approaches.

Like the "new" forms of communication, such as the Internet, some of the very "old" forms—personal communication in markets, in the mosque, and so forth—could also be of importance for development. The Arab world and the Middle East consist of very different societies, some literate and metropolitan, others illiterate and rural. In rural areas especially, people use traditional forms of communication. The idea that traditional communication is affirmative because it transports traditional values confuses the "medium" and the "message." Of course, there is an intimate relationship between the forms and substances of communication, in the sense that the use of traditional communication will more often coincide with traditional conservative views of politics and the world, whereas the use of modern media tends to correspond with modern views. However, there is certainly no predetermined relationship. On the contrary, traditional communication in many countries and regions is the most important source of political information. In many cases where modern mass media became victims of state censorship, traditional communication took care of the distribution of the banned items of information. At the same time, reactionary Islamist groups have begun to use modern print and electronic media as tools for their aims, as was the case with Ayatollah Khomeini's spread of his revolutionary message through videotapes before the Iranian revolution in 1978-79 (Sreberny-Mohammadi and Mohammadi 1994). If these examples show that there is no fixed relationship between message and medium, then it seems quite natural to look at traditional communication as a source of development, especially when combined with modern mass media.

MEDIA, COMMUNICATION, AND CULTURE

S.E. Goodman and J.D. Green argue correctly that it is not so much the capability of the Arab world and the Middle East to deal adequately with information technology but the political, economic, and cultural circumstances that hamper the overall acceptability of these technologies:

> Largely uninformed external coverage of the Middle East tends to project the image of peoples intent upon the eradication of modernization, the abolition of technologies synonymous with the West, and a generalized desire to revert to some earlier epoch of history. In our view, this impression of regional technophobia is oversimplified and exaggerated. (...) [T]here have been important applications of information technology in the region, including some with unique indigenous characteristics. Yet (...) economic, political and cultural circumstances are such that the overall acceptability and value of these technologies remains ambiguous. (Goodman and Green 1992)

Having dealt with political and socioeconomic patterns of media development it is time to consider what Goodman and Green call the "cultural circumstances" of information technology. Although the impact of the media on political and economic development in the Third World was debated in previous decades, the discourse in the Arab and Islamic world has shifted towards culture. Many governments, communication theorists, and Islamist groups agree in their critique of the West's "cultural invasion" via mass media and media imperialism either through direct broadcasting or by means of Western texts and programs in the indigenous media. Governments like that of Saudi Arabia, whose rule is based on religious-cultural legitimacy, employ the invasion paradigm as an ideology to justify restrictions against satellite TV, the Internet, or any other mass media. Likewise, their own media empires are designed to counteract the supposedly detrimental influence of foreign media (which is at the same time a political challenge for those governments). A study of the reactions to direct satellite broadcasting has revealed that the invasion paradigm is widespread not only among governments but also among certain segments of media consumers (al-Makaty et al. 1997: 61). In the last resort, hardline, culturally based media policies in the Arab world and the Middle East aim at cultural separation and the rollback of the achievements of media globalization, markedly of the opening up of censored media spaces (see Table 0.1).

According to Majid Tehranian, Islamic information and communication theory has three characteristics: it is normative, heterogenous, and it is not unique (Tehranian 1988: 191 f.). Although this typology might in itself be simplistic given the large corps of theoretical Islamic writing published in the nineties, there is still evidence for Tehranian's viewpoint:

- Uniqueness of Islamic communication theory: A widespread view among Muslim scholars is that Western communication theory "underestimates the societal function of communication, and ignores the role of social structure and culture"

(Hasnain 1988: 184). This view of Western theory is incomplete, as social interaction has been an integral part of that theory for decades. With respect to interpersonal communication Paul Watzlawik, Janet H. Beavin, and Don D. Jackson, for example, have outlined the difference between communication problems as a result of divergent interpretations of the *content* of a text or spoken message as opposed to problems arising from the *social relationship* of the communicators (Watzlawick et al. 1990: 53 ff., 79 ff.). Heike Bartholy, to mention just one other example, has elaborated this paradigm for the field of intercultural communication, stating that differences in the social position of communicators from different cultural backgrounds—nationals having the status of "citizens" in contrast to many nonnational immigrants, for example—can interfere with their ability to "understand" each other, because the social status factors interfere as hidden messages in the communication process (Bartholy 1992: 174-191). What follows from this is that Islamic communication theory cannot claim uniqueness as the first and only theoretical body to consider social or cultural factors of communication. Although it is surely legitimate and important to reconsider Koranic and other traditional Islamic views to show that Western culture does not have a monopoly on communication thought, all too often "Islamic communications" and "Islamic communication theory" are not as culturally distinct as their titles suggest.

• Normative character of communication theory: The widespread view among Muslim thinkers that Western media is a tool of Western cultural "invasion" is rejected by Western scholars like Sinclair, Jacka, and Cunningham (Sinclair et al. 1996: 7 f.). Indeed, the invasion paradigm seems rather a normative than an empirically based theory. One of the major arguments against the cultural imperialism approach is that national and regional media production in countries like Egypt or India has not been destroyed through Western competition. India produces more films today than Hollywood, and Egypt is still the most important center for films and books distributed in the Arab world. A second argument against the cultural imperialism view is that it ignores the processes of media usage on the part of the consumer. The mass media are not omnipotent. In fact, the messages are manipulated by audiences and the public. Even seemingly standardized fiction like the soap operas *Dallas* and *Dynasty* are filtered by the consumer through structures of meaning construction on a national, local, or individual level. The media therefore seem to have a limited effect on people's minds and thinking (Liebes and Katz 1990). In Germany, *Dallas* was often regarded as an expression of the patriarchal society, which was criticized especially by the political left (Herzog-Massing 1986); in Holland, the soap was welcomed as counteracting the loss of family values (Ang 1985); and in Algeria, *Dallas* was interpreted as a warning against the loss of such values (Stolz 1983). The example of Algeria in particular shows that the consumption of foreign media does not necessarily destroy indigenous cultures, but can easily bring about cultural mixes and new intercultural media spaces and lifestyles, or can even help to revitalize traditional cultures. In this regard, Western satellite TV or Western programs in the national media do not simply "invade" the Arab world and the Middle East, but provide a stimulus for new discourses on culture.

- Heterogeneity of Islamic communication theory: The fact that there are opponents as well as advocates of the cultural invasion paradigm in the Middle East indicates that Islamic information theory is heterogenous in nature. Jamal al-Suwaidi, Director of the Emirates Center for Strategic Studies and Research (ECSSR) in Abu Dhabi, was quoted in the Saudi Arab News with the following statement:

> I don't know how there are people living among us who don't expect political and economic changes given the Information Communication Technology. (...) These people will become museum pieces. (...) The Arab peoples should accept the age of information and discard their fears concerning the cultural invasion as these fears belong to the past and actually widen the civilization gap between Arabs and other nations.[6]

Given these arguments one gets the impression that a considerable amount of Islamic thought on communication and the media, especially ideas on "cultural invasion" by Western mass media, aims at a normative distancing from the West. The culture and the media of the West are deemed to be pornographic, violent, and unsocial in nature and engaged in an "imperialist" crusade against the Islamic world. The cultural invasion paradigm is a simplistic form of Islamic thought on communication that demonstrates that communication and the media have become an integral part of culturalist ideologies—like Samuel Huntingtons *Clash of Civilizations*—that have become fashionable since the end of the Cold

War era. Culturally based criticism is possible, but it must be based on sophisticated theories of global and intercultural communication, solid empirical research, and should address concrete problems such as the often very one-sided view of Islam in Western media (Hafez 2000), the hegemony of Western news agencies in the international information flow, or the growing gap between the information-rich and the information-poor countries.

A second very important aspect is the fact that the cultural discourse on the mass media tends to distract attention from essential problems of the mass media development in North Africa and the Middle East: media freedom and the role of the mass media in political and social development. Insofar as the cultural invasion paradigm is used to justify the banning and censorship of "non-Islamic" thought in Arab and Middle Eastern media, the cultural discourse seems detrimental for political and social development. The reaction of the Arab media to the Salman Rushdie affair was ample evidence for the fact that it is not only governments but sometimes also journalists and intellectuals who adopt censorship and self-censorship in order to protect Islam. Analysis has shown that in most cases journalists in the Middle East did not support Khomeini's death verdict (or religious expert opinion [fatwa], to be more precise), but the argument that Rushdie's book should be banned was very widespread.[7] These traditionalist-culturalist views contradict the abovementioned protests of other Arab journalists against censorship and information control and endanger the future of critical Arab journalism.

THE CHAPTERS

This book covers the basic issues in the context of mass media and society as outlined above. Problems relating to information such as control, ownership, development, and culture are discussed by authors from different backgrounds working in the United States, Europe, and the Middle East as media experts, social scientists, and Arabists.

The book is divided into three sections. Part I (Amin, Boyd, Guaaybess, Najjar) represents case studies in media control and ownership in Egypt, Jordan, Saudi Arabia, and the Arab world at large. Part II (Ayish, Kirchner, Winkler, Rawan) moves from the narrow focus on media and politics to the interaction between mass media and the development of society. Part III (Werner, Glass) concentrates on cultural aspects, mostly on Islamic concepts of information and communication and Islamist approaches to modern mass media.

Hussein Amin argues that the Arab world has reached a critical stage in the modern information evolution. According to the author, nei-

ther the communication infrastructure nor media freedom and ownership meet international mass media standards. The article gives an
overview of the Arab world's print media and broadcasting systems.

Douglas A. Boyd analyzes the impact of ownership on Saudi
Arabian national and Arab regional broadcasting enterprises. The
author points to the basic dilemma resulting from Saudi business having
adopted new broadcasting technologies as a tool for modernization
while at the same time limiting citizens' access to these technologies.
Boyd argues that Saudi Arabia supports foreign-based media enterprises
in order to continue to influence the Kingdom's image in the Arab world
and beyond. In this sense, the basic aim of the Saudi media empire is not
to influence the contents of Middle Eastern media coverage as such or to
uphold Islamic values, but to stabilize the Saudi political system.

Whereas Boyd contends that the goals of Saudi media activities
are limited, Tourya Guaaybess argues that Saudi competition is increasingly felt in neighboring countries such as Egypt. Saudi and Western
programs transgress Egypt's borders and are held responsible for the
Egyptian governments' move towards privatizing the broadcasting system. According to Guaaybess, the government is inclined to keep political liberalization at bay, despite having deregulated the system in economic terms.

The case of the Jordanian press laws discussed by Orayb Aref
Najjar reveals that autocratic regimes in the area are reacting to media
globalization by attempting a rollback of media liberalization. Najjar
shows that although globalization has made it harder for the regimes to
bottle the "genie of press freedom," hopes for an immanent widening of
censored media spaces in the age of global media are unfounded.
International media are merely one (albeit very important) aspect of the
internal development of national media. This needs to be accompanied
by internal coalitions of forces that support liberalization.

Muhammad I. Ayish's chapter sheds light on the extent to
which technological developments in communications are conducive to
participatory development and societal change. According to the author,
technological modernization seems to have outpaced the mass media's
ability to foster a freer exchange of ideas. The mass media have therefore
lost their capacity to enhance national development. Ayish argues that
the loss of the development features of mass communication is only
partly due to political control. It is also the result of increased commercialization. Investment in technological progress has brought about a
media culture that is shaped more by advertising and entertainment
than by development issues. Ayish advocates pan-Arab communications
integration to improve the Arab media's chances of surviving in the
information age.

Henner Kirchner discusses the extent to which the Internet is a source of societal change and development in the Middle East. In terms of the number of Internet connections, most countries in the Middle East (including North Africa) have a much slower speed of growth than (Western) industrial countries. According to the author, language barriers and the attempts of Arab governments to censor the contents of network media are responsible for this development. Only a small part of the population is in a position to use the Net for commercial purposes. In this sense, the effect of the Internet is not to close, but to broaden the information gap between North and South.

Stefan Winkler in his case study of Egyptian, Lebanese, and other Arab book publishing industries, argues that book publishers in the area are often not specialized enough and cannot judge whether a book is conducive to societal development. Although books are still sold in large numbers and are often available in cheap editions at affordable prices, a host of problems from the quality of the raw material and old-fashioned distribution systems to inflexible import/export regulations and copyright problems prevent the Arab publishing industry from expanding.

Many aspects of modern mass communication have been introduced into the Middle East. In his chapter, Shir Mohammed Rawan argues, however, that in countries such as Iran and Pakistan, traditional forms of personal communication in the mosques and market places are still commonplace. A field study carried out in the North West Frontier Province of Pakistan reveals that traditional opinion leaders such as the *khan* or *mullah* carry more credibility than TV or newspapers. In the case of Iran, Rawan argues that the Islamic regime understood the role of traditional communication from the very beginning of the Revolution in 1978-79, and developed means of integrating modern and traditional communication. The author argues that a combination of both forms of communication is vital for societal change.

Karin Werner's contribution on the media practices of Islamist women in Egypt shows how young women are constructing individual sacral spheres with the help of modern media. Whereas Rawan demonstrates in his study that traditional communication is not, in principle, restricted to specific values or cultural meanings, the women in Werner's study explicitly refer to the textual referent system of Islam (Koran, etc.) as a source of inspiration for their personal conduct. They use modern media—recorders, videos, and the like—to perfect their own virtual reality and, at the same time, to protect themselves against the "corruption" of society through the regular mass media.

Dagmar Glass discusses Arab-Islamic information and communication sciences, which have long been ignored by Western academia.

She identifies five different directions of information and communication theory in the Arab world and analyzes the concepts of those calling for either a re-Islamization or a re-Arabization of information. Those advocating re-Islamization search for a reform of the media systems in Muslim countries, which could help to revive communication within the Islamic community (*umma*) and to counteract what is perceived as Western domination of the global flow of information.

ENDNOTES

1. For a review of the history of the Arab press see Ayalon 1995.
2. See reports on the countries of North Africa and the Middle East: Attacks on the Press in 1997. A Worldwide Survey by the Committee to Protect Journalists. http//www.cpj.org/pubs/attacks97/attacks97index.html (August 18, 1998).
3. Ibid.: http://www.cpj.org/pubs/attacks97/mideast/tunisia.html (August 18, 1998).
4. Deutsche Welle Monitor-Dienst, July 10, 1996: 2.
5. Index on Censorship. http://www.oneworld.org/index_oc/ii/iie.html (August 25, 1998).
6. Quoted in Machado 1997.
7. A comparative analysis of European and Middle Eastern media reactions to the Rushdie affair will soon be published by the author. For the time being, see Piscatori 1990.

BIBLIOGRAPHY

Alqudsi-Ghabra, Taghreed. 1995. Information Control in Kuwait: Dialectic to Democracy. *Journal of South Asian and Middle Eastern Studies* 4: 58-74.

Ang, Ien. 1985. *Watching Dallas*. New York: Routledge.

[Atwan, Abdul Bari, and Jihad Khazen]. 1997. "In saudischer Tasche." Abdul Bari Atwan und Jihad Khazen über den saudischen Einfluß auf arabische Medien. *Informationsprojekt Naher und Mittlerer Osten* (INAMO) 12: 8-10.

Ayalon, Ami. 1995. *The Press in the Arab Middle East. A History.* New York: Oxford University Press.

Ayish, Muhammad. 1991. Foreign Voices as People's Choices. BBC Popularity in the Arab World. *Middle Eastern Studies* 3: 374-389.

Bartholy, Heike. 1992. Barrieren in der interkulturellen Kommunikation. In *Transkulturelle Kommunikation und Weltgesellschaft. Zur Theorie und Pragmatik globaler Interaktion*, edited by Horst Reimann, 174-191. Opladen: Westdeutscher Verlag.

Behbahani, Kambiz. 1998. Zeitungen wie Pilze bekämpfen. *Die Tageszeitung*, August 5.

Campagna, Joel. 1998. Press Freedom in Jordan. *Middle East Report* (Spring): 44-47.

Chouikha, Larbi. 1992. Etatisation et pratique journalistique. *Revue Tunisienne de Communication* 22: 37-46.

Ezzeldin, Ahmed S. 1997. Ägyptische Presse: Zur Affäre um das Gesetz 93/95. *Informationsprojekt Naher und Mittlerer Osten* (INAMO) 12: 15 f.

El-Gawhary, Karim. 1995. Friß oder stirb. Einblicke in das arabische Kulturleben. *Süddeutsche Zeitung*, December 12.

Freund, Wolfgang S. 1992. Nieht gerade wielfältig—von gelenkt bis eben frei. Die Arabische Presse. In *Arabien: Mehr als Erdöl und Konflikte*, edited by Udo Steinbach, 321-326. Opladen: Leske und Budrich.

Gerlach, Julia. 1997. Lindenstraße made in Egypt. Unterwandert Saudi Arabien die arabische Welt im Vorabendprogramm? *Informationsprojekt Naher und Mittlerer Osten* (INAMO) 12: 12-14.

Goodman, S.E., and J.D. Green. 1992. Computing the Middle East and North Africa. http://www.sas.upenn.edu/African_Studies/Comp_Articles/Computing_10174.html (February 28, 1997).

[Hafez, Kai]. 2000. *Islam and the West in the Mass Media. Fragmented Images in a Globalizing World*, edited by Kai Hafez. Cresskill, NJ: Hampton Press.

Hasnain, Imtiaz. 1988. Communication: An Islamic Approach. In *Communication Theory. The Asian Perspective*, edited by Wimal Dissanayake, 183-189. Singapore: Asian Mass Communication Research and Information Centre.

Herzog-Massing, Herta. 1986. Decoding Dallas. *Society* 1: 74-77.

Ibrahimi, Hamed. 1997. Die Presse im Würgegriff. *Le Monde diplomatique/Die Tageszeitung* (February): 5 (monthly supplement of *Le Monde diplomatique* (German translation) to the German newspaper *Die Tageszeitung*).

Kazan, Fayad E. 1994. Kuwait. In *Mass Media in the Middle East. A Comprehensive Handbook*, edited by Yahya R. Kamalipour and Hamid Mowlana, 144-159. Westport, CT: Greenwood.

Lahav, Pnina. 1993. The Press and National Security. In *National Security and Democracy in Israel*, edited by Avner Yaniv, 173-195. Boulder: Lynne Rienner.

Liebes, Tamara, and Elihu Katz. 1990. *The Export of Meaning. Cross-Cultural Readings of Dallas*. New York: University of Oxford Press.

Machado, Lawrence. 1997. Satellites explode Myth of Isolation. *Arab News*, January 12.

Al-Makaty, Safran S., Douglas A. Boyd, and G. Norman Van Tubergen. 1997. A Q-Study of Reactions to Direct Broadcasting Satellite (DBS) Television Programming in Saudi Arabia. *Journal of South Asian and Middle Eastern Studies* 4: 50-64.

Möller, Jochen. 1997. a7ibak gidan ya INTERNET. Internet-Zugänge in Kairo und anderswo. *Informationsprojekt Naher und Mittlerer Osten* (INAMO) 12: 25 f.

Mouffok, Ghania. 1997. Algeriens Presse: Das Echo des Chaos. *Informationsprojekt Naher und Mittlerer Osten* (INAMO) 12: 19 f.

Mostefaoui, Belkacem. 1997. Ausländisches Fernsehen im Maghreb—ein Medium mit kulturellen und politischen Auswirkungen. *Wuquf* 10/11 (1995/96): 425-455.

Najjar, Orayb Aref. 1998. The Ebb and Flow of the Liberalization of the Jordanian Press. 1985-1997. *Journalism and Mass Communication Quarterly* 1: 127-142.
Napoli, James J. 1991. Benazir Bhutto and the Issues of Press Freedom in Pakistan. *Journal of South Asian and Middle Eastern Studies* 3: 57-76.
Napoli, James J., Hussein Y. Amin, and Luanne R. Napoli. 1995. Privatization of the Egyptian Media. *Journal of South Asian and Middle Eastern Studies* 4: 39-57.
Piscatori, James P. 1990. The Rushdie Affair and the Politics of Ambiguity. *International Affairs* 4: 767-789.
Pool, Ithiel de Sola. 1983. *Technologies of Freedom*. Cambridge: Harvard University Press.
Rugh, William A. 1979. *The Arab Press: News Media and Political Process in the Arab World*. Syracuse, NY: Syracuse University Press.
Shahak, Israel. 1997. *Open Secrets. Israeli Foreign and Nuclear Policies*. London: Pluto.
Sinclair, John, Elizabeth Jacka, and Stuart Cunningham. 1996. Peripheral Vision. In *New Patterns in Global Television. Peripheral Vision*, edited by John Sinclair, Elizabeth Jacka, and Stuart Cunningham, 1-32. Oxford: Oxford University Press.
Sreberny-Mohammadi, Annabelle, and Ali Mohammadi. 1994. *Small Media, Big Revolution. Communication, Culture, and the Iranian Revolution*. Minneapolis: University of Minnesota Press.
Stolz, Joelle. 1983. *Les Algeriens regardent Dallas. Les Nouvelles Chaines*. Paris: Presse Universitaire de France and Institut Universitaire d'Etudes du Development.
Tehranian, Majid. 1988. Communication Theory and Islamic Perspectives. In *Communication Theory. The Asian Perspective*, edited by Wimal Dissanayake, 190-203. Singapore: Asian Mass Communication Research and Information Centre.
Watzlawick, Paul, Janet H. Beavin, and Don D. Jackson. 1990. *Menschliche Kommunikation. Formen, Störungen, Paradoxien*, 8th ed. Bern: Hans Huber.

I

MEDIA CONTROL
AND OWNERSHIP

1

Mass Media in the Arab States between Diversification and Stagnation: An Overview

Hussein Amin

All of the Arab states are classified as belonging to the developing world, and all grew out of a colonial past, but are still greatly influenced by the Arabic language and by Islam, the main religion. The Arab world occupies a large geographical area that is estimated at approximately 13,738,000 square kilometers; it extends from the shores of the Atlantic Ocean in the west to the Persian Gulf in the east. The term "Arab world" generally refers to the following countries: Algeria, Bahrain, Egypt, Iraq, Jordan, Kuwait, Lebanon, Libya, Morocco, Oman, Palestine, Qatar, Saudi Arabia, Sudan, Syria, Tunisia, the United Arab Emirates, and Yemen. The combined population of these countries was estimated in the 1990s at around 230 million. Media are tied to economic development, and the level of economic development in the Arab world is widely divergent. The World Bank classifies Yemen, Egypt, Jordan, Syria, and Lebanon as lower-middle-income countries; Oman and Iraq as upper-middle-income; and Saudi Arabia, Kuwait, and the United Arab Emirates as high-income oil exporters. Because Bahrain and Qatar have populations below one million, the World Bank does not classify these countries at all. Income is one indicator of media development and penetration, but educational level, journalistic traditions, and the political system are likewise important determinants of media development. The primary functions of the mass media in the Arab world are to convey news and information of general interest, interpret and comment on events, provide opinion and perspectives, reinforce social norms and cultural awareness through the dissemination of information about the culture and the society, provide specialized data for commercial promotion and services, and, finally, entertain.

The Arab world has reached a critical stage in its modern information evolution. As nations around the world privatize, restructure, and align to compete internationally, the Arab world remains impeded by old political divisions, static economic models, and poor media structures and performance. The challenge for the region is to build momentum through revisiting the structure of the mass media and its relation with the state as well as rethinking the role of the mass media in society. Political stability is vital if Arab states are to emerge as competitive economies. As it is, some states in the region are making progress toward opening state-controlled markets, diversifying oil-dominated economies, and allowing the growth of private media.

PRINT MEDIA

Although the Arab states share many common features, including history, culture, language, and religion, a regional press has been slow to develop. The relative importance and penetration of print media in the Arab world is tied to the level of literacy. Generally, where literacy is high, newspaper penetration is likewise high. The illiteracy rate in the Arab world is quite high and therefore print media circulation is very limited. Other factors that have contributed to the underdevelopment of the Arab press include repressive press laws and regulations, severe censorship rules, strong ideological and political tensions, and distribution problems that have impeded free expression and distribution of the print media.

The most negative ratings in the Arab world in terms of censorship were reserved for Iraq and Saudi Arabia. Within the Arab world, censorship is tolerated and even expected as a form of civic responsibility. The development of print media in the Arab world varies widely among the individual countries. The first Arab newspaper printed by Arabs was the *Jurnal Al-Iraq*, dating from 1816. The first Arab daily newspaper began publication in Beirut in 1873. The early Arab press in the nineteenth century was generally an official voice of the ruling party. Furthermore, freedom of the press within the framework of news agencies in the Arab world is limited. All news agencies in the Arab world have one thing in common: all are official agencies and their primary purpose is to convey to the country and the world the achievements of the many sectors of the state. Most Arab news agencies are still in the very early stages of development, and they face many difficulties in areas such as finance, personnel, and facilities (Azet 1992).

In North Africa where Algeria, Tunisia, and Morocco had a long French presence, much of the print media has been influenced by the French in terms of thought and language. In Algeria, a less restrictive information code was introduced by the government in 1990 after the continuous, violent antigovernment riots. The country's six daily newspapers are state-owned. The leading papers are *Al-Shaab* and *Al-Mujahid* and their respective evening counterparts *Al-Masa* and *Horizons*. *Al-Mujahid* and *Horizons* (the only daily published in French) are official organs of the National Liberation Front (FLN). *Al-Jumhuriya* and *Al-Nasr* are published in Oran and Constantine, respectively. Although the official language is Arabic, French is widely used in Tunisia, especially in media circles. A revised press code was introduced in the late 1980s, but many restrictions and limitations on ownership and press freedom remain in place. There are five daily newspapers. *L'Action* and *Al-Amal* are published by the Democratic Constitutional Rally (RCD). *La Presse de Tunisie* and its evening edition, *La Presse-Soir*, are published by the government. *As-Sabah* is published by a private company, Dar Al-Sabah, which also publishes the weekly *Le Temps*. The RCD also publishes a weekly for Tunisian workers abroad, *Al-Biladi*, and a political magazine, *Dialogue* (Drost 1991).

To a certain extent Morocco has a free press system, with a government dominated by pro-royalist parties and an opposition given freedom to criticize the king and the political system as long as the opposition parties respect the official line. The government still exerts control over the media. Morocco has a well-developed press, including eleven daily newspapers and a large number of weeklies. The leading government organs are *Le Matin du Sahara* and its evening companion *Moroc Soir* (Drost 1991).

The press in Egypt is one of the most advanced in the Arab world, and Cairo is considered the largest publishing center. A new press law was introduced in Egypt in 1996, replacing the 1995 law that imposed penalties including imprisonment on journalists for slandering members of the government (Amin and Napoli 1997). The press in Egypt was founded in the late nineteenth century. Now the press is dominated by four publishing houses: Al-Ahram, Dar Akhbar Al-Yum,

Dar Al-Tahrir and Dar Al-Hilal. The three most influential dailies are *Al-Ahram*, *Al-Akhbar*, and *Al-Jumhuriya*. In recent years Egypt has introduced private newspapers such as *Al-Usbua* and the business newspaper *Alam Al-Yum* (Amin and Napoli 1997). The Egyptian government still wants to control the public by controlling the press.

The Libyan press philosophy is organized to reflect Gaddafi's philosophy, and is therefore under the tight control of the government. Libya's official Wakalat Al-Anba Al-Jamahiriya (Jamahiriya News Agency, or JANA) is virtually the single source of domestic news, the sole authorized distributor of foreign news, and the publisher of most of the newspapers and periodicals in Libya, including the main daily newspaper that is the official mouthpiece of the regime, *Al-Fajr Al-Jadid* (The New Dawn) (Mezran 1994).

In spite of being the largest Arab state in terms of geographical size, Sudan still faces many economic difficulties. The press is subject to severe censorship imposed by a military government that banned political parties and imposed a state of emergency. More than forty newspapers and magazines were published in Sudan during the three years of democratic government under Sadiq al-Mahdi. The coup of June 1989 brought to an abrupt end this period of free expression, one of the most liberal and least repressive in recent African history. The new dailies, *Injaz Al-Watan* and *Al-Sudan Al-Hadith*, were established under government supervision in September 1989. In May 1990 the government also launched a new English-language weekly, *New Horizon*. Some of the banned political parties and other organizations circulate secretly published newsletters, but face heavy penalties for doing so (Drost 1991).

Ever since the Baath political party came to power, the structure of the Syrian press has been modeled on that of communist countries, allowing limited freedom of expression and of the press. Many publications are published by political, religious, or professional associations and trade unions affiliated with or controlled by the National Progressive Front, and several are published by government ministries. The two largest publishing companies are Dar Al-Wihdah and Dar Al-Tishrin. There are more than ten daily national and regional newspapers. The three major national dailies are *Al-Baath*, the organ of the party, *Tishrin*, and *Al-Thawrah*.

Following the stalemate in the 1980-88 Iran-Iraq war and the crushing defeat in the Gulf war, the Iraqi media is, understandably, totally controlled by the government. Media philosophy emerged from the Arab Baath Socialist Party (ABSP) that rules the country. All foreign publications are banned. The Iraqi official Wakalat Al-Anba Al-Iraqiya (Iraq News Agency, or INA) is virtually the only source of news for the media. The circulation of newspapers in Iraq is among the lowest in the

Arab world because of a shortage of print paper. The three major dailies, *Al-Jumhuriya, Al-Thawra,* and *Al-Qadissiya,* are organs of the government (Drost, 1991).

Out of necessity, Jordan has been one of the region's most aggressive economic reformers and is aiming for a private media system. The press is relatively free; however, all publications and publishing houses must acquire a license, and the publication of some newspapers in Jordan was suspended by the government. The Jordanian press is partly privately and partly state-owned; the most influential among the country's five daily papers, *Al-Ray,* was founded by the government.

Yemen was created by the contentious 1990 marriage of conservative North Yemen and Marxist South Yemen. The country is ruled by a coalition government that is committed to bolstering the nation's underdeveloped economy. Prior to the union, the press in North Yemen was diverse, unlike in South Yemen, where the press was under the complete control of the regime. Major newspapers are published in Sanaa, Aden, and Taiz and include *Al-Thawra* and *Al-Jumhuriya* (Drost 1991).

Lebanon is considered the most liberal state in the Arab world. Once the "Paris of the Arab world," Beirut and Lebanon are seeking to regain their status after the civil war. With the highest literacy rates in the Arab world, Lebanon's media are significantly superior to other media systems in the region. Over thirty daily newspapers and a large number of news weeklies are still published in Lebanon. The largest publishing houses are Dar Al-Sayad, Dar Al-Nahar, Editions Orientals, Dar Alf Laila and Dar Al-Hayat. The most influential dailies are *Al-Anwar* and *An-Nahar* and its French-language companion *L'Orient-Le Jour.*

The Gulf states include Bahrain, Kuwait, Qatar, Oman, Saudi Arabia, and the United Arab Emirates and have for years represented the Middle East's oil wealth. Politically, the Gulf states are Islamic monarchies where kings and emirs hold sway. They range in terms of conservatism from strict Saudi Arabia to the more liberal Kuwait and the UAE. Now they are seeking to find their way in the post-oil-boom era. Although they are still prosperous, the Gulf states have experienced recessions, budget deficits, and a decline in living standards caused by low oil prices and growing populations. Moreover, political turmoil has manifested itself in bombings and protests by Islamic activists against the region's all-powerful monarchies.

Saudi Arabia is the dominant state in the Gulf states and the Islamic kingdom has the most controlled media system in this region. A censorship committee with representatives from different government ministries monitors all local and foreign publications. Nationally, there are more than ten daily newspapers published in Saudi Arabia, the most popular Arabic ones being *Al-Riyad* and *Al-Bilad*. The leading English language newspaper is the *Saudi Gazette*. The Saudi Press Agency (SPA) is the state news agency and owns big publishing companies such as Saudi Research and Marketing (SRM) (Rampal 1994). Saudi media plays an important role in the Arab world by providing the most widely distributed private pan-Arab newspapers, *Al-Hayat* and *Al-Sharq Al-Awsat*.

Private ownership and reduced government pressure have led to a more diverse press in Kuwait. Kuwaiti print media are popular not only at home but also in other Arab countries. The largest publishing houses are Dar Al-Siyasa, Dar Al-Ray Al-Am and Dar Al-Qabas. The largest newspaper is *Al-Qabas* (Kazan 1994). Qatar's print media matured as a result of specific national policy and the desire of some individuals to participate in public life by publishing newspapers. Qatar's Wakalat Al-Anba Al-Qatariya (Qatar News Agency) is the main source of news in the country. Four daily newspapers are published in Qatar, three in Arabic and one in English. They are *Al-Raya* and its companion *Gulf Times*, *Al-Arab*, and *Al-Sharq*. There are eight daily newspapers in the United Arab Emirates, five in Arabic and three in English. The first daily, *Al-Ittihad*, appeared in 1972 and remains the leading paper of the UAE in Arabic. *Emirates News* is its English-language counterpart. Both are published by the state-owned Dar Al-Ittihad and generally reflect the government's point of view. The official Wakalat Al-Anba Al-Umaniya (Oman News Agency) is the main source of news in Oman, and there are three daily newspapers: *Al-Uman*, its English-language companion the *Oman Daily Observer*, and *Al-Watan*.

In Palestine, a serious debate has been conducted about the advisability of publishing under occupation. Proponents argued that publication would fill a void in print media and would serve to educate both writers and readers. Opponents of publication held that publishing would provide Israel with valuable intelligence about the Palestinian community, would normalize occupation, and would move resistance from the street to the press. The first newspaper to publish under the occupation was *Al-Quds* (Jerusalem), still the most widely circulated domestic newspaper. The opposition at first boycotted the newspaper but then reconsidered and began publishing in 1972. By 1987, there were twenty-two newspapers, twenty-two magazines, and forty press services. Israelis have periodically ceased some of these publications permanently and have restricted distribution of others. Yet Palestine continues to have an active press, with a number of papers founded since the installation of autonomy rule in 1993-94. The press is still openly defined as a political tool for liberation (Najjar 1994). Voices critical of Yasir Arafat's government are often silenced by force.

RADIO AND TELEVISION

Radio and television broadcasting networks in Arab counties are primarily absolute monopolies and usually function under direct government supervision. The broadcasting institutions in most Arab states are owned, operated, and controlled by the governments The main reasons for centralizing broadcasting are: the Arab governments' desire to preserve national unity and the centralized system of government and administration; the Arab governments' utilization of the broadcast media as a political and a propaganda tool; and their interest in keeping these tools out of hostile hands. Radio and television, in particular, are of immense value to these governments because of the relatively high illiteracy rates in the Arab world. Because radio and television bypass illiteracy, they are frequently used as a propaganda arm by Arab governments to control and mobilize the public (Amin and Boyd 1993). Most Arab radio and television systems are subsidized by governments and partially financed by advertising revenues.

Despite the many similarities, there are some significant differences among the broadcasting systems. Most consequential are the political rules by which they play. Arab radio and television systems can be divided into two groups. The first group operates under a national mobilization philosophy, a type of broadcasting system observed in Algeria, Egypt, Iraq, Syria, Libya, Yemen, and the Sudan. These countries have treated radio and television in a very similar manner and exercise total control over the broadcast media. They strongly prescribe the use of radio and television as instruments of political communication to encourage national unity and support. Egypt, which is the most influential state in terms of television development, program appeal, and exports, is somewhat the exception. The second major group operates under a bureaucratic, laissez-faire philosophy, and includes all other Arab states except Morocco and Lebanon. These states have administrative control over radio and television broadcasting, but they are more relaxed than the previous group in the sense that they do not maneuver their broadcast media in a controlled direction in order to gain nationwide support for the government.

Arabs rely heavily on oral culture; therefore the importance of radio is quite substantial. Most households in the Arab world have at least one radio. Radio broadcasting started in many of the Arab states on a commercial basis, funded by individuals or corporations, as in Algeria (1925), Egypt (1926), and Tunisia (1935). All stations were profit-oriented, based on the marketing of program products and radio sets as well as the selling of commercial messages (Labib et al. 1983). Government radio stations were established in these countries after the elimination of

private stations. Many Arab states jump-started their systems by giving
the task to a foreign company. Egypt, for instance, authorized the British
Marconi Company to operate the government system from 1934 to 1948,
and Tunisia authorized the French broadcasting authority to establish
radio broadcasting in 1939. Nearly all of these radio stations are now
government services. However, during the last decade, the region has
witnessed a movement toward commercial broadcasting, such as Radio
Mediterranée Internationale (RMI), established in Morocco in 1982. In
addition, Dubai has commercial radio stations that derive their incomes
from advertisements and exist alongside government stations.

Television is a very important medium in nearly all of the Arab
world. Television broadcasting started in the Arab world in the 1950s. It
was introduced in Morocco in 1954, and in Algeria, Iraq, and Lebanon in
1956. It progressed to other Arab countries during the 1960s and 1970s
(Labib et al. 1983). Arab households are closely knit and self-contained,
especially in the conservative Gulf states, where entertainment is cus-
tomarily confined to the home. Saudi Arabia, the most conservative of
the Gulf states, saw the visual medium as an acceptable alternative to
public cinemas (still not permitted in the Kingdom). Also, state or quasi-
state controlled television is a means of filtering what receivers see. At
least this was the case before video recorders—or other so-called "small
media"—became popular in the region (Amin and Boyd 1993).

Algeria started its radio broadcast services in 1967 as a service to
French colonists. Most of the program services were relayed from Paris,
and the first Arabic radio broadcast channel was introduced in 1940, followed by a Berber channel, Kabyla, in 1948. Politically the main purpose
of these services was to provide propaganda and support for the French
presence. The main impetus behind the development of Algeria's broadcast system was that the country is relatively large in size and its population scattered (Head 1985). The French broadcasting organization
Radio Diffusion Television Francais (RTF) installed radio transmitters in
key cities in North Algeria. In January 1963, RTF became Radio
Diffusion Television Algerie (RTA). The French model of government
control influenced radio broadcasting; from the beginning, RTA was
tightly controlled by the Ministry of Information and Culture. Ahmed
ben Bella, the first Algerian President, began the establishment of state
socialism in Algeria and thought that radio broadcasting would play a
major role in its development. He was followed by Houari
Boumedienne, who came to power in 1965 and strove to orient Algeria's
national identity and cultural independence away from the West, especially France. He also started a mission to Arabize most of the existing
programs (Amin 1997). Television broadcasting in Algeria began in
1956. Algeria relied heavily on transmission from Europe via a relay sta-

tion located on the Balearic islands. As with radio, Algeria started to Arabize the medium, and, by 1969, had established a televised Arabic literacy pilot project carried out by UNESCO (Head 1974). Algeria under President Ben Jadid began to move toward political and economic reform, which resulted in the breakup of RTA into smaller enterprises, thereby decreasing the level of state control and opening the door for private entrepreneurs to get into the broadcasting business. RTA was split into four entities in 1987: the National Enterprise of Television (ENTV), the National Enterprise for Audiovisual Production (ENPA), the National Enterprise for Radio (ENRA) and the Algerian Telediffusion Enterprise (an enterprise managing television equipment). The system is state-controlled, and the programs, particularly the news and news programs, are designed to promote the policies of the current political regime (Mohammadi 1993).

Bahrain started its own radio broadcasting service in 1955. The station increased hours of transmission gradually to fourteen hours by 1980. Bahrain established an English-language radio service in 1977, as the language is widely spoken in both Bahrain and in the neighboring states. Programs are a mix of news, education, and entertainment as well as religion. At the beginning of the 1990s, Bahrain television had two channels with a mix of programs, the most popular of which are the Arabic serials from Egypt. In 1993, Bahrain's main channel was placed on Arab Satellite (ARABSAT), for direct broadcast transmission to the Arab world (Amin 1997). The system has come more under the control of the government in recent years because of political tension between the government and Islamic activists.

Official radio service began in Egypt on May 31, 1934. After the Egyptian revolution in 1952, broadcasting came under complete government control, and radio became the voice of the Egyptian revolution. Gamal Abdel Nasser, Egypt's first president, understood the power of the medium and was able to capitalize on the oral Arab culture and the power and the emotion of the Arabic language. He, therefore, devoted a great deal of the Egyptian administrative energy and extensive economic resources to developing Egyptian radio broadcasting. Most of these radio services and programs were somewhat politicized and promoted the image of the President. Nasser's successor, Anwar al-Sadat, made sure that the government maintained control over the broadcast media after an attempt to obtain control of the radio and television building (Napoli and Amin 1994). In 1971, the Egyptian Radio and Television Union (ERTU) was formed with the objective of exercising complete control over all broadcast material for either radio or television in Egypt. Egyptian radio is now composed of seven networks: the main network, the regional network, the educational network, the religious network, the commercial network, the Arab network, and the beamed international service network (al-Halwani 1984). Egyptian television began broadcasting on July 21, 1960, a date chosen to mark the eighth anniversary of the 1952 revolution. From the very beginning, the most important type of programming on Egyptian television was films, as Egypt had already established the most advanced and sophisticated film industry in the region. American and British programs were also used by Egyptian television until the time of the 1967 war. After the war, the number of Western programs decreased substantially due to the cessation of diplomatic relations between Egypt and the United States and Britain. Programs from the Soviet Union were substituted. This situation continued until the 1973 war. At the conclusion of the war, Egyptian television tended to reflect the changing international political orientation of the country (al-Halwani 1984). Egypt produced most of its own television programming, and also provided television products and talents that other Arab countries lack in creating an indigenous television production industry (Amin and Boyd 1993).

The next major shift in television broadcasting did not occur until the late 1980s and early 1990s. Until that point, Egyptian television services were composed of two national networks covering almost all parts of the state. In 1990, the Egyptian government under President Hosni Mubarak started to decentralize the system by establishing five local television channels covering different parts of the state, in addition to a teletext service information channel (Amin 1997).

At the same time, the Egyptian government began privatizing the medium by introducing the first cable system in Egypt. Cable News Egypt (CNE) was introduced in June 1990 as a joint venture between the Egyptian Radio and Television Union (ERTU) and other investors that carried services like Music Television (MTV) and the Cable News Network (CNN) (Foote and Amin 1993). Satellite television broadcasting was introduced in 1990; Egyptian Space Net started transmission in Arabic with an average of thirteen hours of daily programming including news, sports, entertainment, and religious, educational, and cultural programs to the Middle East, North Africa, Europe, and a small part of Asia. Other transmissions include the Nile TV International television network, which broadcasts in English and French. Egypt recently added two satellite television networks, Nile Drama and Egyptian Spacenet 2, and has launched the new satellite NILESAT (Amin 1997).

The Iraqi government did not pay much attention to the development of radio until it started receiving hostile radio broadcasting from neighboring states, especially Egypt's radio messages against the Iraqi prime minister, Nuri al-Said, who was asking for Arab support for the pro-Western Baghdad Pact (Boyd 1993). A military group headed by Abd al-Karim Qasim took over the country in a military coup in July 1958 and started utilizing the power of electronic media to gain political support internally and to communicate with Arab countries externally. The Iraqi revolutionary regime at that time relied on the former Soviet Union for technical assistance as well as for the establishment of broadcast facilities. Most of the radio services during both the Iran-Iraq war and the Gulf war called for Arab support for the Iraqi regime. Iraqi radio focused primarily on claims and issues such as the historical rights that Iraq has over Kuwait, religious justifications of the invasion, and the occupation of Kuwait. The latter was portrayed as a confrontation between Muslims and non-Muslims. The imbalance of wealth between the rich Gulf states and the poor Arab countries was also emphasized (Amin 1992). Iraqi radio services consist of the main channel, the Voice of the Masses (Sawt Al-Jamahir), Kurdish and other minority language channels, and foreign and beamed programs. Most of these services are mobilized for propaganda supporting the Iraqi political leadership. In 1956, the political power structure realized the importance of television and ordered an increase in the power of the Baghdad station. But this era ended when Abd al-Karim Qasim was overthrown in 1963 and his body displayed on live television. New stations were opened, however, north of Baghdad, namely in Kirkuk, Mousul, and in Basra. At the beginning of the 1970s, a second television channel was introduced. Like radio, television is a heavily political medium (Martin and Chaudhary 1983).

Jordanian radio, which is officially known as the Hashemite Broadcasting Service, was expanded in the 1950s to enable the Jordanian government to counter Cairo's broadcast attacks on the government for taking orders from the British. In 1959, King Hussein inaugurated the Amman Broadcasting Service. The service was never very powerful or influential, as it did not reach the neighboring countries of Syria, Iraq, Israel, and Saudi Arabia. However, because it was a commercial service, the income it generated helped to pay the broadcast service bill until 1967. One result of the 1967 war was the general cooling of the broadcast propaganda in the Middle East. The Jordanian main broadcast service is now composed of the main Arabic program, the English service, and the FM stereo service (Boyd 1993). Television made its entry into Jordan in 1968 with a three-hour transmission on one channel. In the early 1970s, another channel was added carrying foreign programs (Boyd 1993). The Jordanian Radio and Television Corporation started broadcasting the Jordanian Arab Space Channel on February 1, 1993 on ARABSAT. New plans for this channel include the utilization of the second generation of ARABSAT 2-A, engaged by a Ku-band transponder. To transfer political messages across boundaries, plans for future expansion of the Jordanian Arab Space Channel include transmission of the service to Europe and the United States.

Kuwait began making radio broadcasts in 1961 after independence. Because the state of Kuwait is a small country and large terrestrial networks were not required, the introduction of both radio and television broadcasting posed almost no difficulties in terms of financing. Kuwaiti radio broadcast services include the main program, the second program, the English program, the Koran program, the music program, and the Persian and Urdu service. Most of the radio broadcast facilities were destroyed during the Gulf war, but immediately after the liberation of Kuwait, the Kuwaiti government replaced the facilities with advanced state-of-the-art technologies. Television followed radio a few years later and was presented to the country on an informal basis by the end of the 1950s. It was the American company RCA (Radio Corporation of America) that initiated a low power television station in Kuwait City to market and promote the sale of television receivers. Officially, at independence in 1961, the Kuwaiti Ministry of Information took command of the system after changing it to European standards. The television broadcast in Kuwait includes four channels, and programming is a mixture of news and entertainment. Because of the ongoing tension between Iraq and Kuwait and the problems of prisoners of war, Kuwaiti television's programs are heavily weighted with political and public affairs as well as talk shows. In the wake of the war, Kuwait found it necessary to establish its own network despite the damage that was done to the Kuwaiti TV studios. After the 1990 invasion, Kuwait realized the importance of communication and wanted to take its place in the new era of global communication (Amin 1996). After the war, Kuwaiti officials realized the importance of starting satellite broadcasting, and official transmission of the Kuwaiti Space Network began on July 4, 1992. The network is considered a government project, owned and operated by the Kuwaiti Emirate, through affiliation with the Ministry of Information.

The French government in Lebanon established the country's radio broadcast service in 1937. During the civil war, unofficial broadcasting came to Lebanon, and many unofficial stations started to operate. More than fifty of these stations were in use during the war in Lebanon. Lebanese television was launched in May 1959 with one channel. A second commercial channel was introduced in 1962. Tele-Orient was the first television station and was owned by Lebanese interests and the American Broadcasting Company (ABC), which later sold its share to the British Thomson Corporation. Lebanese television is a mix of Western and foreign programming, particularly from the United States, Europe, and Egypt. Nonofficial television broadcasting started during the Lebanese civil war. These networks included Tele-Lebanon, Star of Hope, Fahi Television, and Lebanese Broadcasting Corporation (LBC). Television in Lebanon is a unique case in the Arab world. More than forty private television stations are now operating in Lebanon; however, a decree issued by the Lebanese Cabinet reorganized the country's radio and television broadcast industry by reducing the number of TV and radio concessions.

When Gaddafi came to power on September 1, 1969, the new military regime stopped all foreign broadcasting within the country. The development of radio in Libya was very similar to Egypt's experience, because Gaddafi was greatly influenced by Egypt's Nasser. He admired the broadcast Voice of the Arabs from Cairo and thereafter started to invest huge amounts of money to advance radio broadcasting in Libya. The broadcast enterprise in Libya was restructured on June 2, 1973, when the People's Committees took over control of the radio operation in Tripoli and Benghazi (Katz and Wedell 1977). The National Service of Libyan Broadcasting broadcasts nineteen hours each day. There are now two radio channels: the European program and the Libyan Jamahiriya broadcast, which includes the "Holy Koran" program (Boyd 1993). Libyan television broadcasting started in 1968 with the help of the British Broadcasting Corporation (BBC). Much of the development of the television broadcasting system happened in the 1970s and 1980s. The content of the television broadcast schedules tends to be serious rather than entertaining. News, public affairs programs, and discussion programs represent a good deal of the television schedule. Messages stress Arab unity, pan-Arabism, and Arab integration (Boyd 1993).

Morocco began radio broadcasting in 1928 in Rabat. The system grew during the 1940s and 1950s to offer two radio stations: the A program in French and the B program in Arabic and Berber. Later a C program in Spanish and English was established. In January 1962 after Morocco's independence, an executive order shifted Radio Diffusion—Maroccan (RTM) to the control of the Ministry of Information. RTM radio currently consists of three networks based in Rabat plus nine regional stations scattered throughout the country. The national radio network is the most important service for the lower socioeconomic levels. RTM's programming includes music, news, and public affairs programs and entertainment programs. Television made its entry into Morocco in March 1962. RTM-TV reaches over 80 percent of the population, and in July 1989, the first private television station, 2M International, was introduced. 2M International is scrambled ten hours a day and unscrambled for five hours (Boyd 1993).

The British introduced radio to Palestine in 1936 and broadcast in English, Arabic, and Hebrew from the occupied territories. Palestinians themselves did not have access to radio broadcast stations until the establishment of the PLO. Many of the Arab countries established Palestinian stations. In 1954, Nasser, in his role as informal leader of the Arab world, was the first Arab leader to create a radio program about Palestine. Iraq soon followed Egypt's example, as did Syria and Kuwait shortly after. The first PLO station run by Palestinians started broadcasting from Egypt in 1965. However, this independence was short-lived; in 1967, Egypt assigned an Egyptian censor to the station and then closed it in 1970. The PLO had similar experiences in many of the Arab countries from which it set up broadcasting stations. Palestinians do not control any television stations, and there is as yet no cable television, although projects are underway to train and establish a station in the territories (Najjar 1994).

The Qatar radio broadcasting service started in 1968 when Great Britain announced that it would leave the area, and the system was advanced after independence in 1972. Programming includes the Arabic program, the English services, and the Urdu program which is directed toward Pakistani expatriates. Most of the radio programs are a mixture of news, entertainment, religious, and educational programs. Television was introduced in Qatar in August 1970. The Arabic program telecasts on channels 9 and 11; the second television service, which broadcasts entirely in English, operates on an ultra-high frequency and utilizes more than one channel in the spectrum. The Arabic main channel was put on ARABSAT in 1993 (Amin 1997). The new Emir of Qatar normalized relations with the state of Israel and started *Al-Jazeera* (The Island) network, which is one of the most powerful and openly critical satellite pan-Arab news networks in Arabic language. Qatar closed its information ministry, programmatically entering a new era in the development of the mass media.

Officially, radio broadcasting in Saudi Arabia progressed during the 1950s and was supported in the 1960s because of the government's interest in decreasing the size of the audience of foreign broadcasts. After the October 1973 Middle East war, radio broadcasting witnessed a tremendous improvement due to a greatly increased budget arising from the growth of oil revenues. Radio services in Saudi Arabia are composed of the general program, the "Holy Koran" broadcast, the international foreign language program, and the European service. Radio in Saudi Arabia has a religious tone, as Saudi Arabia is the center of the Islamic world (Boyd 1993). Saudi Arabian television began in 1965. Like radio, it was subject to opposition and rejection and earned the antagonism of conservative religious groups. Saudi Arabia initially operated two national television systems. Television programming in Saudi Arabia is similar to radio in the sense that Saudi Arabia is the heart of the Islamic nations. Therefore, religious programming has special importance in the country, particularly during the month of Ramadan and the season of Haj when censorship is stringently exercised. Saudi private global broadcast media became popular after 1991 through the introduction of satellite packages such as Arab Radio and Television (ART), Orbit, and the Middle East Broadcasting Center (MBC) in 1993, all of which are Saudi-owned networks, operated from outside the Kingdom (Amin 1997).

Radio broadcasting in Sudan was introduced in 1940, but Radio Umdurman was unable to cover the entire state until 1972. However, the advancement of the system faced a similar problem to that faced by Algeria. Sudan is the largest country in Africa, and its population is scattered throughout the state. Sudan gained independence from Britain in 1956, and in May 1969, Jafar Numairi took over the country in a military coup. Radio services in the Sudan are composed of the following programs: the national program, the Koranic station, Voice of the Sudanese Nation, National Unity Radio, and the Juba Local Service (Head 1974). Television began in the Sudan in 1962, with the inauguration of a low-power transmitter in Umdurman, built with the assistance of the Federal Republic of Germany. The expansion of television facilities was delayed due to the lack of funds and personnel. Later, the government realized that it must develop a national system for mass communication. In 1972, a second television station was introduced, soon followed by a third station in the Nile province. Color television was introduced in 1976. In 1978, the first satellite system, SUDOSAT, was established to link the country and to achieve national integration but faced numerous technical, personnel, and operational problems. The one national color channel broadcasts approximately fifty-two hours a week (Head 1974).

The development of radio in Syria started in 1946 when the Syrian broadcast organization was founded. Syria's radio broadcasting was greatly influenced by the country's union with Egypt from 1958-61. Syria's radio employees learned from the Egyptians the philosophy of radio propaganda. Syria's main radio services are the main program and Voice of the People (Boyd 1993).

As a result of its brief unification with Egypt, television started in Syria in 1960. In addition to the main station in Damascus, other stations were introduced during the 1960s in Aleppo and Homs, and these stations were connected in the 1970s to the main station through microwave links. The upgrade and expansion of the Syrian television system was strongly motivated by the availability of television signals from other countries, specifically Israel (with whom Syria was engaged in wars in 1967 and 1973) as well as Iraq and Jordan. In 1975, a decision was made to introduce color television in Syria (Boyd 1993). Television in Syria is directly financed by both the government and advertising sales, and most of the programs such as those featuring news, drama, music, and public affairs are designed to promote the political regime, as in other Arab states under mobilization broadcasting.

Radio started in Tunisia when the Tunisian and the French governments signed an agreement establishing the Radio Broadcasting Service in 1939. After independence, the Tunisian government began to develop broadcast facilities and initiated a plan to modernize the system, especially the Arabic service. Tunisia's radio is utilized as a tool to promote national development, especially in the fields of agriculture, industry and public health (El Gabri 1974). Television was not introduced to Tunisia until May 31, 1966, Tunisia's national day, and offered both information and entertainment. Programs are mixed, in French and in Arabic, and as in Tunisia's radio service, national development issues are given great attention. On November 7, 1992, Tunisia inaugurated its own international television network, TV7. TV7 utilizes one of the Ku-bands on the EUTELSAT IIF3 satellite. The coverage area includes all the European and West Asian countries as well as North Africa. The main objective for launching the service was to develop bridges to improve communication between Tunisian expatriate labor in Europe and the home country (Amin 1996).

Radio was introduced to the United Arab Emirates by British forces, and Abu Dhabi was the first emirate to introduce Arabic radio broadcasting in 1969. Upon independence, Abu Dhabi radio changed its name to United Arab Emirates Radio. The federal government advanced and promoted the service during the mid-1970s and also added an English language program. Television transmission started in Dubai as a monochrome system in August 1969 before the formation of the United Arab Emirates federation. After the formation of the UAE, Dubai's system became the national television channel owned and operated by the federal government. Color television was introduced in 1974. By the mid-1980s, the UAE had added a second national television channel heavily dependent on English programs, especially from the West. Dubai has played a very important role in the UAE in terms of broadcasting services and has offered commercial radio services as well as two color television services that are a mix of Arabic and English.

Radio was launched in Oman in 1970 and was expanded in 1973 with a national Arabic program. In 1980, an English program was added. Television broadcasting began in Oman in 1974 on one channel. Television programs include news, information, and cultural programs with great dependency on Egyptian broadcast television products (Boyd 1993). The Omani television program is mostly in Arabic language.

Radio made its entry to South Yemen, now united with North Yemen, in May 1954, and in August of the same year, Aden Broadcasting Services was officially inaugurated. The radio facilities were greatly expanded in the late 1950s with the help of the British government and, after independence, the Soviet Union. In 1974, a decree was issued establishing government control over all kinds of mass communication. Television was also introduced in South Yemen with the help of the British government. When the National Liberation Front took over power from Aden, the quality of the television service deteriorated due to the lack of technical support. The state has continued to operate a monochrome service, as its main focus is on radio broadcasting. North Yemen radio was developed in 1947. Sanaa's three radio stations broadcast only in Arabic. In contrast, South Yemen developed its radio services in 1954 and relied on the BBC Arabic service. Arabic programming was introduced through the Aden broadcasting service. Television was introduced in North Yemen in September 1975, when the government formally opened the Sanaa-based television broadcast station, and it was broadcast in color. In contrast, in South Yemen, monochrome television broadcasts started early in 1965 with the help of the British. Since the unification, many plans have been developed to integrate the electronic media of North Yemen and South Yemen and are being evaluated for implementation (al-Gamrah 1982).

CONCLUSION

Concern over the information age is original, focusing on issues of culture and religion. Islamic society in general and Arab society in particular are notably defensive of their traditions and values. The Arab world and the Islamic world are inseparable on the this point, and are justifiably proud of the great cultural legacy preserved through the use of the Arabic language, Middle Eastern customs, and media. Arabs have other concerns as well. Some countries are fearful of the political/religious repercussions of this influx of alien values. An anti-Western, Islamic fundamentalist reaction to the sudden easy availability of pop-culture products has been taking place for some time, and the predominant fear of the government is the destabilization of some Arab nations.

 Another political concern has to do with the Arab governments' sensitivity to perceived unfavorable news reporting by international satellite radio and television networks. The lack of skill within governments to cope with what is defined as negative reporting about Arab leadership and Arab governments causes jingoistic responses, such as the banning of satellite dishes in Saudi Arabia, or the refusal to develop telecommunication infrastructures to link Middle Eastern countries with the global information community. Arab media has responded to the cyber era by applying rules of censorship that are imposed by different nations. In the West, freedom of expression is a basic right to every citizen, and is protected at all costs. Within the Arab world, this type of censorship is easily tolerated, and even expected as a form of civic responsibility.

Arab media grows out of and serves the Arab environment. Arab society is slow to change and the media is a reflection of the political, cultural, and economic backgrounds of the Arab people. The Arab world has little or no freedom of expression under the current regimes and the Arab countries thus, lack a liberal heritage to start building their media systems in the new millennium. Many new factors are challenging the traditional setting of Arab mass media such as new communication technologies, satellite broadcasting, and intense competition. These factors will certainly give unlimited options to Arab audiences to access information and entertainment across boundaries. The more Arab media continue to present heavily controlled news and entertainment, the more likely it will become that Arab audiences will seek better content from transnational media. At the beginning of the new century Arab governments must rethink the financing and subsidizing of their media systems. Arab media do not operate apart from the world; globalization processes backed up by democratization and privatization will help stimulate the development of different private media models for the Arab governments to consider.

BIBLIOGRAPHY

Amin, Hussein Y. 1992. The Role and the Impact of Egyptian International Television Network During the Gulf Crisis. In *Media in the Midst of War: Cairo Reporting to the Global Village*, edited by Ray Weisenborn, 15-21. Cairo: Center Press.

Amin, Hussein Y. 1996. Arab Global Television. In *New Patterns in Global Television: Peripheral Vision*, edited by John Sinclair, Elizabeth Jacka, and Stuart Cunningham, 103-125. New York: Oxford University Press.

Amin, Hussein, and James Napoli. 1997. Press Freedom in Egypt. In *Communication and Press Freedom in Africa*, edited by William Jong-Ebot and Festus Eribo. Boulder, CO: Westview Press.

Amin, Hussein Y. 1997. The Middle East and North Africa. In *World Broadcasting: A Comparative View*, edited by Allan Wells, 121-143. Norwood, NJ: Ablex.

Amin, Hussein Y., and Douglas A. Boyd. 1993. The Impact of the Home Video Cassette Recorder on the Egyptian Film and Television Consumption Patterns. *The European Journal of Communications* 18: 77-88.

Azet, Mohamed F.M. 1992. *News Agencies in the Arab World. The Sun Rise for Publication, Distribution and Print* (in Arabic). Jidda: Dar Al-Shuruk.

[Boyd, Douglas A.] 1993. *Broadcasting in the Arab World: A Survey of the Electronic Media in the Middle East*, edited by Douglas A. Boyd, 2nd ed. Ames: Iowa State University Press.

Drost, Harry. 1991. *The World's News Media*. New York: Longman.

Foote, Joe S., and Hussein Y. Amin. 1993. Global Television News in Developing Countries: CNN's Expansion to Egypt. *Equid Novi: Journal for Journalism in Southern Africa* 2: 153-178.

El Gabri, Ali. 1974. Al Maghreb. In *Broadcasting in Africa: A Continental Survey of Radio and Television*, edited by Sydney W. Head. Philadelphia: Temple University Press.

al-Gamrah, Ali Saleh. 1982. *Management and Administration for Radio and Television in Yemen* (in Arabic). Tunis: Arab States Broadcasting Union (ASBU).

al-Halwani, Magy. 1984. *Arab Broadcasting* (in Arabic). Cairo: Dar Al-Fikr Al-Arabi.

[Head, Sydney W.]. 1974. *Broadcasting in Africa: A Continental Survey of Radio and Television*, edited by Sydney W. Head. Philadelphia: Temple University Press.

Head, Sydney W. 1985. *World Broadcasting Systems: A Comparative Analysis.* Belmont, CA: Wadsworth.

Katz, Elihu, and George Wedell. 1977. *Broadcasting in the Third World: Promise and Performance.* Cambridge: Harvard University Press.

Kazan, Fayad E. 1994. Kuwait. In *Mass Media in the Middle East: A Comprehensive Handbook*, edited by Yahya R. Kamalipour and Hamid Mowlana, 144-159. Westport, CT: Greenwood.

Labib, Saad, Hamdi Kandil, and Yehia Abu Bakr. 1983. *Development of Communication in the Arab States: Needs and Priorities.* Paris: UNESCO.

Martin, John L., and Anju Grover Chaudhary. 1983. *Comparative Mass Media Systems.* New York: Longman.

Mezran, Karim K. 1994. Libya. *International Journal of Middle East Studies*, 26(2): 305.

Mohammadi, Yahya. 1993. Algeria. In *Broadcasting in the Arab World: A Survey of the Electronic Media in the Middle East*, edited by Douglas A. Boyd, 2nd ed., 203-220. Ames: Iowa State University Press

Najjar, Orayb Aref. 1994. Palestine. In *Mass Media in the Middle East: A Comprehensive Handbook*, edited by Yahya R. Kamalipour and Hamid Mowlana, 213-228. Westport, CT: Greenwood.

Napoli, James, and Hussein Y. Amin. 1994. Press Freedom in Egypt. In *Communication and Press Freedom in Africa*, edited by Festus Eribo and William Jong-Ebot, 185-210. Trenton, NJ: Africa World Press.

Rampal, Kuldip R. 1994. Saudi Arabia. In *Mass Media in the Middle East: A Comprehensive Handbook*, edited by Yahya R. Kamalipour and Hamid Mowlana, 244-260. Westport, CT: Greenwood.

2

Saudi Arabia's International Media Strategy: Influence through Multinational Ownership

Douglas A. Boyd

Until the early 1960s the Kingdom of Saudi Arabia was seemingly unaware of the importance of domestic or international mass communication. This was before oil sales made this conservative Islamic nation both extremely wealthy and an international economic and political power. During the early 1960s the Saudi government showed initial concern about what it believed to be a radio propaganda threat from other states, primarily Egypt, and started building a domestic electronic media system. Starting in the late 1970s and continuing throughout the 1980s, the Kingdom became aware that it had to be proactive in media affairs if it was to foster its emerging regional and world-wide leadership role. During the 1990s the government and some of its citizens decided to be major actors in what was believed to be a powerful new international communication medium: direct satellite television broadcasting.

This study details the history of Saudi media developments, concentrating on events in the past decade that have made Saudi Arabia a major owner of Arabic-language print and electronic media both in and outside the Arab world. This research is important because through ownership patterns one can better understand the tactics and motivations of Saudi leaders who are the media owners, especially those who are members of or related to the royal family.

Historically, many nations, even those embracing democracy, have tried in some way to limit access of citizens to some information. Ithiel de Sola Pool in *Technologies of Freedom* notes:

> While the printing press was without doubt the foundation of modern democracy, the response to the flood of publishing that it brought forth has been censorship as often as press freedom. In some times and places the even more capacious new media will open wider the floodgates for discourse, but in other times and places, in fear of that flood, attempts will be made to shut the gates. (Pool 1983: 251)

Approximately a decade later, Robert Stevenson similarly said:

> Even the most optimistic assessments of the future would not exclude government efforts to influence the media in the West or government control of the media in other parts of the world, but the legitimacy of government control is gone. The proliferation of faxes, e-mail, DBS TV, desktop publishing and VCRs means that a government monopoly on information—never successful anyway—is no longer a realistic policy. (Stevenson 1992: 546)

This study also concerns communication technology and a particular country's desire to, on the one hand, embrace new electronic media as part of the modernization process, and on the other, limit citizen access to it, even though nonindigenous news and entertainment programming can no longer be effectively stopped from crossing borders. Should they wish to do so, Saudi citizens can see and hear material that, for whatever reasons, the government believes threatens its very existence or what it believes to be its Islamic cultural values.

RADIO BROADCASTING AND TELEVISION IN SAUDI ARABIA

The country's modern history began when Abdul Aziz ibn Saud captured the old walled city of Riad from the Rashid family in 1902; over the next thirty years, he, his sons, and his followers conquered vast sections of the Arabian Peninsula. In 1932 that land (bordering on Jordan, Iraq, Kuwait, Qatar, the United Arab Emirates, Oman, and Yemen) was proclaimed the Kingdom of Saudi Arabia, the only country in the world named after a family.

The two factors that have most influenced Saudi Arabian society are religion and oil. The Kingdom is the most conservative of the Gulf countries, adhering to the basic beliefs of a Sunni Islamic sect that follows the teachings of Mohammed Abd-al-Wahhab. The consumption of alcoholic drinks is illegal; public cinemas are not permitted; censorship is widely practiced; women—who veil from head to foot in public—are not permitted to drive; and the country's legal system is based on the Koran, Islam's holy book. In the 1930s, oil was discovered in the Eastern Province.[1] Petroleum revenue increased steadily during the 1950s and 1960s, but not until the rapid increases in OPEC-inspired oil prices after the 1973 Middle East war did the country accumulate enormous wealth and put into effect its remarkably energetic development plan. An important supplier of oil to the United States, Europe, and Japan, Saudi Arabia is the largest oil exporter of the Arab countries and has the largest oil reserves—261.2 billion barrels—of any country (Amirahamadi 1995). Estimates of the Kingdom's population vary because the government is sensitive about the large non-Saudi work force living there, but as of 1992 the total population was estimated to be 16.9 million; about 4.6 million are foreign nationals.[2]

By the early 1960s two developments occurred that pointed the way to future Saudi media developments. First, although the country was not yet as wealthy as it would become in the 1970s, Saudi citizens started to experience the emergence of a Western-style consumer economy. Second, inexpensive transistor radios became easily obtainable. It was not until the mid-1960s that Saudi Arabia had a viable national domestic radio service over which programming, adhering to conservative Islamic codes, could be heard. A major reason for the establishment of a national Saudi radio service was the attractiveness to Saudi listeners of neighboring radio stations. When Egypt's Voice of the Arabs started, and continuing through the 1967 Six Day War, the Saudi government had almost no radio defense. It had not planned a viable domestic alternative.[3]

Those living in the Kingdom during the 1960s can testify that one did not need a survey to document the popularity of Egyptian radio. The Voice of the Arabs and Radio Cairo could be heard in shops and residences through open windows, during the days before air conditioning became widespread. One clearly defined result of such hostile broadcasts was the realization that the Kingdom could no longer ignore the need to create a viable domestic media system, one that would become one of the best financed and most powerful (at least in terms of transmitter strength) electronic media systems in the Middle East.

Clearly, one of the motivations for the 1963 announcement by then-King Faisal that the Kingdom would start a television system was the realization that some type of home visual entertainment and information that the government could control was needed. Such an announcement was great "symbolic modernization," and practical, too, because many residents had seen television in Egypt, Lebanon, or Europe, and the prospect of having a medium that at the time some neighboring states did not was generally well received. Starting in July 1965, television spread from Jidda and Riad, the first cities with services, to other major populated areas of the Kingdom. In August 1993 the second channel started.[4] Both locally made and imported programming on this channel is only in English, and like the First Channel, it is available nationwide. Television very quickly became popular in the Kingdom with data showing television set ownership to be near saturation.

THE LOSS OF SAUDI GOVERNMENT INFORMATION CONTROL

Two incidents occurred that had a dramatic impact on the Saudi government's media policy. First, in November 1979 a group of 225 well-armed Saudi religious zealots who opposed the royal family took over Islam's most holy place, the Grand Mosque in Mecca (Quandt 1981). It took several weeks to dislodge the Mosque occupants, but by then the information damage was done. As the Saudi Ministry of Information had done in the past (and would do during the August 1990 Iraqi invasion of Kuwait), it at first said nothing, leaving popular Arabic-language international radio stations such as the British Broadcasting Corporation (BBC), Radio Monte Carlo Middle East (RMCME), and the Voice of America (VOA), and regional Arabic services to report on what they believed to be happening. RMCME was especially well listened to at the time and the Saudi government was so concerned about the impact of its reports that they jammed the station.[5] After the incident was over, the Ministry of Information rather skillfully used its domestic television service to examine the incident and the leader of the takeover in an attempt to minimize damage. The government's inability to control information from outside the country became a major source of concern.

Another event made it quite clear that in the increasingly modern electronic world, the Saudi government could no longer control how citizens got information. Videocassette recorders (VCRs) were an almost immediate success in the Arab world when they arrived in the late 1970s, especially in the Gulf states where there is a great deal of disposable income and where at the time there were few alternatives to government-run television. In Saudi Arabia most cassettes of Arabic-language and Western television and feature films are pirated. The efficiency of the cassette pirates is evident from the speed with which the controversial British/U.S. made-for-television film *Death of a Princess* (1980) reached the Kingdom. Purporting to detail the death of a Saudi Arabian princess and her lover for adultery, the film was flown to the Eastern Province the morning after its showing on British commercial television; copies were duplicated and made available in the Dammam area for sale the same day. Though luggage is thoroughly searched by Saudi customs authorities, it is possible for a VHS cassette to be carried through customs in a coat pocket.

In July 1981, the government reorganized by royal decree a commission established in the late 1970s to study and make recommendations about the Kingdom's information problems. Known as the Higher Media Council, it is headed by the Minister of the Interior (who directs internal security), rather than the Minister of Information (in charge of the previous body), in part because of the then widespread belief that it was Ministry of Information officials who were unable to control information and were thus the cause of unfavorable international press. The Council had the responsibility to:

- Outline a clear and well-defined information policy for both internal and external matters;
- Help in the development of radio and television programming by all available measures; and
- Help the Ministry of Information solve the problems hindering the higher information policy from reaching its objectives (Najai 1982: 58 f.).

The government realized, at least temporarily, that it must be more prompt in providing information about internal matters. An example of such a possible change had occurred earlier in the handling of a Saudi Arabian airlines accident at Riad airport in August 1980. Almost immediately after the catastrophe, the state radio and news service released information about the aircraft fire, which killed over 300 people. Film of the plane taken by Saudi Arabian television was fed by satellite to all interested television organizations and quickly appeared on European and American network television news. Subsequently, problems during the annual Haj ceremony in Mecca, such as the death of 1400 pilgrims in a tunnel accident in summer 1990, and the fire at a Mecca tent city for pilgrims that killed or injured hundreds in April 1997, have been handled in a manner that gave Western journalists access to information they requested.

Many members of the royal family and ranking government leaders knew they could no longer control incoming information. Western shortwave and mediumwave international radio has been popular since the 1950s; the videocassette revolution was unstoppable (despite strict government laws to control video rental stores); those living in the Jidda area could see Egyptian television transmitted from across the Red Sea and many in the Eastern Province could view as many as twelve television channels from neighboring Gulf states; and travel to other Middle Eastern and Western countries exposed a large number of Saudi citizens to Western visual material and information—the very "un-Islamic material" against which many in the government and religious community wanted to protect citizens. The increase in conservative Islamic activists in Saudi Arabia is of concern to the government. Their concern with indigenous media is reflected in the following paragraph of a letter submitted to the King in May 1991:

> Reformation of the mass media in accordance with the Kingdom's policy to serve Islam and to reflect the ethics of society, elevating its culture, and purging the media of everything not conforming to these objectives, with a guarantee of its freedom to spread awareness through accurate news and constructive criticism within the limits of the sharia. (Dekmejian 1994: 631)

Fifteen months later, the same Islamic group sent a "Memorandum of Advice" to Saudi religious leader Abdulaziz bin Baz that included this media-related concern. They wanted the government "to censor foreign materials, magazines, and television programs to prevent the dissemination of infidel and secular ideas and nude pictures" (Dekmejian 1994: 634).

At no time has the government attempted to keep communication equipment from Saudi homes. There are 6.5 million radio receivers, 5 million television sets, and 3 million videocassette recorders[6] in 2.9 million Saudi households.[7] Baskerville Communications Corporation and the BBC World Service International Broadcasting and Audience Research office estimate that between 500,000 and 700,000 Saudi homes can receive satellite television.[8] Each new communication-related technology brought a new challenge to the government, but none was greater than home television reception directly from satellites. Direct Satellite Broadcasting (DBS)[9] came to Saudi Arabia, but as it turned out, those providing the most desirable services were Saudi-owned companies.

Saudi Arabia, with a land area the size of the United States east of the Mississippi River, understood very early the value of satellites for communication. The Kingdom was an early member of INTELSAT and used leased satellite time in the early 1970s to connect its television transmitters. As noted in more detail below, both the inspiration and most of the money for ARABSAT came from Saudi Arabia (Abu-Argoub 1988).

The adoption patterns for television reception from satellites in the Gulf states are almost identical to the purchase of home videocassette recorders (Boyd et al. 1989); the first recipients were royal family members and the wealthy. Although Saudis had to get permission from the Ministry of Communication to own a dish, those with money and influence either did so or ignored the regulation. These home dishes were not DBS in the sense that we have come to know them—small eighteen-inch dishes that receive digital signals. Then, and to some extent now, these were relatively large rooftop-mounted dishes that could receive Western programming such as CNN International (CNNI) and U.S. Armed Forces Television. Initially, there were few of these, and thus the government paid little attention until August 2, 1990, the day Iraq invaded Kuwait. Although official Saudi electronic media did not acknowledge the Iraqi invasion for four days, 54 percent of those in the Saudi capital Riad who were interviewed by a research firm hired by the BBC said they knew about the invasion the day it happened (Mytton and Eggerman 1993). Those with access to CNNI from home dishes, or from Ministry of Information offices, could see unfolding the events leading to Desert Shield and Desert Storm.

Egypt's SpaceNet—that country's early satellite television service—played a role in the Gulf crisis by delivering information to Egyptian and other Arab military forces stationed in Hafar al-Batin, Saudi Arabia, and Sharja in the United Arab Emirates. The first Television Receive-Only Down-Link (TVRO) dish was installed in military headquarters, where programs were received and disseminated by cable to several locations. Additional TVROs were placed near where Egyptian forces were stationed in Saudi Arabia; television programs were retransmitted via a low-power VHF transmitter that enabled soldiers to watch television programs on ordinary television receivers (Amin and Boyd 1994).

SAUDI-OWNED NETWORKS: SAUDI ARABIA'S INTERNATIONAL MEDIA EMPIRE

London-based Middle East Broadcasting Center (MBC) is the creation of several wealthy, influential Saudi businessmen. Shaikh Salah Kamal— later to start satellite-delivered Arab Radio and Television (ART), an MBC competitor—owns many businesses in the Kingdom, including a

Jidda-based media production and advertising company. Since the beginning, MBC's principal owner and Chief Operating Officer has been Walid bin Ibrahim al-Ibrahim, not yet thirty years old when MBC started in September 1991; his connection with the Saudi royal family is his sister, King Fahd's wife.

Although Egypt was the first country to utilize satellite distribution in the Arab world with the hope that those with home satellite dishes would pick up the signal, MBC pioneered not only a service designed to be seen free-to-air directly by home viewers; it was also the first to do so on an advertising-supported basis. Whereas the Gulf war had motivated many to purchase home satellite receivers with the hope of receiving more extensive news coverage than was provided locally, MBC's launch date was before Arab world dish sales increased dramatically. One relatively early success for MBC were the agreements with the governments of both Morocco and Bahrain to rebroadcast MBC's signal terrestrially; this was especially important in the case of Bahrain because of the large, affluent audience in Saudi Arabia's Eastern Province just a few miles from this Gulf island nation. The interest of the Saudi government in having MBC available to home viewers can be seen by the negotiations that took place for the service's terrestrial broadcast from Bahrain. Rather than having MBC work directly with Bahrain's Ministry of Information, the retransmission agreement resulted from discussions between Saudi Arabia and Bahrain's Ministry of Foreign Affairs.[10]

At first MBC operated an evening schedule from a converted pasta factory in south London. These modest beginnings changed when British Prime Minister John Major presided over the opening of a purpose-built, state-of-the-art broadcasting facility in London's Battersea area on March 10, 1995, during which he welcomed MBC as a "very distinguished member of the international press."[11] Programming starts at mid-morning in the Middle East and continues until after midnight. There is a teletext service until the start of programming, which then continues with programs for women, children, and the evening offering of news and entertainment. The tendency in the Arab world is for state-run television to be unexciting, but MBC programming uses Western television production values—one of the advantages of being located in London.

Although MBC may be the best known entity of the al-Ibrahim ARA Group International Holding Company, it is not the only one. Over the years, MBC owners have acquired or started various media-oriented ventures that now span four continents. ARA owns United Press International (UPI); ARA International Production Company; ANA Radio and Television, which distributes Arabic-language news and information from Washington, DC; Spectrum 558 AM, which transmits Arabic programming in London and southeast England; MBC FM, which operates a twenty-four-hour per day radio service delivered from the MBC London headquarters via satellite to Saudi Arabia where it is rebroadcast nationally; ARA Media Services (AMS), a Jidda-based advertising sales and media representation agency; and SARA Vision, formed to operate the Multi-Channel Multi-Point Distribution Service (MMDS) wireless cable system in Saudi Arabia.[12] The proposed service (featuring a tape-delay system permitting censorship of objectionable material) could offer up to sixty channels when it becomes operational.[13]

The MBC FM service is unique to the Kingdom because, with the exception of American Armed Services Radio English broadcasts in the 1950s and 1960s and during the Gulf war, MBC is the first non-government radio service to be relayed from Saudi soil. According to a survey done in Saudi Arabia by the Pan-Arab Research Company in 1995, MBC Radio was the Kingdom's most popular foreign radio station with 35 percent of the audience listening.[14]

The short history of DBS television worldwide shows that such ventures are risky—startup costs are high and return on investment can be slow at best. Rome-based Orbit may well be the most costly DBS effort in the world, especially since it is unlikely that Orbit will ever realize a financial return large enough to recoup its initial investment of at least one billion dollars. Orbit had its origins in Hong Kong-based Star TV. Started by Richard Li, son of wealthy and influential Hong Kong businessman Li Ka-Shing, Star TV quickly became a major innovator of television throughout Asia. In 1994, Li sold part, and later all, of Star TV to Rupert Murdoch's News Corporation and it remains an important part of Murdoch's worldwide print and electronic media empire (Cox 1994; Gershon 1997). When Li was first looking for a buyer, one interested party was Saudi Arabia's Mawarid Investment Group, which is headed by Prince Khalid bin Abdullah al-Saud, cousin and brother-in-law of King Fahd.[15] The Kingdom's largest private-sector employers, Mawarid is privately held by members of the Saudi royal family. When they were unsuccessful in investing in Star TV, Mawarid's principals approached Alexander B. Zilo, an American Star TV executive who had worked in U.S. television before moving to Asia. Zilo said that he knew Mawarid's owners were serious when they called him and said that they were sending a plane for him to come to Riad for talks.[16] The decision to start Orbit occurred during a time when there was great interest in DBS in the Arab world and when MBC was the only major DBS competitor. Zilo's background at Star TV proved of great value to the planning of the world's first all-digital DBS service. Drawing on Star TV's experience of planning a digital subscription service, many of the executives and the senior technical staff moved from Hong Kong to Rome to be part of a crash program of guiding many former contractors of Star TV to get the service on the air. Planning started in September 1993 and the service was officially launched in May 1994 (Parker 1994).

Although Orbit at first provided a free-to-air preview channel, the service is now subscription-based because people in the Arab world, especially in the Gulf, had incomes sufficient to purchase the sophisticated Scientific Atlanta receiver, initially priced at $10,000, but later drastically reduced because of a lack of purchasers. This charge is in addition to monthly fees for a variety of program packages.[17] The service was originally planned to have up to twenty-four separate channels, transmission of which was made possible by seven-to-one digital compression, but that number has not been reached. At one time as many as nineteen were being offered, including rebroadcasts of two Egyptian domestic channels, ESPN (Entertainment Sports Programming Network), The Music Channel, The Hollywood Channel, CNN International, C-SPAN, and BBC World Service Arabic Television News.

Why the emphasis on Western entertainment programming in an area of the world that is perhaps most sensitive to such visual entertainment? The European edition of *Newsweek* quoted Zilo on this question: "We are going after a niche market with the most potent, affluent demographics in the world (...). These people travel a lot and watch Western television when they're away. When they come home, there's nothing."[18] Although Orbit had what seemed to be unlimited financial resources, both Western management and Saudi owners initially misjudged the service's customer base; they made a major error in contracting the BBC to operate an Arabic television news service.

The BBC's Arabic radio service was the corporation's first foreign language service and has been a popular one in the Arab world since it started in 1938. In a region where virtually all electronic media are government owned, interest in news from a credible organization such as the BBC is especially valued (Boyd 1993). Zilo had a relationship with the BBC because when he lived in Asia, Star TV featured the BBC's English-language World Service Television on one if its channels. Outwardly, the ten-year, $150 million contract with the BBC was a good decision because it provided the BBC with income for its commercial venture and gave Orbit something MBC and ART did not have: an independent news source from a service that in the Arab world was a credible household news name. Orbit did not foresee two important developments—a Saudi government ban on satellite dishes, and the move to London of Mohammed al-Masari, an outspoken fax-sending, electronic mail-using Saudi Arabian dissident. On March 10, 1994, just as the holy month of Ramadan was ending, the Saudi Arabian government issued decree No. 128, officially banning private satellite dish ownership.[19] Reasons for banning dishes include wishing to keep out Western news and entertainment, "un-Islamic" program material, and anything anti-Saudi. However, aside from isolated instances of the religious police having dismantled a few dishes, the ban has not been enforced and dishes as well as satellite reception equipment are readily available in the Kingdom.

The Saudi government, Orbit soon learned, had no interest in a Kingdom-based company that provided an independent news service. Alexander Zilo said that the eight-hour service became a problem when it started devoting time to al-Masari's specific objections to the way the Saudi royal family was running the country and that he had talked to the BBC about the coverage.[20] Coverage of al-Masari's activities peaked in late 1995 and early 1996 when he fought a successful court battle in Britain to stay there as a political refugee. However, the event that caused Orbit unilaterally to break its BBC contract was a *Panorama* program on the BBC Arabic Television News showing "secretly shot [in Saudi Arabia/D.B.] film of the preparations for a double execution by beheading" (Snoddy and Gardner 1996: 3). The demise of the Orbit-sponsored BBC Arabic Television News service on April 20, 1996, embarrassed the BBC, especially after it was revealed that no other company could take over the service. In the process of concluding a contract in 1994, Orbit had persuaded the BBC to permit it to own, for "tax efficient" reasons, all of the studio and editing equipment used for BBC Arabic news; Orbit would not permit anyone else to lease or purchase it (Richardson 1997).

Orbit was the first Saudi-owned DBS service to take advantage of excess transponder capacity to cooperate with another DBS provider. In 1996 Orbit started featuring some of the Star TV channels, and in January 1997 for $20 per month Orbit offered a package of Star Select channels customized for the Middle East: Star Select International, Star Movies, Star Sports, NBC/CNBC, and the Fox Kids Network.[21]

Of the three Saudi-owned DBS services, ART is the only one to be operated primarily from the Middle East; this is, in part, why relatively little information is available in the West about the multichannel satellite service. ART is part of Shaikh Salah Kamal's Jidda-based Dallah Al-Barakah holding company. As noted earlier, Kamal was a principal founder of MBC. Like the Saudi-headquartered Mawarid Group of companies (Orbit's owners), ART's electronic media interests are relatively recent.

Although uplinked to satellites serving the Arab world and Europe from Italy (where it is establishing a new studio and distribution facility), most ART post-production is done in Cairo because of this city's vast store of film and television talent and available production facilities. In 1994, ART started four free-to-air channels serving the Arabic-speaking world. ART's first four DBS channels were: ART I, a general channel showing films and television programs that appeal to a wide variety of ages and tastes; ART II, all sports; ART III, the children's channel; and ART IV, the film channel, featuring both Arab world and Western films that have been dubbed or subtitled. By mid-1995, ART had added another service, with plans for more programs as well as a subscription service.[22] By mid-1997, ART offered six satellite program services: Variety Channel, Sports, Children's Channel, Movie Channel, Music Channel, and ART Shopping.[23] ART has decided not to telecast any nonsports news, thus avoiding the type of problems with the Saudi government that Orbit had as a result of its former BBC Arabic Television News, or criticism that MBC's news is "Saudized." ART decided to partner the London-based outlet for Viacom's Showtime services. For part of 1996 and 1997, Via PAS-4, Showtime provided a multi-channel service to the Middle East: Bloomburg Information TV, Nickelodeon, Paramount TV Channel, MTV Europe, VH-1, The Movie Channel, and TV Land.[24] However, Showtime and ART decided not to use the same home delivery technology, reflecting the changing nature of technical and programming partnerships among Middle East satellite delivery services.

Although not directly involved in his own DBS business at this time, Saudi royal family member Prince Al-Walid bin Talal bin Abdulaziz al-Saud, a wealthy international investor, is involved in several media-related businesses, including Euro Disney and the television interests of former Italian Prime Minister Silvio Berlusconi (Rossant 1995). He is additionally involved in music-oriented business ventures with Michael Jackson and reportedly is the primary financial backer of ART's Music Channel that he had downlinked to his yacht (formerly owned by Donald Trump) while on vacation in the Mediterranean. In November 1997 he successfully acquired 1 percent of Rupert Murdoch's News Corporation, reportedly making him the single largest stockholder of that company after Murdoch and his family.[25]

Perhaps nowhere else in the world does satellite ownership, technology, and transponder availability play such a key role in the success of DBS services. The primary satellite carrier in the Arab world is ARABSAT, an Arab League-sponsored consortium of Arab states (with Saudi Arabia as the majority shareholder) that owns and operates communication satellites. Most of the first ARABSAT generation, known as the I-Series, had technical problems and a limited number of transponders. The new II-Series generation, starting with II-A, has twenty-two medium- and high-power C-band and twelve Ku-band transponders.[26]

ARABSAT continues to face competition from other satellite organizations, especially from INTELSAT, who in January 1995 launched the 704 satellite used by Orbit and PANAMSAT's Indian Ocean PAS 4 that has a Ku-band spot beam centered on Saudi Arabia.[27] Another major competitor is NILESAT, an Egyptian-owned communications satellite company operational since 1998.

DBS is too new to assess adequately its impact on viewers. However, a few studies have been completed and thus offer a preliminary assessment. Safran al-Makaty, Douglas A. Boyd and G. Norman van Tubergen found three types of Saudi male viewers: those wishing for a government satellite dish ban; those opposing DBS because they saw programming as a cultural threat that would have a negative impact on society; and those that believed that the Saudi government itself should use DBS to advance Islam worldwide (al-Makaty et al. 1996). Khalid Marghalani, Philip Palmgreen and Boyd examined gratifications sought from DBS channels, concluding that seeing news from different perspectives was an important motivation for viewing DBS (Marghalani et al. 1997). On the other hand, the most potent disincentive for viewing DBS was the fact that most DBS channels available to Saudis have a Western flavor that clashes with the tenets of Islam.

In 1997 the Emirates Center for Strategic Studies and Research released preliminary data from their 1996 media usage study of high school and college students. One finding from the United Arab Emirates is that younger people, especially when there are "incidents" in the Middle East, prefer foreign media such as CNNI, NBC, or BBC, over local outlets. In fact 75 percent said that foreign news services were more credible than local news.[28]

It is not only television via satellite that is of interest to those in the Kingdom. Washington, DC-based WorldSpace is the inspiration of Noah Samara, an Ethiopian-born U.S.-based lawyer whose company's mission is to make digital radio signals available to most of the developing world. Even with American and other venture capital backing, the high start-up costs of the organization, especially technical development and satellite construction and launch, have fueled speculation in Europe and North America that a wealthy Gulf state such as Saudi Arabia had a significant financial interest in the venture; WorldSpace's first satellite covers the Middle East and Africa.[29] During a spring 1997 meeting in Toulouse, France (where the satellite is being built by Alcatel Alsthom), organizers would not deny that Saudi financing was involved. *Newsweek* confirms that, "the Bin Mahfouz family, which handles the Saudi royal family's finances, has invested in WorldSpace" (Yang and Johnston 1997).

DISCUSSION

It is clear that satellite delivery of television programming to the Arabic-speaking world is a major development in the relatively short history of Middle Eastern electronic media. There is a tradition of Arab ministries of information wishing to control—or at best influence—information their citizens receive, and governmental ownership of electronic media. The ability of Arabs to receive a variety of television entertainment and news offerings directly from both within the Arab world as well as the West has the potential to eliminate government broadcasters as a major source of visual home entertainment. It is primarily because of the above-noted conditions that Arabs are the world's most enthusiastic international radio listeners (Boyd 1993). Television is accepted by media researchers as a medium that is more powerful than radio. Pictures, after all, are captivating, and programming that meets viewers' needs will find a willing audience.

There is a long tradition of Arab states such as Saudi Arabia attempting to influence what is written about them in the Arab world press. Especially during the years before the Lebanese civil war that started in the mid-1970s, the Lebanese press was known for allegedly accepting money from those states that wanted favorable newspaper coverage. Former Lebanese President Charles Hilu is said to have remarked upon receiving a group of Lebanese journalists: "Now that I have met you in your official capacity, may I learn what foreign countries your papers unofficially represent (...). Welcome to your second country, Lebanon" (Dajani 1977).

Two recent examples of the Kingdom's internationally distributed off-shore newspaper publishing are London-based, Lebanese-owned *Al-Hayat* (leased to a member of the royal family for twenty years), and *Al-Sharq Al-Awsat*, owned outright by another Saudi royal family member. The fact that London-based MBC, Rome-headquartered Orbit, and Jidda-located ART are owned by members of or those close to the Saudi royal family is not accidental. Nor is it coincidental that these businesses are, for the most part, located outside of the Arab world. They, like most contemporary Arab novelists (the most notable exception being Egypt's Nobel Prize winner Naguib Mahfouz), write from outside the Middle East because that ensures them freedom of expression.[30]

Visitors to the Arab world have noticed that the rooftops are becoming crowded with satellite television selections. The Saudi-owned DBS services are no longer unique and now compete with Western programming (via some of the Saudi-sponsored services) and DBS services from other Middle Eastern countries. Iraq is unique among Arab states in not having a satellite television channel because no company will provide it with transponder time. Even Libya has leased a satellite transponder for daily broadcasts (Warg 1997).

There is no doubt that all DBS services hope for a return on their financial investment. The question that continues to be asked is to what extent the Saudi government itself, possibly through the Higher Media Council, is involved with start-up costs for the services, and if this is the case, why a government concerned about outside media influence would position itself as defacto owners of foreign-based media outlets. The answer is, at least in part, to continue influencing Arab world information that is at least somewhat influential in promoting a positive image of the Kingdom. ART has decided to avoid nonsports news altogether and concentrate on multichannel family programming; MBC's news, although generally thought to be credible, is Saudized in the sense that the Kingdom is presented only positively—mention of foreign-based dissidents such as Dr. al-Masari or alleged human rights violations in the Kingdom are avoided altogether. As documented earlier, Orbit's short-lived contract for an Arabic television news service was terminated because the BBC did include issues that were sensitive to the Kingdom as it has always done on its short- and medium-wave Arabic radio service to the area. At the close of the twentieth century, Saudi Arabia has decided that it can most effectively influence television programming through either direct or indirect media ownership.

ENDNOTES

1. There are many sources of information about the early history of the Kingdom, for example: Williams 1933; Philby 1952, 1955; Benoist-Mechin 1958; Rugh 1969; Lacey 1981.
2. *Europa World Yearbook*. London: Europa Publications, 1995: 2638; *Background Notes: Saudi Arabia*. Washington, DC: Department of State, 1994.
3. For a detailed account of this Egyptian radio service see Boyd 1975. For a comprehensive discussion of the electronic media in the Arab world see Boyd 1982, 1993.
4. Personal communication of the author with Ali al-Najai, General Supervisor of the Second Television Channel, Riad, Saudi Arabia, February 12, 1983.
5. Personal communication of the author with J. Regnier, Commercial and Marketing Manager of RMCME, Paris, February 1, 1980.
6. *British Broadcasting Corporation. World Radio and Television Receivers*. London: International Broadcasting and Audience Research Library, 1996.

7. *Saudi Arabia*. Middle East Television. Shrub Oak: Baskerville Communication Corporation, 1995.
8. Ibid.
9. Throughout this discussion, the term *Direct Broadcast Satellite* (DBS), rather than *Direct-to-Home* (DTH), reception is used.
10. Personal communication of the author with Hala al-Umran, Assistant Under Secretary for Radio and Television, Manama, Bahrain, June 4, 1993.
11. John Major Inaugurates MBC's New Headquarters. *MBC News* 3, 1995: 1 f.
12. *ARA Group International*. London: ARA Group International (no year listed).
13. Personal communication of the author with Samir Attia, Business Director, International Operations of ARA Group International, London, July 25, 1997.
14. MBC Top in Saudi Arabia. *Middle East Broadcast and Satellite* (July), 1995: 6.
15. Partner Quit BBC Deal. *The Times*, April 10, 1996; Dispute Ends BBC's Arabic Service. *International Herald Tribune*, April 22, 1996.
16. Personal communication of the author with A. Zilo, CEO Orbit Television and Radio Network, Rome, January 3, 1995.
17. Ibid.
18. 20 More Channels, Inshallah. *Newsweek*, June 6, 1994.
19. Saudi Ministers Council. Authorization for Cable TV and Ban for Satellite Dishes. *Al-Sharq Al-Awsat*, March 11, 1994: 1, 4.
20. Personal communication with A. Zilo (see note 16).
21. Star TV Launches New Six-Channel Package for the Middle East Exclusively on the Orbit Network. *Star TV Middle East Limited News*, January 15, 1997.
22. ART: Arab Network for all Arab Nations. *Middle East Broadcast and Satellite* (July), 1995: 17.
23. ART: Arab Radio and Television. Satellite Middle East. www.sat-net.com/sat-mideast/broadcaster.html (February 1, 1997).
24. *The Time of Your Life*. Dubai: Showtime, 1996.
25. Arabian News Corp. buy-in. Sat-Mideast. www.sat-net.com/sat.-mideast (November 28, 1997).
26. *ARABSAT II-A Transponder List*. Herts: COMSYSTEMS Limited, 1996.
27. *INTELSAT 704 Launched Successfully*. Washington, DC: INTELSAT, 1995; PAS-4 Due for August Launch. *Middle East Broadcast and Satellite* (July), 1995: 6.
28. Local Media Urged to Step up Quality. *Gulf News*, January 6, 1996; personal communication of the author with Jamal al-Suwaidi, Director of the Emirates Center for Strategic Studies and Research, Abu Dhabi, January 5, 1997.
29. *Digital Direct Delivery to Portable Radio Receivers Worldwide*. Washington, DC: WorldSpace (no year listed).
30. Writing from the Arab World: Looking for Mahfouz's Successor. *The Economist*, March 15, 1997.

BIBLIOGRAPHY

Abu-Argoub, I. 1988. *Historical, Political, and Technical Development of ARABSAT.* Ph.D. thesis, Northwestern University, Evanston, Illinois.

Amin, Husein Y., and Douglas A. Boyd. 1994. The Development of Direct Broadcast Television to and within the Middle East. *Journal of South Asian and Middle Eastern Studies* 4: 37-49.

Amirahamadi, Hussein. 1995. *Oil at the Turn of the Twenty First Century: Interplay of Market Forces and Politics.* Abu Dhabi: The Emirates Center for Strategic Studies and Research.

Benoist-Mechin, Jacques. 1958. *Arabian Destiny,* translated by D. Weaver. Fairlawn, NJ: Essential.

Boyd, Douglas A. 1975. Development of Egypt's Radio: "Voice of the Arabs" under Nasser. *Journalism Quarterly* 4: 645-653.

Boyd, Douglas A. 1982. *Broadcasting in the Arab World: A Survey of Radio and Television in the Middle East.* Philadelphia: Temple University Press.

Boyd, Douglas A. 1993. *Broadcasting in the Middle East: A Survey of the Electronic Media in the Arab World.* Ames: Iowa State University Press.

Boyd, Douglas A., J.D. Straubhaar, and J.A. Lent. 1989. *Videocassette Recorders in the Third World.* New York: Longman.

Cox, Meg. 1994. One-Man Show: How Do You Tame a Global Company? *Wall Street Journal,* February 14.

Dajani, Nabil. 1977. *Lebanon: Free Press or Freedom of the Press?* Paper Presented at the Meeting of the International Association of Mass Communication Research, Leipzig.

Dekmejian, R. Hrair. 1964. The Rise of Political Islamism in Saudi Arabia. *Middle East Journal* 48: 628-643.

Eggerman, Mark. 1993. The Role of International Radio as a Source of News in some Middle Eastern Countries during the Gulf Crisis. In *Global Audiences: Research for Worldwide Broadcasting,* edited by G. Mytton, 179-200. London: John Libbey.

Gershon, Richard. 1997. *The Transnational Media Corporation: Global Messages and Free Market Competition.* Mahwah, NJ: Erlbaum.

Lacey, Robert. 1981. *The Kingdom: Arabia and the House of Saud.* New York: Harcourt Brace Jovanovich.

al-Makaty, Safran, Douglas Boyd, and G. Norman van Tubergen. 1996. *A Q-Study of Reactions to Direct Broadcast Satellite (DBS) Television Programming in Saudi Arabia.* Paper Presented at the Meeting of the International Communication Association, Chicago.

Marghalani, Khalid, Philip Palmgreen, and Douglas Boyd. 1997. *The Utilization of Direct Satellite Broadcasting (DBS) in Saudi Arabia.* Paper Presented at the Meeting of the International Communication Association, Montreal.

Mytton, Graham, and Mark Eggerman. 1993. International Radio as a Source of News. In *Global Audiences: Research for Worldwide Broadcasting, 1993,* edited by G. Mytton, 179-200. London: John Libbey.

Najai, Ali. 1982. *Television and Youth in the Kingdom of Saudi Arabia: An Analysis of the Uses of Television among Young Saudi Arabian Viewers*. Ph.D. thesis, University of Wisconsin-Madison.

Parker, Phil. 1994. Orbit Communications: Satellite TV for the Middle East. *Middle East Broadcast and Satellite* (October): 9.

Philby, H. St. John. 1952. *Arabian Jubilee*. London: Robert Hale.

Philby, H. St. John. 1955. *Sa'udi Arabia*. London: Ernest Benn.

Pool, Ithiel de Sola. 1983. *Technologies of Freedom*. Cambridge: Belknap Press.

Quandt, William B. 1981. *Saudi Arabia in the 1980s: Foreign Policy, Security, and Oil*. Washington, DC: The Brookings Institution.

Richardson, Ian. 1997. Anniversary of Arabic TV Closure. *Al-Quds Al-Arabi*, April 20 (English translation provided by the BBC's Office of International Broadcasting and Audience Research).

Rossant, John. 1995. The Prince. *Business Week*, September 25.

Rugh, William. 1969. *Riyadh: History and Guide*. Riad: Author.

Snoddy, Raymond, and David Gardner. 1996. BBC-Saudi TV Row Reveals Raw Spot. *Financial Times*, April 10.

Stevenson, Robert. 1992. Defining International Communication as a Field. *Journalism Quarterly* 3: 543-553.

Warg, Peter. 1997. Live from Libya: Ghaddafy on the Air; Saddam Next? *Variety*, January 13-19.

Williams, Kenneth. 1933. *Ibn Sa'ud: The Puritan King of Arabia*. London: Jonathan Cape.

Yang, Catherine, and Marsha Johnston. 1997. Media Mogul for the Third World. *Business Week*, June 30.

3

Restructuring Television in Egypt: The Position of the State between Regional Supply and Local Demand

Tourya Guaaybess

For a few years now, the Egyptian Radio and Television Union (ERTU) profited from the opportunity offered by new technologies: it broadcasts its own programs abroad through its first satellite network, the Egyptian Space Channel (ESC). Nevertheless, the diffusion of Egyptian audiovisual productions abroad far precedes the dawn of the modern satellite era: these productions have enjoyed great success all over the Arab world for a long time now. From the 1920s onward, Egyptian cinema dominated the Arab market and eventually became the second most important source of national income. No other Arab radio station could compete with Sawt Al-Arab (The Voice of the Arabs), created in 1956 in the aftermath of the Suez crisis. Its main chronicler, Ahmad Said, spokesman for President Gamal Abd al-Nasser, was famous for his rhetorical style and his ability to captivate his millions of listeners (Nasser 1990). Radio was then a mouthpiece of the pan-Arab and anti-imperialist Nasserite ideology. It helped in establishing Nasser's leadership in the region. However, the Arab defeat of 1967 brought the downfall of Ahmed Said and of

Voice of the Arabs. It lost all credibility when it announced the immanent victory of the Egyptian troops while they were actually withdraw-
ing. This example not only reflects the importance of the media but also
shows how they can be used by the regime.

Egypt's media heritage remains a rich source of audiovisual
production, which gives it a central role in the region, although Egyptian
television's part in this—whether in the form of exchanges or donations
of programs—is quite recent. At present, due to the advent of direct
broadcast satellites, Arab television stations are being forced to adapt to
the new trend, globalization. This is the object of our study. Although in
vogue, this term nonetheless constitutes an inescapable reality—the
availability of television networks on the world market, whatever their
geographical origin may be. This internationalization of televisual
exchanges compels the media actors to adopt appropriate strategies.

The ongoing changes in the Egyptian audiovisual sector can be
understood from three different perspectives:

- Firstly, the political: ERTU, a state monopoly, is a tool of state
  power, a mouthpiece of state policies, official Islam, Egyptian
  heritage, and good morals. Through what it reveals and conceals, television reflects a biased societal view.
- Secondly, the economic: the ongoing liberalization process
  jeopardizes the state's monopoly on television.
- Thirdly, the technological: without falling into "technological
  determinism" (Katz 1988) or limiting ourselves to this paradigm, we can hold that the spread of broadcast satellites has
  played an important role in the current changes. Cable networks and satellite channels bypass national borders and
  thereby widen the regional and international market for televisual products.

Our analytical framework will combine these three perspectives
in order to trace both the origins and development of the Egyptian audiovisual sector, and finally to identify the main features of its present evolution. Egyptian state policy regarding television will be examined from a
historical perspective and within a regional framework. There will then
follow a discussion of the causes and consequences of the failure of inter-
Arab cooperation that have led to a centralization of televisual resources.
Since the Gulf war, a new division within the Arab audiovisual field has
emerged: Egyptian television has to compete with a new category of
actors, namely private Saudi businessmen. Finally, we will focus on the
current restructuring of Egyptian television, a process stemming from
President Mubarak's policy of economic and political liberalization,
which has allowed new groups to participate on a private basis.

A CENTRALIZATION OF RESOURCES IN
THE AUDIOVISUAL SECTOR

The current emergence of the private sector is less a token of faith in liberal ideology than a response to the failure of socialism in all of its forms. With regard to television, the decline of leftist ideology can be seen in the rise and fall of developmental theories that praised the spread of this medium to Third World countries, but were later phased out by the prevailing contemporary discourse on free market economy. In the 1960s, advocates of economic and communications development, among them Daniel Lerner and Wilbur Schramm, held that the introduction of information technologies in the Third World would do away with north-south and urban-rural sociocultural gaps (Lerner 1958; Schramm 1964). At the time, numerous studies, many of which were funded by UNESCO and supported by local authorities, served to promote the new medium.[1]

The 1976 UNESCO General Conference in Nairobi announced the birth of the New World Information Order (NWIO), which was to complement the New International Economic Order. The NWIO aimed at rebalancing relations between the "new" countries and the developed ones which, "through the technical power at their disposal, have an impact on developing countries that is not only economic or technological but also psychological or social" (Bourges 1978: 11). At that time, the Arab countries decided to develop their own audiovisual network in order to free themselves from foreign dependency regarding communications and to acquire autonomous means of information.

The idea actually goes back to 1967. A few months after the Arab defeat in the Six-Day War, the creation of an Arab satellite was suggested during the meeting of the Ministers of Information in Tunis. In 1969 the Arab Radio and Television Broadcasting Union was created. In a well-documented and critical article, Hamdy Kandil, director until 1986 of the UNESCO Office for Public Information, recalls the context in which this decision was taken:

> The passionate campaign led by the Utopian experts of the 1960s to use satellites for developmental goals overwhelmed Arab decision-makers. (...) It was believed that satellites would broadcast the same television program and would deliver the same message to every Arab citizen, that it would eradicate illiteracy (...), that it would help peasants to better cultivate their land and that they would be able to harmonize cultures, tastes, and even dialects. (Kandil 1987: 660)

The Arab Satellite Communications Organization (ASCO), made up of the member countries of the Arab League, examined the project and decided in favor of the creation of the ARABSAT satellite system. The French consortium Aerospatiale was commissioned to build three satellites. Two were put in orbit in 1985 and the third in 1986. Saudi Arabia was by far the most important partner in this project, as it was the main shareholder in the operation in 1984 and ASCO's headquarters are located in Riyadh.

After signing the peace treaty with Israel, Egypt was excluded from ASCO, a move that deprived the satellite system of this country's substantial production. Other cooperation projects (MaghrebVision 1970; GolfVision 1977) were established (Ben Mohammed 1988), but their implementation was blocked by political tensions (Zeineddine 1994). In the end, pan-Arab regional broadcasting will remain on a low scale. The agreements have not led to total and definite cooperation and the ARABSAT, the "great tool for development, is not well mastered" (El Emary 1996). This failure may be explained by the relative ignorance of Arab decision-makers regarding satellites, the fact that resources are not centralized, shaky cooperation and, more generally, the pitfalls inherent to "technological transfer."

From the golden age of "television for the people" to today's "schizophrenic" television with programs shamelessly mixing business and development, from Nasser to Mubarak, things have changed considerably in Egypt. One reason behind this evolution is the country's adaptation to the global economic environment, and one of its signs is the current privatization process of the audiovisual sector.

Egyptian public television kept its monopoly on national production and broadcasting until 1973. Before this date, regional external demand remained limited due to the absence of television in half of the Arab countries and of color television in general. It is only from that time on, notes Naglaa El Emary, that an Arab market for "TV series-goods" developed (El Emary 1996). The private sector in Egypt, supported mainly by funds from the Gulf countries but relying on national professional know-how, eventually moved into the production of *musalsalat* (television series), because ERTU could not meet the growing national and regional demand. Nevertheless, the state retains control and imposes its rules through censorship and exclusive rights to export.[2]

Due to the Arab boycott of Egypt following the Camp David agreements, a number of television professionals emigrated and carried their business to the Gulf countries (notably, the United Arab Emirates) or to Europe, whereas others broke free from the state's monopoly by importing the equipment they needed for their own production (El Emary 1996: 253). Both trends led to an overproduction that ruined small national producers to the benefit of investors from the Gulf, all of which in turn led to a paradoxical situation: the Egyptian television industry, which could not fill its own programming, found itself in need of products from the private sector and ended up importing its own productions. In the beginning of the 1990s, another international event played an important role in reshaping the Arab audiovisual landscape, namely the Gulf war.

THE GULF WAR, GLOBALIZATION, AND THE TRIUMPH OF THE AUDIENCE

The Gulf war of 1990-91 had a major impact on the structure of both Egypt's public television and the regional audiovisual field. The American news channel CNN, by accustoming the national audience to a foreign product, was one of the main reasons for the considerable increase of dish antennas in Egypt during the conflict. The Egyptian as well as other Arab media became dependent on CNN for information, thereby vindicating the ideas outlined in the "Mac Bride Report" on the domination of the north in that sector. At the height of the Gulf war, ERTU broadcasted CNN's programs for a total of almost 800 hours between December 1990 and March 1991.[3] Egyptian television viewers were quickly seduced by the novelty and quality of the information of American origin, which contrasted starkly with that of ERTU. It was only later that the Egyptian authorities realized that CNN was actually attracting that part of the public television audience for whom national news reports had lost credibility.

Furthermore, during the conflict a number of transborder Arab television networks were created. Egypt played a pioneering role by introducing Egyptian Space Channel (ESC) in December 1990, a channel originally created for its troops posted in Hafr al-Batin, Saudi Arabia (El-Shal 1994: 68 ff.). Later, Saudis operating from London or Rome were to launch their own private satellite networks, notably Middle East Broadcasting Center (MBC), Arab Radio and Television (ART), and Orbit. They thereby modified the power structure with regard to the geopolitics of the Arab media and played a key role in the repositioning of ERTU within that framework. In September 1991, Walid Ibrahim, King Fahd's brother-in-law, launched MBC, the first independent satellite network, from London. MBC started by broadcasting its programs on the Hertzian network, but these were soon blocked by the Saudi authorities, which considered them to be at odds with the country's ethics. Founded in 1994, ART is owned by Sheikh Salih Kamil, also a partner in MBC. Finally, Orbit was put up by Prince Khalid bin Abd al-

Rahman al-Saud. His company broadcasts no less than twenty-eight television and radio channels from Rome.

Faced with an invasion of foreign programs, ERTU's reaction was to forbid the sale and distribution of decoders; but to no avail, as the owners of MBC, ART, and Orbit then decided not to encode their programs, a move that placed their programming within reach of any Egyptian in possession of a dish antenna (Table 3.1). Today, the increasing accessibility of the dish is setting the stage for a major change in the relationship between state-run television and its national audience in Egypt.

Table 3.1: Arab Satellite/Cable Television Networks in Egypt.

Channel	Year Introduced	Ownership	Languages
ESC	1990	Egypt	Arabic
CNE	1990	Egypt/USA	English
MBC	1991	Saudi Arabia	Arabic
Nile TV	1994	Egypt	English/French
ART	1994	Saudi Arabia	Arabic
ORBIT	1994	Saudi Arabia	Arabic
NileSat	1998	Egypt	English/Arabic

El Shal 1996; Napoli et al. 1995

Regarding the trend towards the globalization of television programs, it is important to recall that the phenomenon is still only affecting a small portion of the Egyptian population, namely those who own a dish antenna. In 1996, the number of such antennas was estimated at around 800,000 in the country as a whole, but they are spreading due to their gradually decreasing price; from 30,000 Egyptian Pounds at the end of the 1980s, the price for domestic-made antennas of 120 cm diameter dropped to 1,750 Egyptian Pounds in 1993. Dish antennas imported from Taiwan or Singapore are even less expensive. Also, the shrinking size of this type of antenna makes it more accessible, and some Egyptian entrepreneurs have even become involved in hand-made and illegal production (Alam 1993). And so the dish antenna is following a pattern similar to that of the transistor radio not too long ago.

In the end, the viewers are the ones greatly benefitting from the expansion of the market for communications. Television in Egypt no longer operates according to a logic in which a monolithic transmitter—the state—imposes its programs on a passive audience. Today, the television medium has an audience sold to invisible but powerful advertisers and to ubiquitous but absentee producers. The feedback effect of the new situation inverts the roles to the benefit of the audience, which can now choose to watch programs from foreign satellite networks instead of those shown on public television. In other words, the ideological relationship linking the transmitter, or state television, to the receiver is being challenged by a new economic relationship represented by the numerous networks presently accessible.

In order to survive, state television must be receptive to the audience's tastes and needs at a time when the gap is growing between what can be seen on the screen and the conservative discourse of the public realm. With the viewer no longer limited to national television, the state's policy of social control through audiovisual media is bound to fail in the medium to long term. The new outline of the regional televisual field compels the state to adopt a policy of seducing its audience and seeking financial support from the private sector.

A SECTOR ON ITS WAY TO LIBERALIZATION

Promoters of liberalization present it as a means to adjust the national economy to the world market, thus following President Mubarak who in May 1990 declared that Egypt would embark upon a structural adjustment program called "1000 days," funded for the most part by the World Bank. Although the program aimed above all at strengthening the private sector (Blin 1992; Clément 1992), privatization did not concern all sectors of economic activity, especially those considered strategic, such as the audiovisual sector.

The new outline of the Arab televisual landscape presents the Egyptian state, sole owner and manager of television, with a double challenge. Domestically, the state must win back the audience's trust in order to face the competition from foreign networks. Externally, it must be competitive on the regional level. A number of steps have already been taken in this regard: for example, the launching of a television broadcasting satellite (NILESAT), a call to private investors to finance the modernization of the audiovisual system, improvement in program format, an increase in the number of productions, and the building of a new studio. Because ERTU's activities are already weighed down by a budget deficit of $200 million (Annuaire de l'URTE 1994), its restructuring can only take place with the help of private investors interested in this opportunity to step into the sector.

The television advertising market, for example, is gradually being taken over by the private sector. The four main state-owned advertising and public relations agencies (Al-Ahram, Al-Akhbar, Al-

Jumhuriya, all three publishing a daily newspaper bearing their name, and the Egyptian Company for Advertising are the first to be affected by this competition at a time when the profits in this field are continually increasing as the consumer market in Egypt grows. The four combined control less than 50 percent of the national market for advertising, because advertisers are turning more and more to the private sector even though these public companies are offering more favorable terms of payment and guaranteed access to the major media (Napoli et al. 1995). Despite this trend, public advertising companies still have priority with regard to television. In this sense, they create an obstacle for private agencies, which are more flexible and better able to adapt to international competition. Tariq Nur, Director of Americana, one of the largest private agencies in Cairo, laments: "As long as the media are going to be controlled by what we call the public sector, and as long as there are weak private sector agencies, we will still be within Third World advertising" (Salim 1997: 16).

Another example is the building of Media-City, a huge production unit located in the October Six City near Cairo, a project in which ERTU publicly invited private investors to participate.[4] Its studios are expected to produce 6,000 hours of television programs annually to face regional competition and to fill the time slots of Arab satellite networks. Among the first productions to come out of these studios is the movie *Nasser 56* and the TV serial *Fursan*, shown during the month of Ramadan 1996.

In June 1990, Egypt decided to introduce a cable television system, Cable News Egypt (CNE). This stemmed from an agreement between ERTU (holder of 50 percent of the shares) and private investors who are partners in CNN and MTV.[5] The CNE initiative sets a landmark in the history of Egyptian audiovisual media: for the first time consumers can subscribe to an audiovisual service (Omar 1995a); in addition, CNE's programs are neither Egyptian nor Arab. Private partners are also entering the televisual scene by sponsoring programs. For example, advertisements for products such as Ariel and Persil detergents or Cleopatra ceramics can be seen in many variety shows.

Finally, let us emphasize that the current process of privatization is not totally contradictory to the state monopoly on television. The recent projects do not stem from a withdrawal of the state, but rather from an opening-up towards the private sector for funds. The challenge to the state's monopoly comes instead from political actors.

It is commonly held that economic liberalization and privatization lead to democratization. The argument is quite simple: a regime that has failed to develop the country economically will resort to a democratic discourse in order to legitimize its continued existence (Abd al-Aal 1992; Salamé 1992). However, is there not a contradiction between the process of democratization initiated by the Egyptian state and its declared intention to keep its monopoly on television? The state's official stand on this issue rests on the classic argument according to which television as well as all other media must not jeopardize national sovereignty or security (Nasser 1990).

Nevertheless, this argument does not carry much weight in an era when media broadcast across borders and the national audience has access to programs coming from outside the country. The political forces that are denied access to television, despite their claim to represent the numerous trends making up Egyptian society, are understandably the first to fight the state's monopoly on the media. Likewise, the opposition parties, for whom democracy only comes with free access to the media, work to protect freedom of expression that is likely to guarantee them political representation. For them, television is an affective means of diffusion, and, like radio, it is one of the most popular media in a country where the illiteracy rate is estimated at 50 percent of the population.

On this issue, the words of Ibrahim D. Abaza, Secretary-General of the Wafd party, are revealing:

> The political struggle between us and the government is lopsided. During the campaign for parliamentary elections, under the guise of pluralism each opposition party was allowed twenty minutes of air time on television. The state's monopoly on information simply kills politics and our aim is to do away with it since it is in total contradiction with democracy. Furthermore, the political parties and forces in Egypt are supporting us.[6]

To the limited definition of democracy as a "process which must lead to an alternation of leadership at the top which does not necessarily result from the physical disappearance (either voluntary or accidental) of the last leader" (Abd al-Aal 1992: 283), Fuad al-Badrawi, Deputy Secretary-General of the Wafd party and member of the People's Assembly, responds: "What defines democracy is alternation of power and freedom of expression."[7]

These criticisms seem well founded in view of the content of ERTU's program schedule. Despite their apparently pluralist nature, programs such as *The Newspapers Say* or *Round-Table* remain illusory platforms for the various political and religious trends making up Egyptian society. *The Newspapers Say* is a daily review of the national newspapers, including the opposition press; but the information given is carefully selected, and it often relates only to sports or miscellaneous news. "The Minister wants to give the impression that there is freedom of information," comments Abaza. The second program, one-and-a-half hours long and shown on a monthly basis, is hosted by two journalists from the Al-Ahram Centre for Political and Strategic Studies in Cairo. What we find here is, according to Pierre Bourdieu, a "falsely true" democratic debate where the opposition is invited to comment on a major political issue (Bourdieu 1996: 32 ff.). Abaza recalls:

> I myself have been invited to discuss the future of the Egyptian economy with a representative of the Tagammu [the leftist National Progressive Unionist Party/T.G.]. The show was totally restructured during editing. Out of four hours of recording, I had merely seven minutes of air time left and my opponent had eight. The remainder went to so-called "members" of the audience who were actually professionals of communication and government agents.[8]

In March 1995, Abaza personally sent a letter to the Minister of Information to get authorization for the launch of a private television station. In an official letter justifying his refusal, the Minister argued that "Law 13" of 1979 does not allow individuals working in the private sector to own television stations. Abaza then brought an action to annul the Minister's decision to the Council of State. All the opposition parties supported his request. In November 1996, he argued for the unconstitutionality of article 1 of Law 13 as amended in 1989 (Law 223), considering it contrary to articles 5, 8, 47, and 48 of the Constitution of 1971.[9] He also underlined the nonaccordance of this article with article 19 of the "Declaration of Human Rights" regarding freedom of expression. Considering the arguments raised to be sound, the Council of State decided to suspend the ruling and allowed the plaintiff to refer the matter to the Supreme Constitutional Court. The latter has not examined the case yet. Fuad al-Badrawi, Member of Parliament, has also brought in a motion to amend article 1 of Law 13 of 1979.

What remains to be seen is if these initiatives really threaten the state's control of the media. The project of amendment does not seem to, in view of the weak support base of the opposition parties. As for Abaza's claim, it might not lead to the anticipated result. Nevertheless, today the state's symbolic and economic control over the media is no longer safe from similar initiatives. In order to escape the constraints imposed by the state monopoly, individuals can launch their own private television stations and broadcast their programs in Egypt from abroad. Such is the intention of Abaza, who confides mischievously: "If Louis XVI had had a television set, there would not have been a French Revolution."

KEEPING AFLOAT ON REGIONAL WAVES
AND LOCAL WATERS

As the second millennium has ended, technologies are playing an ever greater role in the development of a world economy. Nowhere is this more true than in the audiovisual sector. Today, the Hertzian revolution has been supplanted by the advent of the satellite era. National markets are no longer sheltered from foreign competition in the form of satellite networks offering an incredible variety of channels and programs.

This new situation presents the Egyptian state with a triple challenge: economic, cultural, and political. On the economic level, the Egyptian government, although keen on retaining control over the national media, has adopted a strategy halfway between liberalization and privatization. Recent projects stemming from the current restructuring of the audiovisual sector have been carried out with the financial support of private investors. With regard to culture, the "regionalization" of Arab television productions is giving rise to two trends: the imprint of the local on the global in terms of diffusion, and the reshaping of the local according to the global in terms of production.

The plurality of discourses now available to citizens through foreign satellite channels is currently opening the door to a third type of challenge, this one more directly political. Taking the government's talk on democracy at face value, various groups from civil society are claiming their right to have more of a voice in the national media, either by means of increased air time on public-owned media or through outright ownership of private television and radio stations. With regard to television in particular, it remains to be seen how long and to what extent the Egyptian government will be able to at once open up the sector economically and keep political liberalization at bay.

APPENDIX: AN OVERVIEW OF EGYPTIAN TELEVISION

The birth of Egyptian television is marked by the launching of its first channel (Channel 1) on July 21, 1960. Aimed at the general public, it broadcasted three hours of programs daily. The second channel (Channel 2) appeared one year later and aired mostly foreign programs. The third channel, culture-oriented and focusing on urban areas, was launched on October 13, 1962. The total volume of programs was then twenty hours daily. In 1967, one channel (Channel 2) was shut down and the two others remained in operation: the main program schedule is made up of local and Arab productions; Channel 2, which broadcasts

most of the imported shows, reflects a desire to open Egyptian television
to the outside world.

This national coverage was later complemented by a regional
one that sought to offer programs closer to their audience. Thus six
regional channels (Table 3.2) were created, all of which are received in
the Greater Cairo area and in the governorates of Giza and Qaliubiya:

Table 3.2: Egyptian Television Channels.

Channel	Year Created	Main Area Covered	Broadcast Hrs/Day
Channel 1	1960	Egypt	24
Channel 2	1961	Egypt	21
Channel 3	1962-67/1985-	Greater Cairo and bordering areas	15
Channel 4	1988	Suez Canal	12
Channel 5	1990	Alexandria area	13
Channel 6	1994	Delta	11
Channel 7	1994	Upper Egypt	12
Channel 8	1995	Middle Egypt	4

There are also two satellite channels. The first, Egyptian Space Channel
(ESC), was founded in 1990 during the Gulf war and was originally created for the Egyptian troops posted in Hafr al-Batin, Saudi Arabia: it
broadcasts twenty-four hours a day in Arabic (ESC produces 20 percent
of its programs, 80 percent of which is originally produced for national
television (El-Shal 1994)). The second one, Nile TV, began operating in
May 1994 with a daily program schedule of six hours or nine hours during the month of Ramadan. In contrast to ESC, its programs are only in
English (four hours) or French (two hours). Finally, Egypt launched
Cable News Egypt (CNE), a charged-for and therefore less accessible
cable television network that offers viewers seven channels. NILESAT,
an Egyptian broadcasting satellite, was launched in 1998.

All combined, the channels broadcast for a daily total of 137
hours, not including commercials, which were introduced on television
in the 1970s and are continually increasing in terms of air time.
Furthermore, video production is rapidly growing at the expense of film
production: since 1980, ERTU has access to video production studios
where popular television series are made.

In 1976, color television made its debut in Egypt after the adoption of the French standard SECAM which was replaced in 1992 by the
PAL standard. Currently, most of Egypt's inhabitants have access to

television since this entertainment medium is of a collective nature and television screens are found in many public venues (including the subway). In 1995 there were 12 million television sets for a total population of approximately 60 million.

In July 1970, an official decree put all radio and television stations under the authority of the Egyptian Radio and Television Union (ERTU). Although the Nasser era witnessed the spread of such stations, the following period brought no major change. In 1989, an amendment to Law 223 from 1969 reasserted that ERTU was the sole body allowed to create and own radio and television stations. The national media come under the authority of the Ministry of Information, which is currently headed by Safwat al-Sharif. ERTU is a large organization managed by a weighty and slow-moving administration. It is also a huge building called Maspero in honor of the French archeologist of the same name and topped by a tower that in 1994 housed 22,606 employees divided among ten specialized sectors.

ENDNOTES

1. Bourges 1978; *Many Voices, One World*, International Commission for the Study of Communication Problems. London: Kogan Page, 1980.
2. For ERTU, the Gulf market is by far the most important regarding the sale of television series (76 percent of its revenues for 1991).
3. These hours are divided up as follows: 100 in December 1990, 200 in January 1991, 224 in February 1991, and 248 in March 1991 for a total of 772 hours. Weisenborn 1992.
4. Media-City aims to be the largest film production site after Universal Studios. See Omar 1995b; Ayad 1996.
5. According to the contract, ERTU's chief executive officer also manages CNE, which has four members of ERTU (out of a total of seven members) on its board of directors.
6. Personal communication with the author, Cairo, April 16, 1997.
7. Personal communication with the author, Cairo, April 20, 1997.
8. Personal communication with the author, Cairo, April 16, 1997. See also Dessouki 1997a, 1997b.
9. Article 5 allows multipartisanism, article 8 guarantees equal opportunity for all citizens, article 47 protects freedom of expression, and article 48 freedom of the press.

BIBLIOGRAPHY

Abd al-Aal, Mustafa. 1992. Légitimation du pouvoir et démocratisation en Égypte. In *Démocratie et démocratisations dans le monde arabe*, Centre d'études et de documentation économique, juridique et sociale (CEDEJ), 283-289. Cairo: CEDEJ.

Alam, Hasan. 1993. The Next Threat on the Dish (in Arabic). *Akhir Saa*, August 18.

Ayad, Christophe. 1996. Au Caire, télécoran contre écrans sataniques. *L'expansion*, July 25.

Ben Mohammed, Mohammed. 1988. Étude critique de la coopération interarabe par les moyens audiovisuels: de MaghrebVision à Arabsat. Ph.D thesis, University of Paris II.

Blin, Louis. 1992. Le programme de stabilisation et d'ajustement structurel de l'économie égyptienne. *Egypte/Monde Arabe* 9: 13-47.

Bourdieu, Pierre. 1996. *Sur la télévision*. Paris: Liber Éditions.

Bourges, Hervé. 1978. *Décoloniser l'information*. Paris: Éditions Cana.

Clément, Françoise. 1992. Genèse d'une réforme: du disours à la réalité. *Egypte/Monde Arabe* 9: 103-165.

Dessouki, Ibrahim. 1997a. "No, They Will not Learn" (in Arabic). *Al-Wafd*, April 3.

Dessouki, Ibrahim. 1997b. The Opposition and Television (in Arabic). *Al-Wafd*, April 17.

El Emary, Naglaa. 1996. L'industrie du feuilleton télévisé égyptien à l'ère des télévisions transfrontières. *Revue Tiers Monde* 146: 251-262.

El Shal, Ensirah. 1994. *Satellite Television Channels in the Third World* (in Arabic). Cairo: Dar Al-Fikr.

El Shal, Enshirah. 1996. Introduction à la télévision égyptienne: Quelques repères chronologiques. *Revue Tiers Monde* 146: 249-250.

Kandil, Hamdy. 1987. Le satellite d'Aladin. Le système de communication du satellite arabe. *Revue Tiers Monde* 111: 659-670.

Katz, Elihu. 1988. La recherche en communication depuis Lazarsfeld. *Hermes* 4: 77-95.

Lerner, Daniel. 1958. *The Passing of Traditional Society. Modernizing the Middle East*. New York: Free Press.

Napoli, James J., Hussein Y. Amin, and Luanne R. Napoli. 1995. Privatization of the Egyptian Media. *Journal of South Asian and Middle Eastern Studies* 4: 39-57.

Nasser, Munir K. 1990. Egyptian Mass Media under Nasser and Sadat. *Journalism Monographs* 124: 1-26.

Omar, Nadia H. 1995a. Egypt Reaches into Space. *Business Monthly* (Egypt) (July): 6-14.

Omar, Nadia H. 1995b. Media City: Egypt's Hollywood. *Business Monthly* (Egypt) (July): 16-18.

Salamé, Ghassan. 1992. Sur la causalité d'un manque: pourquoi le monde arabe n'est-il pas démocratique. In *Démocratie et démocratisations dans le monde arabe*, Centre d'études et de documentation économique, juridique et sociale (CEDEJ), 49-79. Cairo: CEDEJ.

Salim, Yasmin. 1997. Competition Shakes Egypt's Ad Industry. *Middle East Times*, March 21-27.

Schramm, Wilbur L. 1964. *Mass Media and National Development. The Role of Information in the Developing Countries*. Stanford: Stanford University Press.

Weisenborn, Ray E. 1992. Cool Media, The Gulf War and Then ... CNN. In *Media in the Midst of War*, edited by Ray E. Weisenborn, 3-13. Cairo: Adham Center Press.

Zeineddine, Ahmed. 1994. Dessine-moi un satellite. *Arabies* (November): 53-57.

4

Freedom of the Press in Jordanian Press Laws 1927-1998

Orayb Aref Najjar

In an editorial comment on the Jordanian government's plan to enact the 1997 temporary press law, *Al-Sabil* Islamist paper compared working under the new restrictions to being required to "move between one raindrop and another without getting wet" or else be punished.[1] That sentiment expressed the feelings of journalists who have weathered the tumultuous press changes enacted between 1988 and 1998, as well as by the veterans of the 1950s, 1960s and 1970s press laws.

This study argues that the current status of the Jordanian press law will be understood more clearly if it is compared to previous press laws and viewed in a historical context.[2] Comparison among different press laws over time suggests that even though Jordan's move towards press freedom has not been linear (from repressive to liberal), the press has become more liberal over time due to local, regional, and international developments and because of the advent of new communication technology that was embraced by the Jordanian public. The analytical framework used to compare laws concentrates on four areas:

1. The local, regional, and international political context necessary for understanding the impetus behind the promulgation
   of various press laws: Pete Moore suggests that this context
   needs to be taken into account in the Arab world where external pressures have played "key roles in setting and altering
   the environment (both positively and negatively) in the struggle toward democratization" (Moore 1994: 43).
2. The location of power exemplified in the relationship of the
   press to the government and the judiciary: Legal scholar Lucas
   Powe, Jr., notes that "Sovereignty may seem abstract, but real
   issues such as who makes the laws—and therefore what
   laws—turn on where sovereignty is located" (Powe, Jr. 1991:
   302; Wood 1969: 132). The need to examine the role of the judiciary is also guided by the notion that "Law grants power a
   meaningful status of authority and power grants law a factual
   foundation of enforcement" (Rotenstreich 1988: 43). It is also
   true that legitimacy enhances a ruler's authority (Friedrich
   1958: 94) and the quest for legitimacy sometimes hinders
   rulers from enacting repressive laws.
3. Financial control of the press: The need to examine the
   changes in funding practices and financial requirements
   imposed on the Jordanian press is dictated by the fact that different types of funding impose different constraints on the
   press (Yodelis 1975). Herbert Altschull, among others, asserts
   that the content of the press appears to be directly correlated
   with the interest of those who finance it (Altschull 1995: 374).
4. Technological developments in Jordan and the rest of the
   world: The need to examine the effect of technology on press
   law is dictated by the fact that Jordanian officials are well
   aware of the fact that Jordanians have access to other channels
   of communication and that the government needs to factor
   that access into its decision-making process.

Jordan repealed the martial law imposed in 1967 only on July 7, 1991
(Hawatmeh 1991: 13), and an examination of press freedom is especially
important in this era of new openness. In the post-martial law era,
Islamists vie for political influence with secularists, and the opponents of
peace with an Israel that still occupies Arab land struggle to express
their concerns. The presence of a large Palestinian population in Jordan
placed Jordan at the center of the storm in the 1948 Arab-Israeli war, in
the 1967 war, during and after the 1970 PLO-Jordanian struggle, and
during the 1987 Palestinian uprising. As will be illustrated below, these
events have influenced press legislation. Furthermore, the ongoing

peace negotiations between Arabs and Israelis continue to be especially stressful on the Jordanian polity. Thus, these political developments provide a backdrop for the political Jordanian theater.

JORDANIAN PRESS LAWS OF 1927-1950

When the Emirate was established in 1921, it relied on publications imported from Palestine, Syria, and Egypt.[3] When the first government publication, the weekly newspaper *Al-Sharq Al-Arabi* (The Arab East), appeared in 1923, it published official announcements, government legislation, and regulations.[4] The British formally recognized the Emirate of Transjordan on May 15, 1923 as a national state prepared for independence. The emir [prince] was to rule Transjordan with the help of a constitutional government and British advisors (Salibi 1983: 87-88, 93).

The first amended press law, called "Instructions of the Publications Department and the Official Gazette," of March 12, 1927 lacked detail because it was written mainly with that official publication in mind. The length of the amendments to the 1927 and 1928 laws (six and fifteen lines respectively) attests to their general nature. The fact that *rais al-nuthar*[5] signed the 1927 amendment to the press law and that several ministers signed the 1928 law indicates that authority over the press was still diffuse and did not rest with a specialized body like the Ministry of Information. The fact that the role of the court was not spelled out suggests that the lack of government-press conflict in the modest private press of the time made the detailed description of restrictions unnecessary. By 1933, however, administrative authority over the press became more focused; only the Prime Minister signed the press law (Appendix 1/Table 4.1).

The fear of German and Ottoman influence on Jordan during the Second World War led the government to base the 1939 and the 1945 laws on the 1935 Defense of East Jordan Law. This law gave the government extra powers to waive constitutional guarantees, censor the press inside Jordan, control the entry of publications and mail from abroad, and specify penalties (Appendix 1/Table 4.1).[6]

When Israel was established over former Palestine in 1948, 600,000 to 700,000 Palestinian refugees streamed into the East Bank of Jordan (Flapan 1987: 83). The press law, Defense Regulation No. 5 for the Year 1948, signed by Tawfik Abul Huda, Prime Minister and Minister of Defense, contained more stringent restrictions on press content than previous laws, reflecting war conditions as well as the changed demographic realities in Jordan (Appendix1/Table 4.1) (Shreim 1984: 41).

The 1948 exodus of Palestinian refugees from Palestine into Jordan and the newspapers they brought with them from Jaffa[7] changed the political priorities of the press. The debate after 1948 focused on the identity of Palestinian refugees who were given Jordanian citizenship,[8] on who represents them, on whether different Arab countries, Britain and the United States, China and the Soviet Union were friends or foes.

There was no question that the government wielded administrative and legislative authority over the press. But the press continued to set the political agenda for discussion in the Kingdom. Questions concerning the competence of the Arab defense of Palestine and the role of Britain (faulted by Palestinians for its role in the creation of Israel) were major themes in the Palestinian-owned and run press.[9] On August 1, 1949 two journalists were arrested for accusing Arab leaders of incompetence and intrigues that led to the military defeat of Arabs by Jews in 1948. Newspapers lobbied for more freedom. *Falastin* said that "Tight restrictions and severe censorship (...) create a climate of indolence among people and stifle their creativity."[10] One editorial writer called on "pens" to do their duty freely "to identify the aims people should pursue, and prepare them for practicing freedom or sacrificing for it. (...) Freeing freedom for the sincere and the capable (...) in the context of good democratic rule is a service to the country."[11]

The West Bank was officially annexed to Jordan on April 24, 1950. Palestinians were divided on whether to support the unification. But they were being integrated into the political machinery of the country, whereas this was not happening elsewhere in the Arab world. Activists took advantage of the free Jordanian parliamentary elections in 1950 and made gains that allowed them to join the government (Aruri 1972: 93).

The speech King Abdullah delivered to the second Parliament on April 24, 1950 was liberal in tone. The king promised to revise the constitution to provide for ministerial responsibility. The government set May 11, 1950 for the formation of a judiciary committee to consider unifying the laws and revising the constitution. But when the government was criticized over its military dependence on Britain, and over the wisdom of concluding the 1949 Rhodes Agreement with Israel, it censored the press and the record of the parliamentary debates and ordered the closing of five newspapers (Aruri 1972: 101 f.).

THE COLD WAR AND THE PRESS LAWS OF THE 1950s

Journalist and political commentator Lamis Andoni observes that until recently, the literature of the political groups—except the Muslim

Brotherhood—referred to the Hashemite Kingdom as "a British creation" and called for the establishment of a "national democratic regime in Jordan" (Andoni 1991: 13). Never was the struggle for legitimacy of the ruling authority more intense than in the 1950s. That era saw Palestinian refugees adjusting to their new status in the Kingdom amid the rise of Arab nationalism and the Cold War superpower rivalry (Wright 1951: 453-54, 456). The press was at the heart of the struggle.

The Cold War complicated press-government relations in Jordan. There were some who claimed that such liberalization would open the door to communism.[12] But there were others who called for press freedom and warned against replacing British colonialism with Western influence of any kind.[13] In the end, anticommunist forces prevailed. Two new laws regulated the press of the 1950s: The "Law of Fighting Communism" No. 91, 1953, which made joining the Jordanian Communist Party and the possession of communist literature illegal,[14] and Law of Publications No. 79, 1953, which required newspapers to apply for new licenses under stricter conditions (Appendix 2/Table 4.2). The position of head of the Publications Department was established in 1953 and was tied to the Prime Minister's office, again signifying increased media specialization and government control.

The advent of Gamal Abd al-Nasser, the popular president of Egypt, and his frank Arab nationalism, challenged British hegemony in Jordan, and encouraged the opposition. The Jordanian government reacted to that threat by reviving the Defense Regulations on August 18, 1954, allowing it to cancel newspaper licenses without the necessity of showing cause, to dissolve political parties, and prohibit political assemblies. The government immediately used those new regulations to suspend six opposition journals (Satloff 1994: 95). The 1954 elections were thought to be falsified (Aruri 1972: 111 f.).

In the 1953 press law, administrative authority was vested in the minister of justice and the Prime Minister, whereas in the 1955 law, authority was vested in the Prime Minister, the Ministers of Interior, Justice, and Education, reflecting the government's desire to have the Minister of Education control school wall publications (newspaper tacked on a bulletin board between classrooms), and the Minister of the Interior control demonstrations. In 1953, the Prime Minister's rejection of a license to publish was subject to court review. In 1955 it was not (Appendix 2/Table 4.2). Both laws required printing presses to be licensed independently and also required the owners to supply samples of their typefaces, and to report any changes.[15] Articles regulating printing presses were designed to prevent regular presses from printing secret pamphlets. Both the 1953 and 1955 laws introduced sections spelling out prohibited material, and the government acted on those articles. Six newspapers were closed for six months in early 1955. On December 20, 1955, East Jerusalem newspapers went on strike to protest censorship (Haurani and al-Tarawnah 1986: 159). The government enforced a curfew until January 14, 1956 and imposed press censorship on January 23, 1956 until February 5, when it was officially lifted.

A Jordanian government publication described the press of the 1950s as "flourishing," with more than forty newspapers and magazines in print. But the publication added that political parties "took advantage of [i.e., abused/O.N.] press freedom and laws of that time." It explained that many of the publications were party rather than mass publications. That is why banning them was "the natural fruit" of press delinquency. The government publication accused the press of the 1950s of being "non-Jordanian, with loyalty to foreign ideologies," an allusion to the communist and Arab nationalist publications of that period.[16] In the 1953 and 1955 laws, the government gave itself the authority to demand a yearly breakdown of the budget and the right to order an audit to prevent foreign funding (Appendix 2/Table 4.2).[17] Jordan used the Ottoman press law and amended it periodically until 1955. Although Jordan gained its formal independence in 1946, it ended the services of the most influential of its British advisors only in 1956 and abrogated the Anglo-Transjordanian Treaty in 1957 (Pundik 1994: 301).

By October 26, 1956 results of the election of thirty-five out of forty members of Parliament indicated that the majority would be anti-Western. At least three were communists. The new government of Suleiman al-Nabulsi, the leader of the National Socialist Party, promised to respect the constitution "in text and spirit" (Musa 1986: 73). Al-Nabulsi allowed political parties and their press to operate and publish freely (Musa 1986: 77) despite the law that banned all political party activity. The Prime Minister rejected the January 1957 Eisenhower Doctrine, which promised aid to countries that fought communism (Aruri 1972: 134-36). Al-Nabulsi assured his audience at a rally that contrary to American government claims, there was no vacuum to be filled in Jordan, "The only vacuum is in Eisenhower's head," he said (Musa 1986: 79). Policy differences between King Hussein, who rejected communism both in principle and because Jordan wanted American aid, led to the ouster of al-Nabulsi. At a cabinet meeting on February 18, the King issued instructions that the press should not attack the Eisenhower Doctrine (Satloff 1994: 162). After the demise of the Nabulsi government, the ideological parties were driven underground or fled the country. Censorship was reimposed. All opposition was crushed (Aruri 1972: 150).

In 1962, the government rejected the demands of the Jordanian Bar Association to cease applying emergency laws and to introduce a new electoral law.[18] Jordan had maintained that stance over the years by arguing that with Israel occupying a portion of the Kingdom, parliamentary rule in Jordan was impossible. Another constraint in the 1960s was the competition between the PLO and the Jordanian regime for the loyalty of Palestinians.

THE EFFECT OF THE ESTABLISHMENT OF THE PLO ON PRESS LAW

The establishment of the Palestine Liberation Organization in 1964, in part to reclaim the control of Palestinian affairs assumed by Arabs in the mid-1940s, circumscribed the degree of freedom the Jordanian government allowed the press. About 60 percent of the Jordanian population was of Palestinian origin, and a powerful PLO would encroach on Jordanian authority (Haurani 1986: 95, 108). The Jordanian-Palestinian tension was reflected in the forced amalgamation of West Bank papers ordered by the government against the Palestinian-owned and run press of the West Bank in March 1967 and the introduction of government financial control of the press.

A Jordanian historian, Sulaiman Musa, explained that the position of the papers "was theoretically sound. They belonged to their owners." He added, however, that the government could not get the full cooperation of the Palestinian editors after Syria and Egypt experienced coups and turned their information organs into "trumpets of propaganda" against Jordan. The government introduced partial ownership into the law and the owners of the papers were forced into that arrangement (Musa 1986: 176). According to the March 1967 provisional press law, the papers had to be published by joint stock companies with a minimum of capitalization equivalent to $42,000, of which the government had to provide one quarter. That was the first time the Jordanian government consolidated its hold on the press through partial direct ownership. A reporter for the *New York Times* wrote on March 26, 1967:

> According to the Government, the law is intended to raise journalism standards and to establish minimum educational requirements for writers and editors. But the move is widely regarded as an effort to reduce the predominant journalistic voice of Palestinians. (Brady 1967: 20)

Before the law was promulgated, five papers appeared in the Kingdom. After amalgamating and meeting government conditions, only two remained (Najjar 1997: 64-65). Throughout that period, the government has controlled the entry point into the profession by dictating through licensing who is permitted to practice journalism. In the 1950s, persons who enjoyed immunity, such as members of parliament, could not be licensed as editors-in-chief (Shreim 1994: 149). In the 1967 press law, the editor-in-chief had to produce "a certificate of good conduct" from the intelligence services before being given a license,[19] an article that gave the authorities the power to muzzle the opposition.

The government regarded the growth of the commando movement in Jordan as a challenge to its authority. It closed the PLO paper *Al-Fatah*, which was published without a license in the mid-1970s. At the end of December 1970, it suspended the weekly *Amman Al-Masa* for a few months and withdrew the license of *Al-Sabah* two weeks after it appeared. Older publications were also affected: the government suspended the license of the *Al-Difa* (The Defense) daily in May 1971 and set up the Jordanian Press Establishment, which began publishing the daily *Al-Rai* (The Opinion) in June 1971 (Susser 1994: 158).

The tension engendered by the ouster of commandos from Jordan between 1970 and 1972 was reflected in the 1973 press law, which gave the power of press regulation to the Ministry of Information and the Department of Press and Publications. The ultimate authority rested with the Council of Ministers, which had the power to reject licenses and ban papers without court review. The 1973 press law also deprived the press of some of the legal guarantees it had previously enjoyed when it stipulated that the decisions of the Council of Ministers on licensing were not subject to review "by any quarter." The 1973 press law did not specify that the editor-in-chief needed to be certified by the intelligence services, but required printing presses to submit samples of their fonts to the ministry (Appendix 3/Table 4.3) (Shreim 1984: 141, 154, 177). The law also toughened punishment directed against those accused of incitement that endangers the security of the state. In addition, the new law reintroduced prohibitions against articles and information that libel the heads of friendly states, and forbade publishing political statements issued by embassies or representatives of foreign countries accredited to Jordan (except with permission).

Whereas the 1953 and 1955 laws considered the question of intent in publishing material "likely to endanger public security," the 1973 law did not take intent into account. Prince Hassan of Jordan explained that the designation of the PLO as the representative of Palestinians[20] led Jordan to suspend its parliamentary life and rely on a National Consultative Council as a substitute (Bin Talal 1984: 68).

In the 1985-1989 period, restrictions on political activity led professional associations as well as the Union of Jordanian Writers to act as the country's conscience in human rights issues.[21] They protested the government's proposed 1986 election law on the grounds that it did not respect the principles of the separation of powers and the rule of law.

Associations also resisted "normalization" with Israel because it continued to occupy Arab land. These policies placed them in direct conflict with government policy.[22]

Osama El-Sherif, editor-in-chief of *The Star*, described those days as "the black days of the Jordanian press." He said government frustration with the press reached its peak in November 1988 when it forced newspaper owners to sell them and let them be run by government-appointed staff (El-Sherif 1996). Journalists charged that quasi-ownership by the government of the four dailies made all newspapers uniform, and that the government takeover of the press was unnecessary, because it already owned more powerful mediums of expression such as television and radio.

THE BEGINNING OF THE LIBERALIZATION OF THE PRESS

Several factors combined pushed the country towards liberalization. Both government critics and loyalists saw the 1989 bread riot as an indication of the breakdown in communication between the people and their government and urged the government to liberalize. Laila Sharaf, former Minister of Information, said that after the bread riots, the new government was capable of understanding the implications behind the lack of national debate and would be taking the necessary steps to ensure the "natural flow of communications" (Najjar 1989). The severing of legal ties between the East and West Banks of Jordan in 1988 paved the way for parliamentary elections. The elections of November 1989, the first in twenty-two years, encouraged debate.

The Islamists won one-third of the seats in parliament in November 1989. The Islamists' heavy-handed pressure to turn Jordan into an Islamic state whose laws are based on the Sharia religious rather than on secular law led the King to accuse them of "monopoly" (Andoni 1992: 6-7). The government realized the importance of letting other points of view be heard and repealed most martial law regulations that had been in force since 1967 (Hawatmeh 1991: 13). On December 11, 1989 the government reinstated the former elected boards of directors of the press companies it had taken over in 1988, and "froze" martial law in the same month.

Addressing the question of whether Jordan had a free press, *The Star* editor-in-chief El-Sherif observed:

> Compared to the seventies and eighties, yes the press is free. Compared to neighboring countries, yes the press is vibrant. Compared to western democracies, we are still learning to walk. (El-Sherif 1996)

After the Gulf war, the King felt he needed to find common ground for all political parties, including the fundamentalists. He chose to loosen restrictions on political life to ensure against the domination of any particular group such as the Muslim Brothers over others. In the short period in which the fundamentalists were a strong element in the government, their ministers alienated the population by attempting to segregate mixed schools and even ministry employees by gender, and to enforce a strict reading of Sharia Islamic values. The way to achieve such a consensus came through the introduction of the National Charter. The charter, drafted by thinkers representing all political trends in the country (including the Islamists), is a contract between the regime and the people. It guarantees a pluralistic system in return for allegiance of all political parties to the Hashemite monarchy. From that point on, as in all democracies, the opposition will oppose the *government* but not the *regime*—a very important distinction, especially in Jordan where the legitimacy of the monarchy was often in question.

The Charter was formulated and approved by a sixty-member commission made up of all political groups, and was adopted by a national conference composed of all elected officials in Jordan on June 9, 1991. Although the Muslim Brotherhood had five representatives to the Charter commission, and they all approved it, spokesmen continued to stress their opposition to "any charter other than the Koran." On June 19, 1991 the Prime Minister Mudar Badran was replaced by the more liberal Minister of External Affairs Tahir al-Masri.

King Hussein's letter of appointment to al-Masri made it clear that the time had come for liberal democrats to lead, based on clearly defined progressive and forward-looking programs. On July 7, 1991 Masri repealed most martial law regulations in force since 1967, making the liberalization, promised in 1989, a reality. Al-Masri secured the support of the biggest Jordanian coalition of groups, the Jordanian Arab National Democratic Alliance (JANDA). JANDA was given five ministries in al-Masri's government, making it the first time opposition groups have taken part in the government since the mid-1950s. JANDA stipulated that al-Masri pursue no policies that might infringe on the PLO, and lift the remaining security and legal restrictions on political freedom. The new Prime Minister accepted JANDA's terms. With this type of coalition-building, the issue of the legitimacy of the regime has come a long way since 1921 with the ratification of the National Charter on June 9, 1991.

But Jordan plunged into political crisis once again when fifty members of the eighty-seat lower house of parliament signed a petition on October 7, 1991 calling on the government of Tahir al-Masri to resign. It was widely believed that the twenty-five Islamist deputies and the three leftists (renegades from a larger group in parliament who were partners in the Cabinet) chose this time to embarrass the Prime Minister to show their opposition to the Congress, whose session they saw as an attempt by the King to sidestep parliament and to talk over its head to other representatives to the people in the quest for public blessing of the Arab-Israeli peace process. Ahmed Uwaidi, a member of the newly-elected parliament, described the formation of the committee as a ploy to bypass the Constitution. A coalition of seventeen detractors of the Charter calling themselves "the constitutional block" asked for the Prime Minister's resignation, and al-Masri chose to resign rather than have a showdown.

When the election law was changed to one-man one-vote in the 1995 municipal elections of July 11, 1995 traditional community leaders did better than other political parties, including the Islamists, in most constituencies. The Islamists lost in districts in which they had done well in 1989 and 1993. Thus, the government's efforts to curb the power of the Islamic movement appeared to be working, but the same law cut into the power of political parties, and so consolidated the power of the professional associations the King was trying to control. The "tough nut to crack"—the professional associations—had extended their role in Jordan to fill the political vacuum created with the banning of political parties in 1957, and they were very vocal in defending political and human rights in Jordan. For a fourth time in a year, King Hussein expressed his dismay with professional associations and the "yellow press." Ten of the twelve associations were controlled by the opponents of the Jordanian-Israeli peace treaty and had resisted normalization stipulated in the Jordanian-Israeli treaty through a strong antinormalization committee.

The Political Parties Law was passed on September 1, 1992[23] paving the way for multiparty elections in the summer of 1993 and strengthening democratic rights and public and individual freedoms (Hawatmeh 1992). The new openness led to an explosion of publications that ranged from the serious political to some scandal-driven weekly papers. The Publication Department's own records indicate that, of the publications licensed, eight were given to individuals, nineteen to political parties, fifty-eight to companies, and 355 to specialized publications (Musa 1997: 20).

THE 1993 PRESS LAW

Despite the friction between the government and the press over some articles of the law,[24] the 1993 press law was considered an improvement on older laws because it gave civil courts the power to judge breaches of

the law. Furthermore, whereas the 1950s laws barred political parties
from publishing, the 1993 law allowed them to publish their own papers
and exempted them from the financial deposit requirements imposed on
the commercial press (Appendix 3/Table 4.3).[25] On the other hand, one
condition that hampered the publication of a more vigorous party press
was financial: the Political Parties Law limited the contributions of each
political party member to the party press to 5,000 Jordanian Dinars
annually ($7,000). Given the fact that only three people in every 3,000
belong to a political party, the financial situation of the parties remains
weak and prevents them from taking full advantage of the 1993 press
law (Musa 1997: 5).

The 1993 press law renewed discussions between the government and the press over the issue of press freedom and its limits. It also
generated discussion on how to deal with this bold new press. Papers
like *Shihan*, a weekly paper that was being published in Egypt and
Greece, returned to Jordan in 1990 and tested the limits of the 1993 press
law. *Shihan*'s publisher Riad al-Hroub, a medical doctor, boasted that
before *Shihan*, there was no general weekly press. Before *Shihan*, there
was no stress on social issues, or coverage of the negatives in different
areas of life. As a result of its boldness, said al-Hroub, *Shihan* has paid
the price for discussing these subjects through closure, confiscation,
stopping the publication and its publisher. *Al-Bilad* was licensed for
publication in Amman in July 1993; *Al-Sabil* Islamic paper in 1993; *al-
Majd* in 1994 as an opposition nationalist paper; *abed Rabbu*, a political
satirical newspaper, in 1996 (Musa 1997: 4).

Osama El Sherif, editor-in-chief of *The Star*, admitted that the
weekly press often goes too far in sensationalizing news and writing
about the private life of officials, but observed that the 1993 press law, if
applied, can take care of press excesses. He asserted that any press regulation has to be undertaken in the context of "a Jordanian democratic
formula" whose basic maxims include:

- that democracy is a way of life, not a political decision or a
  tactic;
- that freedom of expression and press freedom are not gifts,but
  fundamental human rights that must be sustained and protected;
- that any reform must be based on the rights and obligations
  granted under the Jordanian constitution, the National
  Charter, and laws of the land;
- that any reform must be preceded by a thorough public
  debate because, after all, the people are the source of legislation (El-Sharif 1996).

There were calls to improve the professionalism of the media to make it worthy of its new role in a more open atmosphere. Hakam Khair, then Secretary General of the House of Representatives, said the changes Jordan needs to make to increase the professionalism of the media were brought about by three revolutions: the technological revolution; the ideological revolution caused by the demise of communist ideology; and the new alliances revolution brought about by the emergence of the European Union and the rise of Japan and other Asian countries on the world scene. Kheir suggested that new technology that makes available other points of view via satellite has rendered governments less capable of practicing the rigorous censorship they imposed in the past, and that professionalism has to substitute for direct governmental control (Kheir 1996: 8-9).

How Free Should the Free Press Be?

After the 1989 elections, and after the passage of the Political Parties Law in 1992, tension between the government and the press mounted over the coverage of several political issues. The press supported Iraq in the Gulf war in 1991 (Musa 1997: 5); it did not support the Israeli-Jordanian peace treaty. The press was accused of causing tension between some Jordanians and Palestinians when it openly discussed what has been euphemistically called "national unity issues," or the role of Palestinians in the Kingdom. The weekly press was attacked for its sensationalism. Even some journalists called for steps to curb excesses.

Just when the press thought that it was facing government restrictions at the end of 1996, King Hussein appointed Abd al-Karim al-Kabariti Prime Minister on January 25, 1995. Minister of Information Marwan al-Muasher, a former columnist, declared his willingness to restructure the Ministry of Information, appoint a government spokesperson, sell some of the government's shares in the media by January 1997, and allow radio and TV to be privatized.[26] Those moves, had they taken place, would have conformed to Article 19 of the fifth publications law (1993 No. 10), which stipulated that the government share of press funding should be decreased to 30 percent by mid-1997 (Musa 1997: 14). But the Kabariti government was replaced by the Abd al-Salam al-Majali government on March 19, 1997. Instead of decreased government control of the press, the government introduced the 1997 amended press law while Parliament was not in session and just before new parliamentary elections were to be held.

THE 1997 TEMPORARY PRESS LAW

The "Temporary Law for the Year 1997" increased capital requirements to the point where thirteen publications were put out of business. The old version of Article 40 forbids publication of news that disparages the King or the royal family, the armed forces, the security forces, and heads of friendly states. The new version expands forbidden subjects to include the publication of "news, views, opinions, analysis, information, reports, caricatures, photos or any sort of publication that disparages" any of them, threatens national unity, or endangers the national currency. Sub-article No. 11 forbids the publication of any confidential government document (Henderson 1997). The law replaced imprisonment for journalists with fines to take account of the concerns of human rights organizations, but increased fines for all "press offenses."[27] Article 50 (2a) allows the government to suspend a publication for three to six months if the publication repeats an offense during a five-year period. If a publication repeats the offense three times, it can be closed.

The law withdrew the rights given to political parties in 1993. Article 26, which reads *"Except for press publications issued by political parties,* the license for issuing a publication shall be revoked by force of law in any of the following cases:" was amended by canceling the words in italic. The law added to Article 13 the provision that an editor has to be Jordanian, live permanently in Jordan, and have worked full time in the press for ten years (provisions that were part of the 1973 but not the 1993 law). In short, the 1997 law increased the number of prohibitions that could get journalists into trouble and decreased court review of government actions.

DID THE "YELLOW PRESS" GO TOO FAR?

There were calls from the government as well as the press for regulating the wayward "yellow press" that was accused of sensationalism, of using unfamiliar linguistic terms, of presenting women as sex objects, and of inaccuracy (Musa 1997: 9). But there were also some defenders of the press who admitted that excesses occurred, but said that their effects "were exaggerated and used to make the last amendments [of 1997/O.N.] in order to close some publications and limit press freedom."[28] *Al-Sabil* Islamic paper editor Atef al-Joulani does not dispute the charge that some papers were damaging to the moral fiber of society by writing about social problems in a sensational manner and by covering sex and crime, but stresses that their numbers were limited. Joulani charges that press offenses could have been handled under the 1993 law. He observed that Jordan television, run by the government, shows photos and programs that are much worse than the material published by the offending papers. He added: "That proves that the target is the freedom of the serious press."[29]

Several journalists rebutted the government's claim for the need for such a law. Columnist Tariq Masarwah of *Al-Rai* rejected the government's charge that press reports were responsible for investors' losing confidence in the Jordanian economy and said that "the homeland is not an egg shell that cracks at the slightest touch." He attributed the currency crisis of 1988 to the fact that the President of Petra Bank ignored Central Bank and put the administration of the bank in his pocket (Masarwa 1997). Alian Alian ridiculed government attempts on TV to depict the new law as if it were introduced to safeguard agreed-upon principles and national unity, or to save workers from the weeklies that could no longer afford to pay their salaries, or to deliver people from tabloid reporting. He called government justifications "information counterfeiting." He reminded the government that the content of the law not only touched on the freedom of publication, but also on freedom in general, and threatened to return the country to martial law days. The real reasons for the amendments, Alian said, was to facilitate normalization, as the Jordanian-Israeli peace treaty requires. Article 11 of that agreement dictates that parties should refrain from engaging in negative publicity, and that all legal and administrative measures be taken to stop the publication of such material by any person or institution. The article ends by saying that "Democracy in any country rests on three laws, election law, parties law and press law, and an attack on any of the laws would gut democracy of its content. Democracy has been hurt by the passage of the temporary election and press law" (Alian 1997). The High Court agreed.

On January 26, 1998 the High Court of Justice ruled that the temporary law passed in May was unconstitutional. According to Article 94 of the constitution, the government can issue temporary laws in the absence of Parliament in times of war or internal strife. Because there was no "necessitating circumstances," and no emergency, there was no need for the government to change the 1993 press law. One lawyer considered the historic decision as one that limits the government's powers to issue temporary laws in the future.

THE 1998 PRESS AND PUBLICATIONS LAW

The temporary defeat of the government's attempt to impose stricter laws led to the reopening of the important issue of who pays the piper: government involvement to sell its shares in the press to speed up the process of privatization and press independence. The government has maintained, via the Social Security Corporation (SSC) and the Jordan

Investment Corporation (JIC), a controlling interest (62%) in the Jordan Press Foundation (JPF)—owner of *Al-Rai* and the *Jordan Times*, and 32 percent in *Al-Dustur*. Furthermore, the government owns 46 percent of JPF's equity through the SSC, and it owns an additional 15 percent through the JIC, the investment arm of the government. According to the original press law, the government should have reduced its equity in the papers by May 17, 1997 but introduced the temporary legislation a few days later, while parliament was in recess (Ciriaci 1998). That law removed the clause that mandated the reduction of the government's share in the press. So the brief period of promises of privatization under the government of Kabariti did not materialize. The government has retained its control of the press via its finances.

Control of press funding has been a constant since the 1950s. The 1953 and 1955 laws allowed the government to require papers to submit their budgets to the government. In 1973 it required papers to hire professional auditors and gave itself the right to review audits; that clause was amended in 1993 to require publishers to provide a copy of the paper's annual budget as well as a statement about its revenues, its assets, and financial structure. The clause was kept in the 1998 law in which publications are required to provide the government with a copy of their annual budgets. On the other hand, the government is no longer required to sell its shares in the press as it was in 1993.

The 1998 law (Appendix 4/Table 4.4) imposes strict controls on Jordanians who write for the foreign press, requiring them to become members of the Jordanian Press Association. This article in the law is an indication of the government's attempt to control Jordan's image not just in the Jordanian press, but also its image beamed into Jordan by satellite by controlling the licensing of Jordanian journalists working as freelance writers for the foreign press. After all, satellite technology allows those Arab and foreign publications to bypass Jordanian censorship of content and to transmit right back into Jordan.

CONCLUSION

An examination of press law between 1927 and 1998 illustrates that the location of power has not shifted over time from the government to the press association. In fact, if anything, government licensing of the profession of journalism is much more stringent in 1998 than it was in 1993. Furthermore, government control of press financing has let up only for brief periods. The government promised to sell/reduce its shares in press companies but reneged on that promise. Jordan has attempted to liberalize the press at various points in its political history, but the government has allowed the stresses of many internal and external events to curtail freedom of expression. The Palestinian-owned press was prevented from fully assigning responsibility or blame for the Arab defeat of 1948. It was hampered from discussing whether alignment with the West was a good idea, given the history of the West's support for Israel.

The press was censored in the 1960s and 1970s as the government waged a power struggle with the PLO over Palestinian representation. The government took control of press finances in 1988, a year after the Palestinian uprising, but relented in 1989. Jordan's changed relations with the Palestinians and the willingness of the Palestinian National Authority of Yasir Arafat to talk peace with Israel enabled the Jordanian government to liberalize without the danger of losing power. But the most important factor that contributed to press liberalization was the revival of the political life through the return to a parliamentary system and the enactment of the Political Parties Law of 1992. Numerous new publications invigorated debate in the Kingdom. But the government feared the forces freedom unleashed and attempted to control them, first in 1997 and again in 1998. Yet paradoxically, even when the government introduced the 1997 amendments and when it cancelled the 1993 law and replaced it with the more restrictive 1998 law, the genie of press freedom was already out of the bottle. It was helped by satellite technology and the Internet.

Over time, press liberalization proceeded in fits and starts. But there were gains made at every turn as the Jordanian Bar Association sided with the press in several important cases. The forces for liberalization may, in the end, gain some headway: the presence of a constituency of disparate forces intent on liberalizing Jordan means that any government that tries to restrict freedom will run into trouble. The former Minister of Information, now in the Upper House of Deputies, voted against some articles in the press law; former Prime Minister Taher al-Masri has become very vocal about press freedom; former Minister of Information Ibrahim Izziddin now heads the Shuman Institute and has institutionalized intellectual discussion through series of lectures and prizes for academics and others. University professors are more vocal about freedom. Seminars on press freedom are held regularly by coalitions that range from local universities and human rights groups, to foreigners who work in the press or the human rights field. In short, it is much harder to roll back freedom than it was in the 1950s when the left was stronger, and King Hussein, very popular in the last few years of his life, was weaker.

The paradox of the Jordanian press is that laws that allow people to enter the profession are strictly controlled by the Ministry of Information and are much stricter than the 1993 law. Furthermore, huge financial deposits are required to enter the profession. But the press that makes it through the licensing process is much more daring and is willing to take on government corruption.

Appendix 1
Table 4.1: Jordanian Press Laws, 1927-1948.

Location of Power for Licensing and Regulation	Recourse to Court	Financial Control
Law of 1927 (March 12) Inspector General	•Current [Ottoman] laws will be used for the issuance of licenses.	•Funding: private. •Law requires deposit to cover law suits against publications.
Law of 1928 (April 23) Chief Justice Inspector General Minister of Education General Secretary Head of Antiquities Head of the Treasury	•Ottoman law will be used.	•Funding: private. •Law requires "insurance" of 150 Palestinian pounds for political publications and 100 pounds for political periodicals.
Law Amending Publication Law of 1933 (March 26) Prime Minister	•Refers to Article 11 of the Ottoman law dealing with assignment of responsibility for infractions.	•Funding: private. No mention of conditions for starting a paper. •Assumes previous laws apply.
Law of 1939 (August 30) Minister of Interior Prime Minister (who appoints inspector of publications)	•Reference is made to Law of Defense of the East of Jordan, 1935. Law for the Inspection of Publications. Inspector has the authority to issue an order to prevent publications from publishing, to issue an order to authorize pre-censorship of any publication, may issue an order to prevent	•Private funding. No mention of any conditions for starting a publication.

the publication of certain subjects, in one or more issues for a certain period of time. Inspector also has control of mail and telephone communication and controls materials at the borders by land or sea.
•Inspector has the authority to order police, in writing, to inspect any place they suspect at any time, and to use force if necessary.
•People who disobey any regulations are subject to penalties outlined in the Defense Law of 1935.

Law of 1945 (October 17) Minister of Interior Prime Minister	•Temporary Law, amending Ottoman Law of 11 Rajab, 1327, 16 July 1325. •Additions relate to orders for every publication to print the name of its publisher under penalty of a fine or imprisonment or both. If a publication publishes material subject to penalties described in Articles 16, 17, 19, 26, 27, 28 of the Ottoman Law, the Minister of Interior may order the banning of distribution of the issue that published the offending material, and the Council of Ministers may ban the paper for any period. Although penalties are specified for every offense, the courts determine guilt or innocence, according to Article 31 of the Ottoman Law.	•Private ownership.
Law of 1948 (May 10) Minister of Defense	Reference is made to Law of Defense of the East of Jordan, 1935.	•Private ownership.

Appendix 2
Table 4.2: Jordanian Press Laws, 1953-1967.

Location of Power for Licensing and Regulation	Recourse to Court	Financial Control
Press and Publications Law of 1953	•Minister of interior approves license application. Refusal to license is subject to court review.	Private ownership.
Minister of Interior Minister of Justice Minister of Education	•Applicant must possess "a good reputation," must not possess parliamentary immunity, and must not combine work as a journalist with any government job.	Fixed deposit required for a license "to cover damages awarded in law suits against a publication."
•New position of Director of publications is created Aug. 25 and tied to the Prime Minister's office	•Application includes the make of the printing press to be used. •Minister of Interior may ban publication for 3 days and ask court to extend ban until trial date, but the court determines if publication should be closed for good. Court considers intent when it rules on libel and defamation.	Detailed budget has to be submitted [to guard against foreign subsidies].
	•Publications director may order an audit of a publication's finances at any time, but court determines penalties.	Publications director may order an audit at any time, but court determines penalties.
Press and Publications Law of 1955	•Minister of Interior accepts license, forwards it to the Council of Ministers, which has the right to reject it. Refusal to license is not subject to court review.	•No change from 1953 laws.
Minister of Interior Minister of Justice Minister of Education Prime Minister	The Council of Ministers may also cancel a license; decision not subject to court review. •Applicant must be Jordanian; if not, may be allowed to practice if there is a reciprocal agreement	

Law / Officials	Provisions
Press and Publications Law of 1967 (Feb. 1) Minister of Information Prime Minister •Article 37: "The Prime Minister and the Minister of Justice are entrusted with the application of the articles of that law.	with country of origin. Applicant must get the approval of the Council of Ministers. Those who work for foreign institutions will be treated like foreigners in this context •Applicant must reside primarily in Jordan, possess "a good reputation," must not possess parliamentary immunity, and must not combine work as a journalist with any government job. Application includes the make of the printing press to be used. Court considers intent when it rules on libel and defamation. •Minister of Information accepts license, forwards it to Prime Minister who has the right to reject it. Refusal to license is not subject to court review. Council of Ministers may also cancel a license; decision not subject to court review. Applicant must prove s/he possesses "a good reputation," by providing a certificate (from the intelligence services). Applicant must not possess parliamentary immunity, and must not combine work as a journalist with any government job, or any other job. •Application should include the make of printing press to be used, and the type of font used. Font samples of all the letters used in the press should be presented to the Ministry of Information. Printed copies of fonts should be sent every time they are changed. •Minister of Information determines whether libel has occurred and sets penalties for libel. Court not mentioned in articles dealing with libel, although mentioned in articles dealing with forcing publications to publish rebuttals. •Fixed deposit required for a license for a daily publication, or ownership of printing equipment, or both. •Owner required to hire a professional auditor to audit finances of each publication. •Minister of Information has the right to review all audited accounts. •Each publication is required to contract the services of at least two international press agencies.

Appendix 3
Table 4.3: Jordanian Press Laws, 1973-1993.

Location of Power for Licensing and Regulation	Recourse to Court	Financial Control
Press and Publications Law No. 33, 1973 (June 13) Prime Minister Minister of Culture and Information	•Decisions of the Council of Ministers on licensing not subject to court review. •If publication refuses to make corrections, minister will go to court to exact other penalties. Intent is considered in cases of libel or defamation.	•Fixed deposit required for a license of a daily publication, or ownership of printing equipment, or both. •Owner required to hire a professional auditor. The Minister of Information has the right to review all audited accounts but has to respect the secrecy of those accounts. •Minister of Information sets the guidelines for the price of newspapers and the cost of advertising after consulting with the Journalists Association. •The law specifies penalties for accepting foreign funding or advocating policies harmful to the country.
Press and Publications Law No. 10, 1993 Prime Minister Minister of Information	•Court determines all infractions to offenses listed in the law.	•License is guaranteed "only if the registered capital of the paper is not less that JD50 000, 50 percent of which has to be paid." •Political Parties are allowed to publish their own publications. •All official proclamations are to be published free of charge.

•Financial deposits are required only of the commercial press but not of the press of political parties.

•The publisher has to provide the Director of the Publications Department with a copy of the paper's annual budget, including statements about its revenues, its funding sources, and its financial status.

•The shares the government owns must not exceed 30 percent of the capital of a press company. The government is directed to sell its extra shares in a period not exceeding two years, renewable for only another two.

Appendix 4
Table 4.4: Jordanian Press Law, 1998.

Responsibility for Licensing and Regulation	Recourse to Court	Financial Control
Press and Publication Law of 1998 (Sept. 1) • The Council of Ministers, based on the recommendation of the Minister (of Information) licenses local journalists as well as Jordanian journalists working for foreign publications (Article 9). Both need to belong to the Jordanian Press Association to practice journalism. • Specific periods of training are mandatory for the practice of journalism. Experience of eight years is mandatory for occupying the position of editor-in-chief, so is membership in the union for at least three years. That person should work full time and should be Jordanian and a permanent resident of Jordan. • Directors of press publications mentioned in Article 15 must be Jordanian with full-time residency in Jordan, must manage only one institution, and work full time (Article 16: 1-3). Directors also have to	• The periodical and journalist have a right to keep their sources secret unless the court decides otherwise during its review of criminal cases, or to protect state secrets, to prevent crimes, or to achieve justice (Article 6: d). • The Council of Ministers is required to issue its decision regarding the request to license a press application within 30 days of the request being made. The council gave itself 15 extra days to inform the publication of its decision, but removed the line about its decisions being subject to court review (stipulated in the 1993 Press Law). • The ministry may revoke the license of a paper that does not "rectify its position" (i.e. meet the licensing and financial requirements of the new law) within a period of 90 days. There is no mention of the decision being subject to court review.	• The capital of the daily publication must not be less than JD500,000; the capital for a non-daily not less than JD 100,000 and for a specialized publication not less than JD5,000 (Article 13). Government, university publications, and publications issued by political parties are exempt from these requirements (Article 14). • Article 20 forbids publications and specialized publications from receiving funds from non-Jordanian countries or parties. It also requires the owners to provide the ministry with a copy of their annual budget and all tables related to its revenues, sources of funding, and financial status annually. • Centers of study and research or polling centers and anyone who works for them are prohibited from accepting any aid,

possess academic qualifications in line with regulations to be issued by the minister for that purpose (Article 16: 4).

•Article 19 regulates conditions under which a license becomes "null and void," including for nonregular publication and publishing outside area of specialization (political party publications are exempt from those requirements)

•Article 23 sets conditions for being an editor-in-chief, including having experience for 8 years, residency in Jordan, working for only one publication (editors of political parties are exempt from those requirements).

•Article 25 sets conditions for the licensing of editors of specialized publications, including qualifications for their workers. The law also lays down terms of distribution.

•Article 26 (a) forbids specialized publications from running articles outside their line of specialization without permission from the minister.

•Newspapers that publish "incorrect information" are required to publish a retraction the next day in the same place or must print the correction received from the party concerned in the same place

grants, or financial help from Jordanian and non-Jordanian parties, excluding funds for joint projects, studies, and research approved by the Minister of Education.

•Article 45 requires owners of printing presses, publishing and distribution houses, and study and research and polling centers to hold joint responsibility for paying the legal fees and paying fines levied against their employees.

Appendix 4
Table 4.4: Jordanian Press Law, 1998 (con't.).

the original article was printed Article 27 (b). This regulation also applies to foreign publications distributed inside Jordan. •Article 29 gives the government the right to prevent the entry for a minimum of two weeks, to be extended if necessary, of any foreign publication that refuses to print a correction.		•The article in the 1993 law requiring the government to decrease its shares in press establishments was deleted.
•Articles 35 and 36 prohibit the publishing, import, or distribution of books and publications without prior censorship before printing, and before presenting copies of the work before importation. Two copies of every publication that enters the kingdom have to be reviewed by the director of publications before being allowed distribution rights.	•Minutes of court proceedings shall not be published before a final ruling is issued except if permission is obtained from the court.	•Article 30 requires publications to identify advertisements from other copy.
•Article 37 lists fourteen content areas that are out of limits for journalists (including publishing "any news that (negatively) touches on (*tamis bi*) the King or the royal family." In addition to the prohibition against publishing news on the number and location of troops, the law prohibits "any news items, cartoons or comments that might harm the Jordanian	•The court which made the ruling (against) the owners of the printing press, publishing, and distribution houses, and study and research and polling centers) orders the accused to print the final verdict in full and for free or to run a summary of it in the first issue of the periodical after being informed of the verdict and in the same	•Article 46 levies a number of fines for various offenses. The fines range from JD 100 to JD 10,000. It requires offenders to publish retractions at their own expense. •Owners of printing presses, publishing and distribution houses, and study and

Armed Forces," and "any information that may infringe on the independence of the judicial system," "news that disparage one of the religions whose freedom is guaranteed by the constitution," "news that disrupt national unity or sow the seeds of hatred, and division (...) among members of society," news that disparage heads of friendly Arab and Muslim countries or friendly countries or worsen the relations of the Kingdom with friendly countries, provided those countries reciprocate; news that encourage vice or contain unsubstantiated false rumors, include secret proceedings of parliament without permission, publish secret government documents, publish news that lead to the loss of confidence in the national currency, medical product ads without permission from the Ministry of Health; news that instigate people to gather or stage public sit-ins that are unlicensed.

place the article in question was printed. The court can also decide on publishing the verdict in two other newspapers if it sees a necessity and at the expense of the accused (Articles 44 and 45).

research and polling centers are considered jointly responsible for the financial damages and court fees assessed against their employees in court cases (Article 44).

ENDNOTES

1. Majali Government Prepares Its Weapons to Impose Temporary Press Law (in Arabic). *Al-Sabil*, May 31, 1997.
2. Press laws examined include: The Ottoman publications law of 1329 A.H. and 1331 A.H. (on which some Jordanian legislation is based), the Jordanian press and publications laws of 1927, 1928, 1933, 1939, 1945, 1948, 1953, 1955, 1967, 1973 (Shreim 1984: 117-185), the 1993 press law, the 1997 amended press law, and the 1998 press law.
3. *Mass Communication Media in Jordan*, The Jordanian Ministry of Information, Amman, 1978.
4. It became a government publication with issue 139, published three days after the establishment of the Emirate.
5. *Rais al-Nuthar* translates as manager, director, superintendent, administrator, principal, chief, (cabinet) minister (now obsolete) according to *The Hans Wehr, Dictionary of Modern Written Arabic*, edited by J.M. Cowan, 977. Ithaca: Spoken Languages Services.
6. References to press laws between 1927-1973 are based on the examination of the original text of the press laws in Shreim 1984, analysis is mine.
7. The newspaper *Falastin* started publishing again in Amman on April 4, 1949, after an interruption of nine months and fifteen days. Daud al-Issa, Managing Editor, wrote an editorial in which he said: "(I)ssuing daily papers in a new country like Jordan is not easy, but thank God we have overcome difficulties." He then praised several Jordanian government officials for responding to readers' insistence that the paper be reopened (al-Issa 1949).
8. Nine Members of Parliament spoke on the general subject of freedom and on preserving it by forming a committee that would meet with the Prime Minister to discuss issues in general and the freedom of the press in particular. Preserving the Rights of Refugees and Private Property. A Committee to Meet His Excellency the Prime Minister about Freedoms (in Arabic). *Al-Difa*, June 8, 1950.
9. The writer of an editorial noted that Arab leaders should know that "repressing Palestinian freedom and stifling their voices and preventing them from taking part in self- determination" would not work with people who have "nothing to lose except their chains. Arab politicians understand that our freedom is a condition to every rescue." From the Heart of Palestine: Our Freedom Is a Condition for Any Rescue (in Arabic). *Falastin*, August 9, 1949.
10. The Relationship of the Individual to the Administration. *Falastin*, August 8, 1949.
11. Ibid.
12. This camp was represented by John Baghot Glubb, Commander of the Arab Legion. For his views on the need to suppress freedom of expression to guard against communism, see Glubb 1957: 347-348, 352.
13. This camp was represented by Jordanian Prime Minister Sulaiman al-Nabulsi. In his biography, he boasted that no one has ever gone to prison for political or ideological reasons on his watch (Musa 1986: 89).

14. Text of the Communist Control Act is reprinted in *Official Gazette* 1164, Amman, 1953 (December 16).
15. Article 55 of the 1953 press law, and article 54 of the 1955 press law (Shreim 1984: 146, 157).
16. *The Jordanian Press. Its Origin and Development.* Ministry of Information, Department of Publications. Amman (no year listed): 30.
17. Article 32 of the 1953 and 1955 press laws (Shreim 1984: 141, 154).
18. *Filastin,* January 13, 1963, quoted by Asher Susser 1994: 63; *Al-Manar,* January 13, 1963, quoted by Susser 1994: 65.
19. Article 16(1) 1967 (Shreim 1984: 163).
20. The decision of the Arab Summit Conference at Rabat, Morocco, in October 1974 was to recognize the PLO as the sole legitimate representative of the Palestinian people.
21. Memo [II] from the Representatives of the Different Intellectual, Professional and Union Groups on the On-going Arrest Campaign in the Country (in Arabic). *Al-Urdun Al-Jadid* 3, 1986: 211 f.
22. Memo [I] from the Professional Associations and the Jordanian Writers Association about the Project of the New Election Law for Members of Parliament (in Arabic). *Al-Urdun Al-Jadid,* 3, 1986: 51 f.
23. Set back for the King's Vision. *Middle East International,* December 19, 1992.
24. Journalists objected to Article 5 (d), which forces journalists to reveal their sources if asked by judicial authority; Article 8, which prohibits the publication of news items that contradict the principles of freedom, national responsibility, and human rights; Article 13, (d) which prohibits editors-in-chief from holding other jobs; Article 16, which states that the directors of various journalistic and publishing institutions must have university degrees and "have sufficient experience *as evaluated by the minister of information*" (italics added); Article 40 (2), which bans the publication of items that impinge upon the armed forces; and Article 42, which bans the publication of court proceedings before the final verdict had been passed. Journalists Criticize Press Publications Law. *Jordan Times,* January 9, 1993.
25. Text of Press, Publication Draft Law (in Arabic). *Sawt al-Sha'ab,* March 15, 1993.
26. Al Mua'asher Says There Will Be Major Restructuring in Media. *The Star,* April 11, 1996.
27. Untitled Editorial (in Arabic). *Al-Hadath,* May 19-26, 1997.
28. Fax to the author by Adel Ziadat, July 28, 1997.
29. Fax to the author by Atef al-Joulani, July 27, 1997.

BIBLIOGRAPHY

Alian, Alian. 1997. Al-Majali Government Prepares its Weapons to Impose Temporary Press Law (in Arabic). *Al-Sabil,* May 28.
Altschull, Herbert. 1995. *Agents of Power: The Media and Public Policy.* White Plains, NY: Longmans.

Andoni, Lamis. 1991. Legitimizing the Monarchy. *Middle East International*, June 14.

Andoni, Lamis. 1992. The Dilemma of Jordan. *Middle East International*, January 24.

Aruri, Naseer H. 1972. *Jordan: A Study in Political Development (1921-1965)*. The Hague: Martinus Nijhoff.

Bin Talal, Hassan. 1984. *Search for Peace: The Politics of the Middle Ground in the Arab East*. London: Macmillan.

Brady, Thomas F. 1967. Press Law Shuts Jordan's Papers. *New York Times*, March 26.

Ciriaci, Francesca. 1998. Court Verdict Casts Shadow on Fate of Government Equities in Daily Newspapers. *The Jordan Times*, January 27.

El-Sherif, Osama. 1996. The Press, Government and Future Challenges. *The Star*, December 28.

Flapan, Simha. 1987. *The Birth of Israel*. New York: Pantheon.

Friedrich, Carl. 1958. Authority, Reason and Discretion. *Nomos I: Authority*. Cambridge: Cambridge University Press.

Glubb, John Baghot. 1957. *A Soldier with the Arabs*. London: Hodder.

Haurani, Faisal. 1986. The PLO and the Jordanian Regime: The First Phase 1964-1976 (in Arabic). *Al-Urdun Al-Jadid* 3: 95-111.

Haurani, Hani, and Salim al-Tarawnah. 1986. Here Is How the Baghdad Pact Fell (in Arabic). *Al-Urdun Al-Jadid* 3: 113-160.

Hawatmeh, George. 1991. Masri's Dilemma. *Middle East International*, July 12.

Hawatmeh, George. 1992. Now for Liberalization. *Middle East International*, August 7.

Henderson, Amy. 1997. Press and Publications Law Boasts Stiffer Penalties on Newspapers and Journalists. *Jordan Times*, 18 May.

al-Issa, Daud. 1949. A Greeting and a Promise: Palestine Newspaper in its New Era (in Arabic). *Falastin*, April 4.

Kheir, Hakam. 1996. Jordanian Media and New Developments. Paper Presented at the Jordanian and Islamic Center for Studies and Information, 4-5 May, Amman, Jordan: 8-9 (in Arabic).

Masarwa, Tariq. 1997. And We Flog Journalists. *Al-Rai*, June 21.

Moore, Pete. 1994. The International Context of Liberalization and Democratization in the Arab World. *Arab Studies Quarterly* 3: 43-66.

Musa, Sulaiman. 1986. *Notables From Jordan: Hazza al-Majali, Sulaiman al-Nabulsi, Wasfi al-Tal* (in Arabic). Amman: Dar Al-Sha'ab.

Musa, Issam. 1997. Problems of the Jordanian Press during the Democratic Era (1989-1997). Paper Read at the Conference on "Communication and Diplomacy: New Horizons in the Information Age," September 6, Amman, Jordan.

Najjar, Najwa. 1989. Journalist Cited on Freedom of Press. *Jordan Times*, May 18-19.

Najjar, Orayb. 1997. The 1995 Palestinian Press Law: A Comparative Study. *Communication Law and Policy* 1: 40-103.

Powe, Lucas, Jr., 1991. *The Fourth Estate and the Constitution: Freedom of the Press in America*. Berkeley: University of Berkeley Press.

Pundik, Ron. 1994. *The Struggle for Sovereignty: Relations Between Great Britain and Jordan, 1946-1951*. Oxford: Blackwell.

Rotenstreich, Nathan. 1988. *Order and Might*. Albany: State University of New York Press.

Salibi, Kamal. 1983. *The Modern History of Jordan*. London: Tauris.

Satloff, Robert. 1994. *From Abdullah to Hussein: Jordan in Transition*. New York: Oxford University Press.

Shreim, Omaima. 1984. *The Jordanian Press and its Relation to Publications and Publishing, 1920-1983*. Amman: Press Workers Cooperative.

Susser, Asher. 1994. *On Both Banks of the Jordan: A Political Biography of Wasfi al-Tal*. Illford: Frank Cass.

Wood, Gordon. 1969. *Creation of the American Republic*. Chapel Hill: University of North Carolina Press.

Wright, Esmond. 1951. Abdallah's Jordan: 1947-1951. *Middle East Journal* 5: 458-595.

Yodelis, Mary Ann. 1975. *Who Paid the Piper? Publishing Economics in Boston, 1763-1775*. Columbia: AEJMC.

II

MASS MEDIA AND DEVELOPMENT

5

The Changing Face of Arab Communications: Media Survival in the Information Age

Muhammad I. Ayish

Recent political, economic, and technological trends in the Middle East and around the world seem to have induced remarkable transformations in the Arab mass communications scene. Giving rise to technologically sophisticated media outlets, these developments have provided Arab audiences with more diversified and interactive access to information materials reflecting indigenous and Western-style contents and formats. Data from the early 1990s shows significant rises in broadcast and print media exposure rates among Arab populations[1] and a growing willingness to join the information superhighway on the part of governments, organizations, and individuals. To some degree, digitally based communication media technologies seem to have catapulted modern Arab societies into the eye of the globalization storm, placing further pressures on them to cope with the imperatives of the new information age.

As in other world regions, the digital communications revolution sweeping through the Arab world has stimulated intellectual and political debates, spawning numerous views on the social, economic, and cultural implications of the new media. For their part, Arab governmental policies on information issues have generally been characterized as reactive, ambivalent, and lacking clarity of vision (Ali 1995). Policy debates on information issues took place only after new technologies had been transferred to Arab societies, as evident in satellite television and the Internet. Oblivious to the economic benefits of highly developed communications services, public discussions have been preoccupied with the potential negative effects of information and communication technologies on social values and traditions as well as on existing political arrangements. In addressing these issues, Arab policy makers have chosen to focus more on individual and institutional technology users than on industries. Thus, satellite television reception has been either banned or allowed on a selected basis in some Arab countries, while access to the Internet has been controlled through the installation of filtering devices.

The question addressed by this chapter relates to the implications of this communications revolution for the Arab media of communication in the 1990s. It sheds light on the extent to which technological developments in communications seem to bear on Arab world media contributions to free and substantive debates conducive to participatory development. As forums of free public discourse, the media are potentially capable of setting agendas of public discussions on national issues ranging from intellectual freedom, to political democratization, to social and economic equity. It is argued here that although new information and communications technologies would enable the mass media to reach a wider audience and produce more polished messages, they may not necessarily lead to the mass media fulfilling their functions as social institutions to be reckoned with. In the new information age, increasing communications commercialization and transnationalization are likely to induce further Arab media detachment from national development issues as the media join evolving political and economic structures in the search for global solutions to local problems.

THE HISTORICAL CONTEXT OF ARAB MASS MEDIA DEVELOPMENT

Although the history of Arab media has been a topic of discussion by scholars representing a wide range of academic and ideological orientations, there seems to be a general agreement that Arab communications owe their historical development to an interaction of external and domestic factors (Ayalon 1995; Abd al-Rahman 1996; Boyd 1993; al-Jammal 1995; Kamalipour and Mowlana 1994; Mrowwa 1961; Rugh

1979). On the one hand, it has been noted that the introduction of modern mass media into Arab societies took place during early encounters with Western colonial powers dating back to Napoleon's expedition to Egypt in 1797. Christian missionaries as well as Turkish rulers of Arab lands were also instrumental in establishing print media outlets to achieve religious and political objectives. According to the editors of a recent volume on mass media in the Middle East, Arab communications are viewed as intrinsically external (mostly Western) value-laden phenomena transferred to an alien Arab world setting (Kamalipour and Mowlana 1994: XVI).

On the other hand, media outputs originating in the West took on local social, cultural and political colorations upon their transfer to Arab countries. Indigenous traditions had a substantial bearing on the uses to which communications technologies were put. Newspapers turned into important outlets of literary expression by poets, novelists and other men of letters. Likewise, radio became an ideal tool of communication in the orally oriented Arabian culture. In structural terms, although media ownership patterns in the Arab world had originally been shaped by European models, local political and social arrangements in the post-independence era produced highly centralized communication systems geared exclusively toward nation-building goals. Characterized by pervasive government ownership and operation of broadcast services and a close scrutiny of privately owned print media, those systems have been rationalized by invoking the need for political stability and social harmony in the "march for national development" (Rugh 1979).

Arab cultural and political traditions dominant during the colonial and immediate post-independence eras were also instrumental in setting early professional standards for modern Arab media practices and in defining their relationships with social and political institutions (Hamada 1994). The first Arabic printing press was established by Christian missionaries in Aleppo in Syria in 1706, and by Mohamed Ali Pasha in Egypt in 1819 (the Bolaq Printing Press). Official publications began to appear in Morocco (1820), in Egypt (1828), in Tunisia (1838), in Syria (1865), in Iraq (1869), and in Libya (1866) (Abd al-Rahman 1996: 16-22). As for broadcasting, Douglas A. Boyd notes that Egypt was the first Arab country to start a radio service in the 1920s (Boyd 1993: 17). New radio stations began to emerge in Tunisia (1924), Morocco (1928), Iraq (1936), Jordan (1936), Saudi Arabia (1930s), Lebanon (1937), Algeria (1937), and Syria (1946). Post-independence radio services were established in countries such as Kuwait (1961), Bahrain (1955), Oman (1970), Qatar (1968), United Arab Emirates (1969), and Sudan (1971). Television, on the other hand, was launched as early as the mid-1950s, oddly enough as a private enterprise, on a limited basis in Morocco, Iraq, Kuwait, and Lebanon. The introduction of mass media during the colonial era was accompanied by a heightened sense of nationalism that equated good journalism with antagonism to the West. Freedom as liberation from "imperialism" continued to be a defining theme of some Arab media. In this regard, Adib Mrowwa notes that "Arabs have taken journalism as a tool of struggle, war and strife, and as a tool of revolution and liberation from foreign political domination as well as from outdated traditions" (Mrowwa 1961: 162).

Although Arab media systems have developed in similar historical and cultural environments, they seem to exhibit substantial variations. Faruq Abu Zaid classifies Arab press systems into two ownership categories: public media ownership in Iraq, Syria, Yemen, Libya, and Algeria; and mixed ownership in Egypt, Sudan, Saudi Arabia, Kuwait, UAE, Oman, Tunisia, Jordan, and Morocco (Abu Zaid 1986). In the 1970s, William Rugh identified three press models in the Arab world: the mobilization press, the loyalist press, and the diverse press (Rugh 1979). The mobilization press was dominant in countries with single-party political systems that placed a high value on the role of communications as tools of mobilization. This model was evident in the cases of Nasser's Egypt, Libya, Syria and Iraq, and the former South Yemen. The Egyptian daily *Al-Ahram* under the editorship of Mohammed Hasanain Heikal was a notable example of the mobilization press (Nasser 1979). Under this typology, media are owned and operated by the government and are expected to serve as mouthpieces for official policies and positions. On the other hand, the loyalist press typology describes communication systems operating in an environment where private ownership of print media outlets is legalized, as in the cases of Saudi Arabia, Jordan, Sadat's Egypt, Tunisia, and the United Arab Emirates. Yet the press in this category is not expected to criticize government policies, as it is often subjected to subtle political and economic pressures. Finally, the diverse press category describes media systems in countries with a relatively greater degree of diversity and freedom of expression, such as Kuwait, Morocco, and Lebanon. In this category, the press is owned and operated by private-sector organizations with the freedom to criticize the government.

Variations among Arab media systems in the 1970s and 1980s seem to have produced numerous thematic orientations. Awatef Abd al-Rahman notes that three issues had dominated the Arab press agenda in the 1960s and 1970s: Arab unity and the liberation of Palestine; development and social justice; and freedom and democracy (Abd al-Rahman 1996: 51). These issues may be considered in the context of Rugh's three typologies of the Arab press. Whereas the mobilization press was very much preoccupied with the issues of Arab unity and the liberation of Palestine, national development and social equity were central themes in loyalist press discourse. On the other hand, freedom of expression and the abolition of political controls were a major concern echoed by the diverse press. In the radio and television sectors, issues facing government-controlled broadcasting included poor financial resources, inadequate skilled personnel, foreign media imports, and limited autonomy. In comparing Arab and Western press systems, the editor of the London-based *Al-Hayat* newspaper notes that the former is plagued by scarce financial resources and limited freedom. Under these conditions, Arab media operate within the context of vague and mostly unwritten laws and regulations, often vulnerable to government interpretations of communicators' rights and duties.[2]

An important feature of the Arab press in the 1970s and 1980s was the emergence of what was termed the "migrating Arab press," mainly print media that chose non-Arab countries as bases of operation. According to Rasim al-Jammal and Abu Zaid, the "migrating Arab press" is of three types: first, newspapers established by Arabs who emigrated and settled abroad, establishing their own communities and media of communication, such as the Yemenis in Indonesia and the United States, and the Lebanese in Latin America (Abu Zaid 1985; al-Jammal 1995: 135); second, newspapers that were subsidized by Arab governments as part of international communication ventures or propaganda operations, such as the London-based *Al-Arab Al-Dawli*, and *Al-Sharq Al-Awsat*; and third, publications that were forced to emigrate under political pressures, such as *Al-Hawadith*, and *Kul Al-Arab* magazines. Such publications seemed to have benefited from free speech and advanced communication technology environments in host countries, and have produced some of the finest Arab-world publications, thus setting new standards of excellence in modern Arab journalism.

THE ARAB MASS MEDIA SCENE: TECHNOLOGICAL FEATURES

The technological development of Arab mass media may be divided into three historical phases: the colonial phase, the post-colonial phase, and the 1990s phase. Whereas the colonial phase was characterized by externally induced efforts to introduce media technologies to serve colonial political and missionary objectives, the post-colonial phase was associated with the "dominant paradigm" of development thinking, which envisaged a vital role for the mass media in national transformation. It is at this stage that the basic communications infrastructures like broadcast and publishing facilities were established. It was also a phase marked by

rising literacy rates, increasing urbanization, and political institutionalization. That phase, extending into the late 1980s, was also characterized
by ceaseless endeavors to modernize existing communication and information structures (Sardar 1982). To meet the growing demands of an
expanding Arab media market in print and broadcast communications,
academic and professional training schools and centers were also established in most Arab countries.

The second phase was characterized by the proliferation of new
media technologies that were effective in circumventing strict government controls over information flows in the Arab world. In the 1960s
transistor radio receivers were used by the population to listen to international radio broadcasters transmitting from North America and
Western Europe, drawing on them for news and other information,
especially in times of crises (Ayish 1991). In the early 1970s, audiocas-
sette recorders also made it possible to record uncensored programs and
other materials, especially those with nationalist and fundamentalist
political leanings. By the late 1970s, videocassette recorders were also
gaining popularity in the Arab world, especially among audiences tired
of dull official television programming (Boyd 1993).

The third phase of Arab media technology development began
in the early 1990s in a post-Cold War climate characterized by a global,
digitally based information explosion and sweeping market-oriented
thinking. Regionally, this phase witnessed the outbreak of the second
Gulf war and the launch of the Middle East peace process, two developments with repercussions likely to be felt in the Arab world beyond the
year 2000. A key feature of this phase has been the launch of numerous
commercial media projects inside and outside the Arab region, mainly
as part of Saudi Arabia-based media conglomerates.

Broadcast Communication Technologies

In the field of broadcasting, the Arab world seems to be undergoing a
sweeping electronic media revolution, featuring the launch of satellite
and cable television delivery systems, and the digitization of production
equipment and facilities (Lubbadeh 1995-96). Traditionally, Arab radio
and television organizations were state-controlled operations, rendering
governments solely responsible for technological investment decisions
and policies on the basis of political rather than marketplace considerations. Yet, the past few years have seen a growing involvement of the
private sector in the Arab broadcast industry. For the first time, commercial interests seem to be competing with political ones in the introduction of new technologies to the Arab broadcasting sector.

Arab countries' first-hand experience with unconventional broadcast technologies dates back to the early 1960s, when prospects for setting up a joint satellite communications venture were discussed by Arab information officials. Yet, due to political differences and poor technical and financial resources, the project remained a mere ambition until 1976, when the Arab Satellite Communications Organization (ARABSAT) was established. It took ARABSAT one more decade to launch its first satellite into outer space. Since 1985, more than five satellite systems have been sent into geostationary orbits, serving Arab countries in the areas of telecommunications, direct broadcasting, and television news exchanges (Ayish and Qassim 1995). By the end of 1997, ARABSAT was operating two satellites, namely, ARABSAT 1-C and 2-A, and beaming sixty channels (twelve Ku-band, forty-seven C-band, and one S-band channel). ARABSAT has also contracted for the manufacture of a third satellite, ARABSAT 2-C, due to offer twenty additional Ku-band channels (Arthur 1997: 1, 10).

Around the year 2000, the Arab world will also witness the launch of another satellite system—THURAYYA in the United Arab Emirates; NILESAT in Egypt was launched in 1998. Owned by the Emirates Telecommunications Corporation (Etisalat), THURAYYA is due to be launched in 2000 and will provide telecommunications and broadcasting services to governments and private organizations in the Middle East (Ayish 1997). The Egyptian satellite system NILESAT was launched in May 1998 in cooperation with the European Matra Marconi Space.

Broadcast technological developments in the Arab world have also included television delivery systems through direct broadcast satellites and cable networks. Arab satellite channels have mushroomed at high rates in the past seven years, with all Arab governments (except Iraq and Somalia) sponsoring at least one satellite television channel (Ayish and Qassim 1995). By the end of 1997, there were sixty Arab satellite television channels airing programs on a subscription or free-to-air basis. A key feature of this development has been the increase of private television services, which draw their finances from commercial sources. In 1999, there were seven private Arab satellite televisions networks and channels broadcasting to the Middle East. They include the Middle East Broadcasting Center (MBC) in London, Orbit Television and Radio Network in Rome, Arab Radio and Television Network (ART), Future Television International (Lebanon), the Lebanese Broadcasting Corporation (LBC), Qatar-based AL-Jazeera, and the London-based Arab News Network (ANN). The Arab world also falls within the range of over 100 satellite television channels transmitting from Asia and Europe.

As for cable networks, the wireless Multi-Channel Multi-Point Distribution Service (MMDS) version of this television delivery system is making some headway in the Arab world despite its novelty. In Egypt, the Cable Network of Egypt (CNE) distributes television program materials to subscribers and so does Dubai Cablevision in the United Arab Emirates. MMDS systems have been established in Qatar, Bahrain, Kuwait, Jordan, Lebanon, and in Saudi Arabia, where satellite television reception was banned by the government in 1994. Used on a subscription basis, MMDS systems allow for the prescreening of satellite television programs before their distribution.

Investments in Arab broadcasting have gone beyond the expansion of radio and television transmissions to include the modernization of production equipment and the Arabization of studio software, including the development of Arabic-language character generators and prompting systems. Big international firms in digital technology such as Sony, Avid, Silicon Graphics, and Quantel are becoming household names in Arab television stations. For example, the Qatari satellite television broadcaster Al-Jazeera chose Avid Technology's digital nonlinear news editing and disk-to-air playback system to prepare and transmit news, sport, and documentary programs to the Middle East. Digital technology has been an important component of ART facilities, which comprise production centers in Cairo, Jidda, Riyad, Dubai, Beirut, Amman, Tunis, and Damascus (Lubbadeh 1997). Furthermore, automated newsrooms have been introduced at TV stations in Jordan, Egypt, Kuwait, Bahrain, the United Arab Emirates, and Lebanon in addition to the London-based MBC (Lubbadeh 1996).

Egypt, traditionally viewed as the Hollywood of the Arab world, especially in terms of television drama production, seems to have made notable investments in the television and cinematic production sector. As part of joint French, Japanese, and Egyptian efforts, a film production city is being established on a two million square meter area of land in October Six City, southeast of Cairo. The project aims at establishing a media center capable of competing on an international scale, with a potential production capacity of 100 movies and 3,500 television production hours a year. The city is made up of a studio complex, open-air shooting areas, indoor and outdoor theaters, a service complex, film laboratory, a hotel, a training center, and an employees club (Aldham 1997).

Print Communication Technologies

Since the introduction of the first printing press to the Arab world in the early part of the seventeenth century, the Arab publishing industry has undergone notable transformations (al-Musa 1986: 233). Although traditional hot-metal typesetting techniques continued to be the mainstay of

Arab publishing into the early 1980s, the integration of the computer into print media production marks a big transition in the Arab printing industry. The acquisition and adaptation of new technologies would not have been possible had it not been for the Arabization of computer hardware and software by major computer makers. Since the mid-1990s, desktop publishing software in Arabic has been in full use at most national newspapers in the Arab world. It includes Arabized versions of English-language layout and design software such as Design Studio (Arabized as *Nasher Sahafi*) and Ready. Set. Go! (Arabized as *Nasher Maktabi*), Quark Express, and Page Maker. Software Arabization has also led to the development of scores of Arabic fonts, faithful to the originality of Arabic calligraphy.

Studies carried out on the use of desktop publishing technologies in the Arab world seem to suggest a fast-developing industry. In their survey of desktop publishing (DTP) applications in six Kuwaiti publishing firms, Nabil al-Jerdi and Muwaffaq A. Majid found that the majority of employees believe DTP makes publishing more accurate, adds further effects to the product, improves quality, increases profit, and saves time (al-Jerdi and Majid 1997). In his study of the technological features of the Egyptian press, J. al-Labban notes that the Egyptian magazine *Kul Al-Nas* was the first publication to introduce desktop publishing in 1990, followed by the leading elite newspaper *Al-Ahram* and the opposition *Al-Wafd* newspaper in 1993 (al-Labban 1997). In the United Arab Emirates, Ibrahim al-Rashed notes that all nine Arabic and English-language newspapers in the United Arab Emirates have adopted new desktop publishing and printing technologies. Typical problems facing UAE print media professionals include insufficient training and outdated and incompatible software (using Macintosh and PC platforms) (al-Rashed 1997: 62).

A notable outcome of new high-capacity publishing technologies in the Arab world has been a multiplication of print media outlets to meet a growing readership associated with rising literacy rates. It is projected that over 250 daily and weekly publications will be produced in the Arab countries of the Middle East and North Africa by the late 1990s and this figure is four times the number of publications a decade ago.[3] General and specialized publications catering to certain age and professional groups have been common at newsstands in the Arab world. In the mid-1990s, two publishing groups based in Saudi Arabia invested heavily in new technologies to produce a wide range of those publications. They include the Saudi Marketing and Research Group, which produces fifteen publications ranging from *Al-Sharq Al-Awsat*, *Arab News*, and *Al-Muslimun* to *Al-Iqtisadiya* and *Al-Riyada*. The other group is the London-based Al-Hayat Publishing Ltd., which publishes *Al-Hayat* newspaper and *Al-Wasat* magazine.

New digital technologies have also enabled Arab newspapers to go international by publishing regional editions catering to readers in different regions around the world. For example, the Egyptian *Al-Ahram* and the London-based *Al-Hayat, Al-Sharq Al-Awsat,* and *Al-Quds Al-Arabi* newspapers publish via satellite numerous editions targeting readers in Arab countries, Europe, and North and South America. These papers utilize state-of-the-art news gathering technologies, which allow them to receive news from major international news agencies as well as from their worldwide correspondents and store it on computerized data bases for convenient editing and future retrieval (al-Arif 1997).

An important feature of the increasing use of the Internet as a medium of communication has been the establishment of electronic websites for a large number of Arabic publications on the global network. By the end of 1997, Arabic electronic publications included over thirty online daily newspapers, eighteen weekly magazines, and thirty monthly professional and general mass publications. Some of these publications offer special electronic versions to Internet subscribers and others publish the full paper version, albeit on a subscription basis, as in the cases of *Al-Sharq Al-Awsat* and *Al-Hayat* newspapers (see appendices).

Digital Communications Technologies

The Arab world's gradual integration into the global economic system seems to have prompted huge investments in generally backward telecommunications infrastructures. For example, Egypt allocated $700 million to its 1992-1997 five-year plan for the development of communications using a combination of microwave, satellite, and submarine fiber optic lines. Egypt has increased switching capacity from 160 lines in 1981 to 8,066 in 1996 (Adams 1997). The United Arab Emirates has also taken the lead in telecommunications development, becoming a key telecommunications and information technology center. The UAE telecommunications provider, Etisalat, has invested heavily in the modernization of the country's telecommunications sector. The corporation has been involved in a series of regional and international telecommunications projects seeking to upgrade the UAE's connectivity with other countries using state-of-the art technologies. Such projects include the aforementioned FLAG project (Fiber Optic Link Around the Globe) project, the FOG (Fiber Optic Gulf) link (connecting Kuwait, Bahrain, Qatar, and the UAE) and the THURAYYA satellite system. THURAYYA will provide direct broadcast television as well as a range of telecommunications services to governments and private businesses in a region extending from Southeast Asia to the Western coasts of Africa (Ayish 1997). Other Arab countries have also launched multimillion dollar telecommunications projects with foreign service providers as partners.

Ongoing developments in telecommunications have paved the way for Arab countries to go online and join the global information superhighway club. Abd al-Qadir Kamali and Adnan al-Husaini note three categories of Internet providers in the Arab world: countries with a single provider, most often a government PTT (post, telegraph, and telephone), such as Jordan, the UAE, Bahrain, Qatar, Kuwait, Oman; countries with multiple providers, such as Lebanon, Egypt, and Morocco; and countries where Internet services are confined to research centers and universities or are not available at all, such as Iraq, Syria, Sudan, and Libya. Yet, it was found that although the Arab world has started to go on-line at an impressive pace, the Internet rate of diffusion seems to be far lower than in the United States. In 1997, there were 15,250 Internet subscribers in the United Arab Emirates making up 20.9 percent of total subscribers in the Arab world. The percentage of Internet subscribers in other Arab countries compared to total Arab world subscriptions is as follows: Saudi Arabia and Bahrain (17.8%), Egypt (16.5%), Kuwait (13.7%), Jordan (5.5%), Oman (5.3%), and Qatar (3.8%). It was also noted that the Internet user rate in the Arab world is two per 1,000 persons, whereas in the United States it is one user per nine persons. They concluded that Internet use in the Arab world is hindered by high costs, low data transfer speed, and limited service availability (Kamali and al-Huseini 1997: 25).

Data on computer markets in the Middle East shows a remarkable growth in user rates, which seems to auger well for the integration of the Arab world into the information age. Information technology spending in the Middle East is put in late 1997 at $1.5 to $2 billion a year, and 400,000 to 500,000 personal computers are estimated to be sold in the region annually. The development of Arabized software has significantly contributed to the flourishing computer market spearheaded by pan-Arab computer software developer Sakhr. Starting in 1982 as a hardware and software integrator for regional markets, Sakhr shifted its focus to Windows-based software design and manufacture. Some of its best-selling products consist of a multilingual searchable program that includes a fully vowelized Arabic text, a 62,000-word Hadith encyclopedia, educational software, and a series of Arabized Internet applications. Yet, despite such achievements, software piracy in the region remains the world's highest, with revenue losses estimated at $551 million in 1996.[4]

THE ARAB MASS MEDIA SCENE: SOCIAL ROLES

The question that needs to be addressed in this section relates to whether the technological modernization of Arab mass media in the

1990s has been a mere "surgical change of face" or has given rise to a more active social communications role in modern Arab societies. In other words, if the importation of new technologies is presumed not to be an end unto itself, but rather a means of achieving a set of social goals, how does this "change of face" seem to affect media relationships with individuals and social institutions in Arab countries? The following section surveys Arab media as tools of free public debates pertaining to the realization of participatory development in its general sense.

Media as Fora of Free Discourse

Since their inception in the mid-nineteenth century (newspapers) and the early twentieth century (radio), Arab mass media have been placed under a range of social and political controls that adversely affected their freedom. During Turkish and Western colonial eras, newspapers were used as mouthpieces of ruling authorities, seeking to propagate their views and policies (al-Musa 1986). At the same time, a growing legalized and underground opposition press was evolving in parallel lines, serving as an alternative outlet of expression. Broadcasting, on the other hand, was launched from the very beginning exclusively as a government operation, making it virtually impossible for opposition groups to start their own radio and television services.

In the post-colonial era, successive Arab governments have consolidated their grip on the press through sweeping inhibitive press laws and codes, favoring official definitions of media rights and duties. From the Arab governments' point of view, according to Munir Nasser, press freedom has been sacrificed in the interests of national unity (Nasser 1983: 64). To many Third World officials (including Arab states), it is more important to speak with a national voice than to encourage dissent. It is argued that press freedom endangers national security and the welfare of the state. In a situation where a large segment of the population is illiterate, and where loyalties are drawn along family and tribal lines, conditions that justify a free press do not exist. Like other Third World leaders, Arab statesmen often argue that freedom is a relative concept that has to be carefully applied in the context of responsibility, and Western free press may not necessarily be replicated in the Arab world (Weaver et al. 1990: 115).

By the early 1990s, the Arab governments' tight hold on media operations began to loosen, primarily in response to economic and political globalization trends. The break-up of the Soviet Union, coupled with a sweeping digitally based communications revolution, has opened the way for the diffusion of free market orientations manifested in the rise of privatization as a defining concept of emerging national and global realities. The globalization of national economies has also implied the institutionalization of more liberal and democratic schemes of governance around the world, including the Arab region. Parliamentary elections organized in the past decade following years of martial law-based regimes in Egypt, Jordan, Morocco, Kuwait, Yemen, and Lebanon seem to reflect more relaxed political environments. In traditionally conservative Arab societies where elections are not a common practice, national consultative councils entrusted with advisory functions have been set up in Saudi Arabia, the United Arab Emirates, and Qatar. In the rest of the Arab countries, parliamentary elections are periodically organized under a ruling party platform, producing legislative bodies powerful enough to cause the ouster of a cabinet minister on corruption charges, yet too weak to question certain national policies.

Liberal political developments have spawned numerous amendments to century-old communication laws, making them relatively more responsive to the accelerating changes experienced in the Arab world. New press laws introduced in the early 1990s in Jordan, Egypt, Yemen, the United Arab Emirates, Morocco, and Qatar seem far more liberal than their predecessors. Such laws provide for the individual's rights to free speech and expression, albeit on the basis of governments' perceptions of those rights. In some Arab countries, new laws allow for the establishment of an opposition press, as in Jordan, Egypt, Morocco, Lebanon, and Kuwait. The new developments seem also to have a significant effect on traditionally government-controlled broadcasting. More autonomous radio and television corporations have been established in Jordan, Bahrain, Kuwait, United Arab Emirates, Qatar, and Egypt. Though newly reformed broadcast organizations continue to act as government bodies, they operate more independently of ministries of information, especially in financial and some editorial matters.

The aforementioned political liberalization developments have also been accompanied by a growing role of the private sector and an increasing state disengagement from social and economic sectors. Backed by international organizations like the World Bank and the International Monetary Fund, Arab privatization programs have gone a long way in Morocco, Oman, Jordan, and Egypt despite heavy social costs (Feigenbaum et al. 1997). To some degree, economic privatization in the Arab world seems to have spilled over to the communications sector, especially telecommunications markets, some of which have already been opened up to foreign service providers in Jordan, Egypt, Lebanon, and Morocco. The conventional mass media sector has also been affected by this trend, with the expansion of privately owned print media and book publishing outlets and the launch of commercial broadcast operations inside and outside the Arab region.

The proliferation of government-controlled and privately owned print, broadcast, and electronic media has provided Arab audiences with more diversified access to news, entertainment, and other information. What used to be a single TV channel environment with a maximum of three newspapers has turned into a multiple media outlet. By the end of 1997, there were sixty Arabic and over 100 satellite television channels in addition to scores of terrestrial services covering large portions of Arab lands. Media content has also been affected as competition-wary newspapers and broadcasters seem to have become keener on fostering closer ties with audiences. Print media content critical of domestic government policies is common in the press systems of Egypt, Morocco, Kuwait, Jordan, and Lebanon. More space is being devoted to readers' views and to those of intellectuals on issues ranging from Arab solidarity, to the stalled Middle East peace process, to the rehabilitation of Iraq. Issues of this critical caliber are also being boldly tackled by certain satellite TV programs such as Orbit's *On the Air*, Al-Jazeera's *Opposite Direction*, and MBC's *Dialogue With the West* and *Beyond Events*.

But despite these advancements, a survey of communication realities in the Arab world suggests that press freedom remains an elusive goal for media practitioners. In as much as Arab communication laws recognize the individual's right to free expression, they also embody institutional penalties for what would be interpreted as media transgressions on societal and state rights. They generally range from prosecution of journalists to censorship of information perceived to be harmful to national interests (security and unity), religious beliefs, social norms, the leadership, neighboring countries and their leaders, the integrity and honor of private citizens, and others.[5] The situation is best exemplified by the following observation from Abdullah Zain on press freedom in Yemen:

> Although freedom of expression is guaranteed by the Press and
> Publications Law, the Yemeni press is virtually unprotected as both
> the constitution and the National Charter view this freedom as a
> precious and sacred right (...) Censorship has been tailored to fit the
> interpretations of the Ministry of information and officials seem to
> be narrow-minded in their views and oblivious to the prevailing
> mentality in the nation's institutions. (Zain 1992: 516)

To a large extent, media laws in the Arab world seem not only to favor government interpretations of national interests, but are also vulnerable to frequent government revisions. For example, the 1993 Jordanian press law was hailed as a liberal attempt to institutionalize a greater margin of freedom; yet its May 1997 amendment requiring the press to maintain a minimum $450,000 capital led to the closure of ten weekly publications and to widespread protests from the journalistic community. As the editor of a Jordanian daily newspaper notes, the press in the country's democratic phase continues to be hindered by legal restrictions and a lack of structural changes in ownership patterns (Hawatmeh 1995: 8).

Likewise, the Egyptian government's 1996 June amendment of a series of restrictive legal provisions governing the press (known as "Law 93" of 1995) in response to a one-year campaign by journalists was too minimal a step compared to the remaining inhibitive components of the existing press law, dubbed by journalists as the "Press Assassination Law." The bill imposed lengthy prison terms together with hefty fines for journalists convicted of libel and a host of other ill-defined publication crimes.[6] Amendments included the repeal of a provision granting authorities the right to detain journalists without charge. Mauritania's 1991 restrictive "Press Ordinance" gives power to the Minister of the Interior to ban the distribution and sale of any newspaper or periodical that is likely to harm Islamic principles, state authority, or that jeopardizes public order. Finally, Algeria's media seem to be experiencing the most critical conditions in the Arab world as they grapple with the dual challenge of surviving restrictive government controls and ceaseless intimidation from dissident groups. Sixty-nine media professionals were killed in Algeria since 1993 in acts of domestic strife and scores of others were kept behind bars on security charges.[7]

Restrictive media regulations even dominate countries classified by William Rugh as having diverse press systems (Rugh 1979). In Lebanon, a 1996 cabinet decision, later passed by parliament as the "Audio-Visual Law," granted licenses to four television and eleven radio stations, resulting in the voluntary and forced closure of dozens of others dubbed as "pirate stations." Forty-seven stations, mainly from the opposition media, were denied licenses after submitting applications to the government. In Morocco, a press code gives authorities the right to seize newspapers or other publications believed to contain materials threatening "public order."[8] The press in Kuwait, among the freest in the pre-Iraqi invasion era, has also suffered numerous setbacks as the country recovered from the military conflict.

Inhibitions on information flow in the Arab world seem also to embrace computer-based electronic media of communication. Although many Arab countries are coming on-line in increasing numbers, many governments are doing their best to control what they perceive as morally destructive and politically subversive information. Whereas some countries have restricted access to the Internet, confining it to educational institutions, others have chosen to install screening devices to filter out unwanted materials. The latter case applies to Morocco, Jordan, Bahrain, Kuwait, and the United Arab Emirates. As Joel Campagna notes, creative initiatives to utilize advances in technology such as the Internet promise to facilitate the free flow of information to all citizens of the Arab region, thus rendering government censorship practices irrelevant (Campagna 1997). In many countries, however, the success of these efforts will depend largely on the willingness of governments to relinquish their control over the distribution of information services.

Media as Tools of National Development

The historical development of Arab communications in the context of restrictive settings was instrumental in the rise of "development communication" as a defining concept of media work in the post-colonial era. Originally conceived to denote an active media role in stimulating free public debates pertaining to national development issues in their comprehensive sense (Aggarwala 1979), development communication has come to represent an intellectual and political tradition of communication that precludes freedom of expression as a prerequisite for media involvement in nation-building efforts. Common in Arab societies with varied political orientations, this view draws on the notion that a free press is a luxury Third World nations can do without. Proponents of this view argued that given the conditions of scarce resources, a colonial legacy, a poorly educated population, tribal and ethnic rivalries, and a subservient position in the world economic and information system, a free press can easily lead to an inability of the government to function and to internal chaos (Weaver et al. 1990: 102). According to this view, media dependency on foreign sources is likely to rise as communications lose sight of domestic social, political, and cultural transformations (Abd al-Rahman 1986).

In its basic configuration, the "development communication" perspective incorporates a prescribed media participation in discussing (and therefore promoting) national development activities and projects in the health, agriculture, banking, education, population, and environmental sectors. Originally associated with the "old paradigm" of social and economic change, "development communication" has undergone remarkable transformations in its theoretical underpinnings and implications. Two of its key elements include a realistic view of the power of communications in bringing about desired social change and an emphasis on horizontal communication with grassroots participation. Based on development communication experiences around the world, researchers have come to conceive of the media as playing a supportive rather than an independent role in national development processes. Media contributions to national development are contingent on numerous variables, the most outstanding of which are the institutional social and political arrangements in which the media operate and the availability of human and technical resources (Rogers and Kinkaid 1981).

To these developmental areas Arab mass media have devoted substantive portions of their airtime and print space. Yet, it was found that development materials carried by the Arab media were personality-centered, protocol-oriented, superficially treated, and overwhelmingly positive, lacking critical discussions of issues relating to public policies (Ayish 1989; al-Inad 1994; Kazan 1993; Nuwaisi 1981; Palmer 1993; al-Sarayrah 1986; Shalabieh and Ayish 1991; Sharif 1996; Talat 1987). Furthermore, it was found that development coverage in national print and broadcast media was restricted to urban centers to the exclusion of rural populations whose social and economic woes need the greatest amount of attention. It was also noted that media coverage of develop-ment news was biased in favor of timely events with little investigation of crucial issues and trends underlying social and cultural transforma-tions in modern Arab societies. The media also devoted little attention to women and in most cases have sought to reinforce traditional stereo-types incompatible with impressive advancements achieved by Arab women in social and economic spheres.[9]

In addition to regular coverage of development news, the Arab media also carried out systematic and timely information efforts imple-mented within the concept of communication campaigns. During the past two decades, a good number of those campaigns have been success-fully implemented with high ratings from international organizations. Scores of documented cases provide accounts of mass media uses to educate the public on issues pertaining to health, agriculture, the envi-ronment, and population in Egypt, Tunisia, Morocco, Jordan, Sudan, Iraq, and Saudi Arabia (Abu Laban et al. 1990; Ayish and Rifai 1991; al-Kamal 1989; Nasr 1997; Palmer 1993; al-Sarayrah et. al. 1994). Most of those activities involved planning and carrying out communication cam-paigns targeting specialized or general audiences to increase their knowledge and shape their attitude on issues like family planning, liter-acy, drug addiction, AIDS, and breast-feeding.

Regular and campaign-oriented media involvement in develop-ment in the Arab world has been plagued by numerous problems that seem to have limited the integration of communications into national development strategies. They include loosely formulated development plans, insecure external financing, limited media resources, and foggy communication policies. Rasim al-Jammal notes that communication policies in the Arab world have failed to be properly integrated into development policies and have not been accorded an appropriate status (al-Jammal 1995). In his study of the impact of the mass media on moder-nity in the Arabian Gulf states, Fayad Kazan notes that media participation in national development is hindered by limited freedom of expression, poor integration into overall development plans, and low level two-way interactive communication with audiences (Kazan 1993: 213).

Inasmuch as nondemocratic arrangements, values, and practices have hindered the realization of free media discourse in the Arab world, they have also militated against communications contributions to participatory development. A report by the Arab League Commission for the Study of Communication and Information Issues (1989) in the Arab world stated that:

> There is a shortage of space and airtime in Arab media devoted to development either in terms of explaining its plans and strategies or stimulating dialogue on it, or in terms of the methods of its implementation and evaluation (...) It is noted that Arab mass media are very interested in reporting timely day-to-day activities in a propagandistic fashion rather than in presenting debates on comprehensive long-term issues pertaining to development.[10]

CONCLUSIONS

The preceding discussion shows that in recent years, Arab mass media have experienced substantial transformations in their production methods and delivery systems. The transfer of new technologies into print and broadcast media organizations continues unabated in the 1990s, and is seen primarily as a means of expanding outlets of expression and diversifying sources of information for Arab audiences. The Arabization of computer software and hardware has contributed to the digitalization of Arab communications. Further developments in telecommunications infrastructures in the Arab world have also paved the way for Arab societies to join the global information superhighway. From a technological point of view, satellite systems launched or due for launch into outer space on behalf of ARABSAT and other national organizations are likely to make Arab countries' integration into the global village smoother. Such systems are also expected to expand the media audience, allowing, more than ever before, for a more diverse and varied exposure to communication contents. They are also expected to increase the average daily information intake for individual Arab citizens, though a good deal of that dose would consist of foreign materials from foreign sources or transmitted by Arab media, especially television.

However, the technological modernization of Arab mass media seems to have far outpaced constructive media social roles in modern Arab societies. The study shows that regardless of the approach taken to evaluate Arab media performance, the reality of mass communications remains dismal. On the one hand, the impressive technological stature of modern Arab media in the 1990s has not been conducive to a freer exchange of ideas and to critical debates on major domestic and pan-Arab issues facing modern Arab societies. Relationships between media institutions and political establishments in the Arab world continue to be described in terms of acquiescence, submission, intimidation, and imbalance (Badran 1989; Hamada 1993). Attempts by the media to establish themselves as independent bodies have often been circumvented by restrictive government-sponsored laws and regulations, often favoring official perceptions of realities. Arab media experiences in the 1990s have generated countless cases of media suppression even in countries known for their liberal outlooks. Annual freedom survey reports published by Arab and international organizations seem to testify to the fact that the 1990s were not much different from the 1970s and 1980s when it comes to the ability of the media to criticize governmental practices.[11]

On the other hand, Arab media also seem to have lost substantial ground in playing their traditional role as tools of participatory development. The concept of national development has often turned into a euphemism for the political repression of opposition views, leading to uncritical and one-way flows of information regarding economic and political programs and policies. Even when serious initiatives were taken to highlight developmental achievements, media presentations would be couched in formalities that reflected only the bright sides of the issues. In the 1990s, the imposition of tighter governmental controls over broadcast structures and the enactment of more restrictive legislation to regulate print media have severely curtailed media contributions to participatory development.

The introduction of new technologies seems to have further strained the financial conditions of a large number of the media organizations in the Arab world, as it requires huge investments in equipment purchases and training. Unable to provide the necessary needed financial resources, Arab-world broadcast and print media alike have turned to advertising as an additional source of income to cover spiraling production costs and equipment purchases. In turn, this development has led to further commercialization of media content, and hence to more detachment from national development issues.

The globalization of Arab societies in the 1990s seems to militate against both the realization of a free media environment and a substantive media role in national development. Richard Hawkins notes that in the era of globalization, many political as well as economic problems are now perceived to be global in origin, thus suggesting that only "global solutions" to these problems are optimal, or even possible (Hawkins

1997: 177). As national agendas continue to be externally inspired, media agendas are likely to be affected, with issues of interest to the indigenous Arab populations put on the back burner.

These developments have serious implications for the media in the Arab world. Left with limited options, Arab media either have to join the global bandwagon and phase out their national agendas, or they must seek to walk a tightrope by striking a balance between national and global issues and concerns. Although this role seems the safest, it also carries with it the risk of taking on a paradoxical character with negative consequences for national identities and social values and traditions. On the other hand, an isolationist role would also be more devastating, as it represents a suicidal attempt to hold out in the face of a sweeping external communication blitz. Both roles seem to hinder long-term Arab media survival in the information age.

A modest proposal for Arab media survival in the new information age draws on the concept of pan-Arab integration in political, economic, cultural, and communication spheres. The Arab world, rich in its traditions and moral values as well as economic resources, has the potential to bring about a solid media system that ensures continuity of communications functions in the context of cultural distinctiveness and global interactivity. The role of the media as preservers and perpetuators of Arab cultural values and as carriers of Arab contributions to human civilization would be strongly emphasized. In the coming information age, media battles would be cultural rather than political and their grounds are bound to be global rather than local. In the context of pan-Arab communications integration, media functions stand a better chance of success.

The conception of the media in pan-Arab rather than individual state terms is, of course, contingent on the degree of political and economic integration achievable among Arab countries. Communications, as we have come to realize, are both products and reflectors of sociopolitical, cultural, and economic realities. They could not, and should not, be viewed independently of those realities. Hence, the survival of the Arab media in the new information age does not seem to be solely a function of massive transfers of state-of-the-art technologies, but also of the nature of social, political, and economic pan-Arab contexts in which communicators would operate.

Appendix 1
Table 5.1: Daily Electronic Publications.

Publication	Language	Country of Origin
Al-Dustur	Arabic	Jordan
Al-Rai	Arabic	Jordan
Jordan Times	English	Jordan
Al-Sharq Al-Awsat	Arabic	Saudi Arabia
Al-Hayat	Arabic	Great Britain
At-Watan	Arabic	Kuwait
Al-Ayam	Arabic	Bahrain
Al-Anwar	Arabic	Lebanon
Khaleej Times	English	UAE
Al-Ittihad	Arabic	UAE
Kuwait Times	English	Kuwait
Al-Safir	Arabic	Lebanon
Al-Ayam	Arabic	Palestine
Al-Quds	Arabic	Palestine
Al-Nahar	Arabic	Lebanon
Al-Watan	Arabic	Qatar
Al-Sharq	Arabic	Qatar
Gulf Times	English	Qatar
Al-Raya	Arabic	Qatar
Arab Net	Arabic	Australia
Al-Jumhuriya	Arabic	Egypt
Al-Messa	Arabic	Egypt
Al-Sahafa	Arabic	Tunisia
Al-Bayan	Arabic	UAE
Cairo Press Review	Arabic	Egypt
Gulf News	English	UAE
Petra News Agency	English	Jordan
Al-Khalij	Arabic	UAE
Bahrain Tribune	English	Bahrain
Al-Jazira	Arabic	Saudi Arabia
Al-Qabas	Arabic	Kuwait
Al-Madina	Arabic	Saudi Arabia
Al-Watan	Arabic	Oman
Quds Press Service	Arabic	Great Britain

Source: http://www.liii.com/~hajeri/newstand/daily-news.html (November 1997)

Appendix 2
Table 5.2: Weekly Electronic Publications.

Publication	Language	Country of Origin
Al-Sabil	Arabic	Jordan
Shihan	Arabic	Jordan
Abd Rabbu	Arabic	Jordan
Al-Hadath	Arabic	Jordan
The Star	English	Jordan
Jordan Antiquity	English	Jordan
MELAD	English	Jordan
Al-Mustaqbal	Arabic	Canada
Al-Mirat	Arabic	Canada
Libanorama	Arabic	Canada
Al-Watan	Arabic	USA
Beirut Times	English	USA
Al-Itidal	Arabic	USA
Jerusalem Times	English	Palestine
26 September	Arabic	Yemen
Kul Al-Arab	Arabic	Palestine
Yemen Times	English	Yemen
Middle East Economic Digest	English	Cyprus

Source: http://www.liii.com/~hajeri/newstand/daily-news.html (November 1997)

Appendix 2
Table 5.3: Monthly Electronic Publications.

Publication	Language	Country of Origin
Al-Sirat Al-Mustqim	Arabic	USA
Byte-Middle East	Arabic/English	Jordan
Computer News Middle East	English	USA
Al-Akhbar	English	Palestine
PC-Middle East	English	USA
Business and Technology	Arabic	Jordan
Economic Perspectives	English	Jordan
Al-Nafitha	Arabic	Canada
Issues	English	Jordan
Lebanon News Wire	English	Lebanon
Al-Moharar	Arabic	Australia
Libyan News Agency	English	Great Britain

Appendix 2
Table 5.3: Monthly Electronic Publications (con't).

Al-Muntada	Arabic	USA
Al-Shahr Online	Arabic	USA
Arab View	Arabic	Great Britain
Alamouna	English	USA
Tair Al-Shamal	Arabic	Norway
Nida'il Islam	English	Australia
Al Shindagah	English	UAE
Al Jadid	English	USA
Egypt Today	English	Egypt
Jordan Today	English	Jordan
Jordan Economic Monitor	English	Jordan
Palestine Times	English	Great Britain
Bahrain IT	English	Bahrain
Update	English	UAE
Business Today	English	Egypt
Sudan Views and News	English	Great Britain

Source: http://www.liii.com/~hajeri/newstand/daily-news.html (November 1997)

ENDNOTES

1. *World Media Handbook*. United Nations. New York: UN Department of Public Information, 1995.
2. Index on Censorship. "Press Law 93, 1995." carry.on.oneworld.org/index_oc/issue295/Saudi.html (October 1997).
3   *World Media Handbook* (see note 1).
4. Mideast Computer Mart Expands Fast. *Gulf News*, October 31, 1997.
5. *Press and Publications Laws and Regulations in the States of the Arab Gulf Cooperation Council*. GCC General Secretariat. Riyadh: GCC General Secretariat, 1993 (in Arabic).
6. Committee for the Protection of Journalists. http://CPJ.Org./news/attacks96/countries/Middle Eastlinks.html (November 4, 1997).
7. *Now the Newspapers Are Dying in Algeria*. International Press Institute (IPI Report: First Quarter), 1997.
8. *World Press Freedom Review*. International Press Institute (IPI Report: November/December), 1996.
9. Abd al-Rahman 1994; *The Image of Arab Women in Mass Media and Arts of Expression. A Series of Studies on Arab Women and Development*. Economic and Social Commission for Western Asia (ESCWA). New York: ESCWA, 1996.

10.   *Towards a New Arab Information and Communication Order: Final Report.*
      Arab League Commission for the Study of Communication and
      Information Issues in the Arab World. Tunisia: Arab League Educational,
      Scientific and Cultural Organization (ALESCO), 1985 (in Arabic).
11.   *Now the Newspapers Are Dying in Algeria* (see note 9); *Annual Report.* Arab
      Human Rights Organization. Cairo: Arab Human Rights Organization,
      1997.

BIBLIOGRAPHY

Abd al-Rahman, Awatef. 1994. Arab Women and the Media: Between Reality
      and Response (in Arabic). *Dirasat Ilamia* (April-June): 94-113.
Abd al-Rahman, Awatef. 1996. *The Arab Press: Confronting Dependency and Zionist
      Penetration* (in Arabic). Cairo: Dar Al-Fiqr Al-Arabi.
Abu Laban, A. S. Bahous, K. Abdul Rahman, and Judith McDivitt. 1990.
      *Breastfeeding Knowledge and Practices in Jordan: An Evaluation Report of the
      Health Campaign* (in Arabic). Amman: Nur Al-Husain.
Abu Zaid, Faruq. 1985. *Migrant Arab Press* (in Arabic). Cairo: Madbuli.
Abu Zaid, Faruq. 1986. *Press Systems in the Arab World* (in Arabic). Cairo: Alam
      Al-Kutub.
Adams, April. 1997. Arab FLAG Vase Telecom Opportunities. *Christian Science
      Monitor*, August 22.
Aggarwala, Narinder. 1979. What Is Development News? *Journal of
      Communication* (Spring): 180-185.
Aldham, John. 1997. Media Production City: The Jewel in the Middle East
      Broadcasting Crown. *Middle East Broadcast and Satellite* (November): 34-35.
Ali, Nabil. 1995. *The Arabs and the Information Age.* Kuwait: National Council for
      Culture and Arts.
al-Arif, Mohammed. 1997. *The Impact of Satellite and Computer Technologies on
      Arab Mass Media* (in Arabic). Abu Dhabi: Emirates Center for Strategic
      Studies and Research.
Arthur, David. 1997. Stunning New Developments in Industry. *Khaleej Times*,
      Supplement, March 5.
Ayalon, Ami. 1995. *The Press in the Arab Middle East: A History.* New York:
      Oxford University Press.
Ayish, Muhammad. 1989. Newsfilm in Jordan Television's Arabic Nightly
      Newscasts. *Journal of Broadcasting and Electronic Media* 4: 453-460.
Ayish, Muhammad. 1991. Foreign Voices as Peoples Choices: BBC Popularity in
      the Arab World. *Middle Eastern Studies* 3: 374- 389.
Ayish, Muhammad. 1997. *Telecommunications Policies and Trends in the United
      Arab Emirates and their Implications for National Development.* Paper
      Presented at the Conference on the Information Revolution and its Impact
      on State and Society in the Arab World. Abu Dhabi: Emirates Center for
      Strategic Studies and Research.
Ayish, Muhammad, and Ziyad Rifai. 1991. The Effects of Communications
      Campaigns on Levels of Knowledge, Attitudes and Practices Pertaining to

Family Planning in a Northern Jordanian Town (in Arabic). *Abhath Al-Yarmuk* 3: 23-62.

Ayish, Muhammad, and Ali Qassim. 1995. Direct Satellite Broadcasting in the Arab Gulf Region: Trends and Policies. *Gazette* 56: 19-36.

Badran, Badran. 1989. Press-Government Relations in Jordan: A Case Study. *Journalism Quarterly* (Summer): 335-340.

Boyd, Douglas A. 1993. *Broadcasting in the Arab World: A Survey of the Electronic Media in the Middle East*. Ames: Iowa State University Press.

Campagna, Joel. 1997. Online Website of the Committee for the Protection of Journalists (CPJ). http://CPJ.Org./news/attacks96/countries/MiddleEastlinks.html (November 4, 1997).

Feigenbaum, H. et al. 1997. *Privatization Programs in the Arab World: An Occasional Paper*. Abu Dhabi, UAE: Center for Strategic Studies and Research.

Hamada, Basyuni. 1993. *The Role of Mass Media in Decision Making in the Arab World* (in Arabic). Beirut: Arab Unity Studies Center.

Hamada, Basyuni. 1994. The Relationship Between Media Practitioners and Politicians in the Arab World (in Arabic). *Alam Al-Fikr* 2: 166-223.

Hawatmeh, George. 1995. The Changing Role of the Jordanian Press in the Democratic Era. In *The Role of Jordanian Media in Democracy*, edited by George Hawatmeh, 1-5. Amman: Jordan Center for Strategic Studies/University of Jordan.

Hawkins, Richard. 1997. Prospects for Global Communication Infrastructure in the 21st Century: Institutional Restructuring and Network Development. In *Media in Global Context: A Reader*, edited by Annabelle Sreberny-Mohammadi, Dwayne Winseck, Jim McKenna, and Oliver Boyd-Barrett, 177-193. London: Arnold.

al-Inad, Abd al-Rahman. 1994. First Page News in Daily Saudi Newspapers (in Arabic). *Dirasat Ilamia* (January): 61-75.

al-Jammal, Rasim. 1995. *Communication and Information in the Arab World* (in Arabic). Beirut: Arab Unity Studies Center.

al-Jerdi, Nabil A., and Muwaffaq A. Majid. 1997. The Impact of Desktop Publishing Technology in Six Major Printing Firms in Kuwait. *Journal of Gulf and Arab Peninsula Studies* 84: 245-271.

al-Kamal, Farag. 1989. How the Egyptian ORT Communication Campaign Succeeded (in Arabic). *Majallat Kulliyat Al-Iam* (Cairo University) 1: 103-143.

Kamalipour, Yahya, and Hamid Mowlana. 1994. *Mass Media in the Middle East: A Comprehensive Handbook*. Westport, CT: Greenwood.

Kamali, Abd al-Qadir, and Adnan al-Huseini. 1997. Arab Countries Take Off into the Internet Age. *Arab World Internet* 3: 24-30.

Kazan, Fayad. 1993. *Mass Media, Modernity, and Development: Arab States of the Gulf*. Westport, CT: Praeger.

al-Labban, J. 1997. Desktop Publishing Technologies in the Egyptian Press. *Egyptian Journal of Communication* 1: 33-48.

Lubbadeh, Fares. 1995-96. Introduction of Digital Services in the Arab World (in Arabic). *Al-Majalla Al-Tunisia L-Ulam Al-Ittisal* (December-January): 187-197.

Lubbadeh, Fares. 1996. Home-grown Broadcasting in Jordan. *Middle East Broadcast and Satellite* (March): 13-18.

Lubbadeh, Fares. 1997. Modern ART: The Transition to Digital. *Middle East Broadcast and Satellite* (November): 12-15.

Mrowwa, Adib. 1961. *The Arab Press: Its Inception and Development.* Beirut: Al-Hayat Bookshop.

al-Musa, Issam. 1986. *Introduction to Mass Communication* (in Arabic). Irbid: Al-Kittani.

Nasr, Issam. 1997. The Informational Role of A Television Campaign Against AIDS: A Case Study from Saudi Arabia (in Arabic). *Majallat Al-Ulum Al-Insaniyya Al-Ijtimaiyya* 2: 63-120.

Nasser, Munir. 1979. *Press, Politics, and Power: Egypt's Heikal and Al-Ahram.* Ames: Iowa State University Press.

Nasser, Munir. 1983. News Values versus Ideology: A Third World Perspective. In *Comparative Mass Media Systems*, edited by L. John Martin and Anju Grover Chaudhary, 44-66. New York: Longman.

Nuwaisi, Abdullah. 1981. *Mass Media and National Development* (in Arabic). Abu Dhabi: Al-Ittihad Foundation.

Palmer, Edward L. 1993. *Toward a Literate World: Television in Literary Education—Lessons from the Arab Region.* Boulder, CO: Westview.

al-Rashed, Ibrahim. 1997. *Journalism and Publishing Technologies in the United Arab Emirates.* Abu Dhabi: Al-Ittihad Publishing.

Rogers, Everett, and D. L. Kinkaid. 1981. *Communication Networks: Toward a New Paradigm for Research.* New York: Free Press.

Rugh, William. 1979. *The Arab Press: News Media and Political Process in the Arab World.* Syracuse: Syracuse University Press.

al-Sarayrah, Mohammed, Muhammad Ayish, and Sima Bahus. 1994. Communication and Birth Spacing Programs in the Context of the Social Marketing Approach: The Case of Jordan (in Arabic). *Dirastat* 6: 373-407.

al-Sarayrah, Mohammed. 1986. Foreign News in two Jordanian Newspapers. *Journalism Quarterly* 2: 363-365.

Sardar, Ziauddin. 1982. *Science and Technology in the Middle East: A Guide to Issues, Organizations and Institutions.* New York: Gale Research.

Shalabieh, Mahmud, and Muhammad Ayish. 1991. Population Communication on Jordanian Radio and Television: An Analytical Study (in Arabic). *Abhath Al-Yarmuk* 1: 129-151.

Sharif, Sami. 1996. Arab News in Gulf Newspapers: A Comparative Study (in Arabic). *Majallat Al-Ulum Al-Insaniyya Al-Ijtimaiyya* 1: 107-153.

Talat, Shahinaz. 1987. *Mass Media and Rural Development in Egypt* (in Arabic). Cairo: Maktabat Al-Anglu Al-Misriyya.

Weaver, David, Judith Buddenbaum, and Ellen Fair. 1990. Press Freedom, Media, and Development, 1950-1979: A Study of 134 Nations. In *Current Issues in International Communication*, edited by John Martin and Ray Eldon Hiebert, 101-110. New York: Longman.

Zain, Abdullah. 1992. *Communication and Freedom of Expression in Yemen: 1974-1990* (in Arabic). Beirut: Dar Al-Fikr Al-Muassir.

6

Internet in the Arab World: A Step Towards "Information Society?"

Henner Kirchner

Information technology, or the global networking of information and communication systems, is seen as the single most significant technology of the future. Catch phrases such as "information society," "global networking," and "global village" describe the utopian visions associated with it. The political, social, and economic potential of information technologies is continually debated as are the risks and conflicts inherent in these technologies. One particularly controversial aspect of this discussion is the development towards a global information society and its possible social and political ramifications, which find radical critics as well as euphoric supporters. Some see the "electronic democracy" as a key to the future functioning of complex communities (Bangemann 1997: 2), whereas others remain skeptical of the great "illusion of the democratic Internet" (Torres 1995: 4). The Arab region is confronted with local rather than global problems in the development of networking; for example, with restrictive media policies and a lack of acceptance of the new media by state authorities.

Information is one of the most important resources, along with the three other crucial economic factors—labor, capital, and natural resources. International organizations such as the World Bank or UNESCO therefore advise Third World countries to invest in modern information technologies in order to improve their people's standards of living. However, what perspectives, what political, economic, and cultural advantages does the "information age" offer these countries? Will access to the "network of networks" take these countries one step farther on the way to democracy and free access to information, or will it foster the development of an "information elite" on a regional as well as an international level?

The recent development of the network communication sector will be discussed in this article with respect to the Arab countries, as well as the political and socioeconomic impulses that originate from the use of modern communication technologies and from the newly established access to the Internet in this region.

META-MEDIUM INTERNET

Apart from this technical dimension, the Internet makes possible certain forms of communication that go beyond the unidirectional pattern characteristic of the traditional media. Uni-, bi- and multidirectional forms of communication exist side by side and converge. E-mail offers direct communication similar to letter writing plus a medium for discussion via mailing lists. The discussion forums (newsgroups) offered by the Usenet, similar to mailing lists, provide for joint and simultaneous discussion between numerous participants. The best-known service, often confused with the Internet, is the World Wide Web (WWW). But the Internet is also a meta-medium. To classify it as a completely new medium, however, is to overrate the possibilities connected with it: "The Internet does not pioneer new forms; it gives some forms new reach, impact and scope" (Anderson 1997a).

Such overrating led to the myth of the Internet as being democratic and promoting democracy, a myth propagandized especially by those benefiting from this development, like Bill Gates:

> Only few of the advantages of online interactivity are of such potential significance (...) as the improvement of democracy as aided by the Internet. Personal computers connected with interactive networks will provide citizens with the opportunity to participate easily and immediately in democratic processes. (Gates 1996)

It is true that the characteristics of computer-transmitted network communication are relevant from a political and distinctly democratic perspective. Barriers to access to information are removed when decentralized data become available. Digitalization has made it feasible to reproduce information *indeterminately*. There is a seeming equality of information suppliers. The thinning out of communication hierarchies moderates the filter that is typical for traditional media. Top-to-bottom communication is supplemented by bottom-to-top and horizontal communication. Interactivity and a multidirectional format emerge beside primarily distributive forms of political communication (Rilling 1996).

In addition to this, Jon W. Anderson, Professor of Anthropology at the Catholic University of America, Washington, D.C., stresses two other characteristics of network communication:

> The most striking feature of the Internet in this regard is spontaneous, unofficial representation. What this activity marks is an increasingly public, unmoderated (and not infrequently immoderate) representation that additional participants can join on their own authority and interest plus ability to use the technology. (...) By comparison to the asymmetrical arrangements of broadcasting, on the Internet barriers to access are only slightly higher for senders than for receivers, and those are coming down all over. (Anderson 1997a)

These features provoke high expectations for democratic development. The use of those services on the Internet that best represent the multidirectional component mentioned above, namely E-mail and Usenet, also nourishes these expectations: between 1.5 and 2 million messages are exchanged daily in approximately 75,000 mailing lists[1] and almost 20,000 newsgroups[2] and are read by numerous users. This makes the Internet an ideal medium for political activism, particularly for small groups and those who are denied access to other mediums. The Internet offers them the opportunity to present themselves to a wide audience at little cost.

THE NORTH-SOUTH DIFFERENTIAL IN INFORMATION TECHNOLOGY

The number of host computers, that is, of computers permanently connected with the Internet, has multiplied over the past several years. Whereas there were only 500 hosts in 1983, their number had risen to 5 million in 1995 (Afemann 1996a). In 1996, the Bellcore Internet Architecture Research Laboratory had 14.7 million host computers registered, a number which had supposedly risen to 26 million by September 1997. Other sources estimate nearly 20 million computers connected with the Internet.[3] About 70 percent of these computers are used in the United States, 25 percent in Europe and Japan (Afemann 1996a). The remaining 5 percent are allotted to the rest of the world. Considering that even these remaining Internet connections are concentrated in only a few countries,[4] these figures show an extreme difference between the north and the south in terms of accessibility of the Internet.

Furthermore, only about one-fifth of the world's population has access to the basic resources (electricity, telephone, etc.) necessary for network communication (Rilling 1996). This is particularly obvious when looking at the worldwide distribution of telephone lines. First World metropolitan areas such as Tokyo have as many connections available to them as the entire African continent (Afemann 1996a).

It is not only infrastructure and finance that exclude the overwhelming majority of the developing countries' populations (and therefore the greater part of humanity) from the opportunities offered by network communication. The general social conditions in those countries (e.g., illiteracy, lack of resources) also contribute to this fact. The comparison of north and south shows a significant feature of the electronic media that is also apparent within the industrialized ("information") societies: inequality. The Internet, currently available to 1 to 2 percent of the world's population, predominantly represents those who already have a strong socioeconomic standing and who are able to mobilize resources even without the new medium. Consequently, it is the members of local Third World elites living and working abroad who are their home countries' pioneers of the network communication sector.

About half of the Internet is used commercially, and this percentage is increasing. The development is not homogeneous in the Third World. The proportion varies from 10 percent in Mexico to over 70 percent in India. Apart from the communication of local branches with their corporate headquarters in Europe and the United States, the shifting of office work from the industrialized to the threshold countries is a significant factor in this development. One example is the expanding Indian software industry, which has numerous well-trained programmers (70% of the U.S. capacities) and, for a fraction of the costs, takes on orders from large companies in the industry (Afemann 1996b: 30). This, however, leads to the creation of "high-tech islands" (Boldt 1997), which aggravates the structural imbalance within the developing countries.

The Internet allows easy access to the information supplied by other countries. This not only has educational and commercial effects but is also politically controversial in countries with limited freedom of speech. Despite all limitations, this shows the potential for democratization that the Internet has to offer. For authoritarian regimes, censorship only works on a short-term basis, as it requires close observation of all the Internet ports in a country, which again is only possible if the number of users is very limited. However, in order to draw any profit at all from the Net, whether in the commercial or educational sector, the elite must have access to it. This renders all attempts at censorship prohibitively expensive and obsolete on a medium-term basis.

Another significant factor in the south's disadvantage within the "global information society" is the fact that English is the language of the Internet and will continue to be for the foreseeable future. Languages such as Arabic, which do not use the Latin alphabet, need the appropriate software to be reproduced on the users' computers. Suppliers often choose graphics to solve this problem, but this causes longer transmission intervals and higher costs.

In short, the employment of the Internet in the Third World does enlarge the scope of communication and information possibilities. However, only the elites have access to them. A "trickle down" effect is highly unlikely due to various factors such as high cost, lack of resources, or illiteracy.

THE DEVELOPMENT OF NETWORK COMMUNICATION IN THE ARAB WORLD

Many of the problems connected with the north-south differential in information technology are apparent in the Arab region. However, the level of development cannot be assumed to be homogeneous, as individual countries differ greatly in educational standards, financial strength, and willingness to innovate. The level of political acceptance of the new medium also varies. As a result, some relatively wealthy countries with a large high-tech potential only have a few Internet ports, whereas the number of users is growing much faster in other, structurally weaker countries.

Another reason for these discrepancies among the Arab countries lies in the heterogeneity of the infrastructure necessary for data communication. In most cases, this infrastructure is the responsibility of state-run telecommunication companies, with the capacity and quality of the different networks varying from country to country. In 1995, the number of telephone connections per 100 inhabitants in the Arab countries averaged four, one-tenth the amount in most industrialized countries. However, several Middle Eastern countries, for example Syria, have thoroughly reformed their telephone networks or ordered extensive expansions during the past decade. Countries such as Egypt or

Oman were consequently listing the highest increase in telephone connections world-wide (Kamal 1995).

Based on the differences in infrastructure and political situation,
the Arab world can be divided into three zones with differing degrees of
development: the Maghreb countries, the Arab heartland, and the Gulf
countries. In the following section, I will examine the distribution of
country codes, that is, top-level domains, as these indicate the degree to
which a certain country is connected with the Internet. These country
codes for the Internet are distributed by a central institution in each
country, which in turn indicates the extent to which domestic Internet
access is institutionalized.

The Maghreb Region

In mid-1997, Libya was the only Maghreb country not connected to the
Internet,[5] whereas Morocco, Algeria, and Tunisia were registering an
increasing number of host computers. However, only those computers
or networks can be assigned to one particular country which are connected under the appropriate country code, that is, the top-level domain.
Morocco's top-level domain is .ma, for Tunisia it is .tn, and for Algeria
.dz. Compared to international standards, these domains show the following development (Table 6.1).[6]

These specifications show that the region is experiencing an
above-average growth of the number of Internet connections. Morocco
appears to be a true "Internet boom country," whereas Tunisia seems to
be registering a decline. However, such detailed data is only available
for the specific top-level domains. The allotment of "international" top-
level domains such as .com or .net in that region can only be guessed at,

Table 6.1: Connectivity Development in the Maghreb.

	Total	Country		
		Maghreb total *Hosts*	Morocco (.ma) *Hosts*	Tunisia (.tn) *Hosts*	Algeria (.dz) *Hosts*
July 1996	12,881,000	544	477	39	28
July 1997	19,540,000	934	888	15	31
Up in %	51.7	71.7	86.2	-61.5	10.7
January 2000	72,398,000	1,903	1,655	20	228
Up in %	270.5	103.7	86.4	33.3	635.5

as their distribution does not depend on geographical borders.[7] This also explains the decline of Tunisian hosts connected under the top-level domain .tn. Many Tunisian submissions, for example the homepage of the semiofficial TUNESIENET, use the .com domain.[8] This is also true for Morocco, where even Hassan II's homepage is registered under the .com domain, which was originally reserved for commercial use.

In its August 1, 1997 issue, the Casablanca newspaper *La Vie Economique* provided more detailed specifications for Morocco. Although the country was not connected to the Internet until November 1995, network communication is now also booming in the commercial sector. Twenty-nine private Internet providers offer net access including the common services (E-mail, Telnet, WWW, Usenet, FTP, Chat). Seventy-five Moroccan companies, thirty official institutions, and six daily newspapers are presented on the WWW. Forty private web-servers and 4,700 Internet addresses show that the Internet is widely used even beyond specialist and administrative circles.

Internet experts in the region think that Tunisia, connected with the Internet since the end of year 1991, will play a central role in the future development of network communication in North Africa (Kamal 1995). There, the lines providing connections to the Net are not owned exclusively by state-run telecommunication companies, as is the case in Morocco and other countries. Furthermore, the Tunisian experts' high level of experience and training gives their country an advantage in the region (Goodman and Green 1992).

The Mashreq Region and Egypt

In the central Arab region, which includes the Palestine territories, Jordan, Syria, Lebanon, and Iraq, only the latter has no connection with the Internet. Saddam Hussein does have his own homepage, but it is presented on a Jordanian server. Iraq has declared the Internet illegal (Gruhler 1997: 134). Syria, which was not represented on the Net at all in 1995, was not granted its own top-level domain (.sy) until mid-1996. However, no intensive activities have been noted there so far. The country's only official presentation on the Internet is found on an Austrian server. Presently there is an effort to indirectly include Syria through a regional network (RAITNet) that is to serve as a gateway to the Internet. It is currently also possible to employ the services of Internet providers in Jordan and Lebanon, but the costs are very high. Only recently has it become possible in Syria to access Compuserve, an international online service. Permission to use this service has to be requested at the Damascus telegraph office, although it is not yet clear whether the Internet can also be accessed via Compuserve.[9]

The Palestine regions hold a special position in this study, as the telecommunication structure there is still in its infancy and moreover highly dependent on Israel (Zougbi 1995). It is true that the market for cellular phones is booming in the autonomous territories and that the Palestine telecommunication agency TELPAL, founded in May 1995, is one of the beneficiaries of the recent economic development. For access to the Net, however, the Palestinians still depend on Israel's connection. For this reason and because the unclear status of the territories is delaying the distribution of their own top-level domain, Palestinians mostly use "international" domains. Even the Arafat administration presents itself under the top-level domain originally reserved for international organizations (.org). Palestinian educational institutions, such as Birzeit University, that are connected with the Internet use the code of U.S. colleges and universities (.edu). The Israeli top-level domain .il is generally avoided.

Those countries of the region which have their own full access to the Net and their own top-level domains (Egypt, Jordan, and Lebanon), show the following connectivity development (Table 6.2). As shown, this region does not quite reach the other nations' average level of development. Egypt's and Jordan's rates of increase are considerably below average, whereas Lebanon has almost doubled its capacities. The reason for this development is the fact that the required infrastructure has only recently been created there. As a consequence of its "straggler" position, Lebanon is only now reaching the rapid growth that is characteristic of this early stage.

Egypt not only plays a crucial role in the Mashreq, but thanks to its central geographic location it is also at the cutting edge for the networking of the whole Arab region. Its state-run Internet agency, the Regional Information Technology and Software Engineering Center (RITSEC), administers a state of the art network that offers broad Internet

Table 6.2: Connectivity Development in the Mashreq.

	Total	Country		
	Region total *Hosts*	Egypt (.ma) *Hosts*	Jordan (.jo) *Hosts*	Lebanon (lb) *Hosts*
July 1996	12,881,000	2,356	1,615	140	601
July 1997	19,540,000	3,192	1,894	170	1,128
Up in %	51.7	25.5	16.9	21.4	87.5
January 2000	72,398,000	6,160	2,231	250	3,679
Up in %	270.5	92.9	17.8	47.1	226.2

access to a large number of users. In order to clearly separate the various uses connected under the same top-level domain .eg, it was divided into codes for commercial and private use (.com.eg), government agencies (.gov.eg), and educational institutions (.sci.eg and .eun.eg).

Jordan officially presents itself under the top-level domain .jo. Internet submissions by other providers such as newspapers can usually be found on foreign servers under the .com or .org domains. One of the most frequently used Net services in Jordan is the Internet Relay Chat. It is noticeable that a (relatively) high percentage of the users are women (Anderson 1997b). Hoping to speed up the development of the Internet structure in that country, Jordan is participating in a unique joint venture with Israel that aims to train 200 Jordanians IT specialists.

The Gulf Countries

The Gulf region has its own special conditions. Their oil reserves provide these countries with the financial strength necessary for the installation and use of modern network technology. Thanks to long-standing trade relations with other countries, they also have a telecommunications infrastructure available to them that meets international standards. All countries on the Arab Peninsula have their own top-level domain. However, Yemen (.ye) and Oman (.om) can be excluded from this study, because in July 1997 Yemen had registered two and Oman had no host computers registered under their respective top-level domains. Notwithstanding, Oman has been connected with the Internet since 1996. The other countries show the following development (Table 6.3). It is striking that this region has the slowest speed of growth, despite its financial advantages. One of the main reasons for this is the fact that Saudi Arabia, the largest and strongest country, has been relatively passive in developing its use of the Internet and has thus slowed down the progress. Public distribution of top-level domains only started there in 1997.

Table 6.3: Connectivity Development in the Gulf States.

	Total	Country					
		Region total Hosts	Kuwait (.kw) Hosts	S. Arabia (.sa) Hosts	Bahrain (.bh) Hosts	UAE (.ae) Hosts	Qatar (.qa) Hosts
July 1996	12,881,000		5,584	2,920	0	841	1,802	21
July 1997	19,540,000		7,083	3,555	293	896	1,994	345
Up in %	51.7		26.9	21.8	—	6.5	10.7	1,542.9
January 2000	72,398,000		36,861	4,811	5,077	1,507	24,410	1,056
Up in %	270.5		420.4	35.3	1,632.8	68.2	1,124.2	206.1

The most highly developed telecommunications infrastructure is found in Kuwait and the United Arab Emirates. Both the Emirates' semi-private telecommunications company, ETISALAT, and the state-run Kuwaiti, PTT, own technology that, with digital transmission and glass fiber wires, is "state of the art" (Kamal 1995). Internet access in Kuwait is also offered by the university as well as by private local providers, all of whom use rented lines. In mid-1997, ETISALAT is still the only provider in the UAE, serving more than 13,000 users (Krafsig 1997).

It is furthermore remarkable that the smaller Gulf countries (Kuwait and the UAE) have the largest numbers of host computers registered under their own domain. Together with the existence of private Internet providers, these numbers indicate the Internet's high acceptance and the broad user spectrums in these countries. This is a development towards the connected society that is likely to continue.

To sum up, the developments in the three Arab regions have to be evaluated separately. This heterogeneous picture of the "Arab Internet" is not only due to the different levels of technical development in those countries and the fact that they entered the Net at different times. Varying political premises and dissenting ideas about how the new medium should be used also account for the difference.

REGIONAL NETWORK PROJECTS AND THE PROBLEMS OF REGIONAL NETWORKING

There have been several attempts to establish a regional Arabic data communications network, all of which failed due to the lack of standards and public networks. Nevertheless, the rise of the Internet and the TCP/IP (Transmission Control Protocol/Internet Protocol) structure underlying it have considerably altered these conditions.[10]

As a consequence, RAITNet (Regional Arab Information Technology Network) was founded in Cairo in December, 1994. This amalgamation of Arab Internet experts aims to foster the networking of the region:

> The Regional Arab Information Technology Network (RAITNet) is a regional, non-governmental and not-for-profit organization, founded by member and participating institutions of the Regional Information Technology and Software Engineering Center (RITSEC, Egypt) and supported by the International Telecommunication Union (ITU) and United Nations Educational, Scientific and Cultural Organization (UNESCO).[11]

RAITNet's goals include the promotion of the infrastructure necessary for regional and international communication within the Arab region. Although RAITNet claimed NGO status in 1995, these goals (which immediately concern state interests) as well as the list of the founding members show that it is, in fact, an international organization.[12] These mostly state-controlled institutions form the heart of the Arab communication network. Although the region was still an empty quarter on the world map of the Internet at the time RAITNet was founded, this situation has since changed considerably. The rising access numbers prove that the Internet, at least in terms of dealing with technical problems, has established itself in the Arab world.

The problems this region experiences in connection with the Internet are beginning to shift from the technical and structural towards the political and cultural. In particular, the problems created by the "language barrier" as well as by censorship and control are very significant. All countries in the region have to deal with the language barrier, as has been previously observed. The reason for this barrier is the fact that the Internet is predominantly English-speaking. Although the use of the Arabic alphabet is possible, certain prerequisites have to be met:

- The Arabic text is transmitted in the format of a graphic file. The provider needs the appropriate software as well as hardware (e.g. a scanner) to generate a graphics file from a text. The user has to deal with a longer transmission process and therefore with higher costs. This also overtaxes the network capacity.
- Another possibility for the transmission of texts incorporates the use of special file formats (for example PDF (Portable Data Format from Adobe)), but additional programs are needed to decipher these formats. In this case the transmission process also takes considerably longer than an English text in ASCII format.

Both of these alternatives are mainly used by Arab print media that present their current editions on the Internet in one form or the other. *Al-Hayat*, for example, uses the PDF format, whereas the Jordan paper *Al-Sabil* employs graphics. Apart from these possibilities there are some genuinely Arab solutions, including Arabic language SMTP (Send Mail Transfer Protocol) software for mail transport or Arabic browsers (Internet navigation programs) such as "Sindbad" which can be used on both English and Arabic-speaking operating systems. "Sindbad" manufacturer Sakhar and ART (Arab Radio and Television) are partners in a project launched by Prince Walin bin Talal, a Saudi telecom tycoon who is planning to set up a separate Arab WWW that is to present pre-censored materials only.

The plans for the creation of an exclusively Arabic computer standard are older than the region's connection to the Internet. The Arabization Coordination Bureau, which is affiliated with the Arab League, established the Arabic Computer Standardized Code ASMO-449 as early as 1985. These plans to create a parallel Arabic standard seem neither promising nor, with regard to the Internet, desirable. By following them through, the Arabic countries would create a network increasingly separated from the Internet and would thus lose the advantages that global network communication has to offer. The issue continues to be on the agenda of regional Internet conferences such as the ones held in May 1997 in Tunis[13] and Marrakesh. A new standard for the depiction of writing characters (UNICODE) might offer a solution to the problem (Afemann 1996a). It allows any operating system to interpret texts not based on the Latin alphabet. Nevertheless, the language barrier will remain in existence until UNICODE becomes an international standard.

Besides the language barrier, there seem to be several different ways of managing the Internet that hamper its development. Government attempts to control the new medium and its employment are among the more sensational and controversial approaches. Censorship and control have never been limited to authoritarian regimes; efforts in this direction also occur in countries with democratic constitutions. However, certain specific problems arise in the dealings of Arab countries with the Internet. As in the case of other countries facing a restrictive information and media policy, the Internet confronts the Arab countries with new challenges: "On the Internet, local events are projected onto the stage of global politics and return to the local stage as events of global significance" (Fandy 1997). The opposition, whether inside the country or in exile, also finds new possibilities of communication and independent information at its disposal. Furthermore, citizens living abroad have more opportunities to influence important domestic affairs in their countries. The Internet also allows for a new form of Islamic networking beyond the reach of traditional governmental control. This shapes the way the Internet is perceived in the Arabic region significantly: "The main focus in many developing states is with the loss of control over information that accompanies the information revolution" (Rathmell 1997).

As a consequence, Arab governments make different attempts to censor the contents of network media. The events accompanying the introduction of the facsimile to the Arab region provide evidence of the strong interest of regional governments in finding an effective way to control new forms of communication. Syria, for example, has placed strict restrictions on the possession of facsimile machines, and PC owners must register with a military authority (Goodman and Green 1992).

The Internet, however, cannot be controlled so easily. Having decided to procure access to the Net for their countries, governments can no longer rely upon time-tested censorship techniques. The Internet renders customary methods such as wire-taps for telephones or intermediate memory for facsimiles ineffective.

The structure of the Net allows for three possible options of control: technical control, economic control, and access control (Coy 1996). Technical control, that is, control via the way the Internet operates, is not feasible for the governments of the Arabic countries, as they are not represented on the appropriate committees. Access control to the Internet is one feasible option. As Wolfgang Coy argues:

> Internet access is easy. The only prerequisites are a PC, a modem, the appropriate software and a provider, i.e. a service company which acts as the connection to the Internet. These are the conditions as well as the limits of access. (Coy 1996)

These conditions drastically diminish the size of the group to be controlled. Starting points for censorship are local suppliers of information, local Internet service providers (ISP), telecommunications companies, and the users. It is relatively easy to issue reprimands against domestic webpage writers and server operators. The following deliberations will focus on information and information suppliers from abroad. Opposition groups in exile will receive special attention.

The ISP are the eye of the needle of communication in the Arabic countries, as they are mostly government agencies or at least government-dependent. State-run telecommunications companies frequently act as ISPs, as exemplified by the UAE. These providers can deny their customers access to certain Internet addresses by using so-called filter software or presenting only the "cleaned" contents of the intermediate memory (Proxyserver). The idea of the Internet as a medium that networking has made uncensorable, usually overlooks the fact that the Net is, in most cases, based on the telephone network. Even when a former state-run telecom company is privatized, the government still has the ability to control its network, as certain laws allow for such censorship.

Each telecom company can exert influence over Internet access in two different ways. Individual users can be obstructed specifically by blocking their telephone lines. There is also the possibility of economic control over Net access. The providers (ISP and telecom) can use their price structure to formally limit open access to certain socioeconomic classes or user groups. In some industrialized countries, those costs are already at a level affordable by the middle classes (Coy 1996). The initiators thus hope to secure the commercial use of the Internet by domestic companies without having to risk broad repercussions.

Because technical measures of censorship are difficult to realize on a broad basis without considerably diminishing the benefits of the Net, network censorship in the Arab countries is not only handled as a question of content control, but also of Net access. The political objectives are obvious: "Their main concern is to balance the economic and educational benefits of Internet access with their desire to control the flow of information" (Rathmell 1997).

The degree to which the "security of the Internet," as censorship measures are dubbed (Kamal 1997), is indeed guaranteed, varies from country to country. The most radical step is the "evacuation" of domestic Internet presentations to other countries (Libya, Syria, Iraq). A blockage through high access costs, which is an "acceptable model to reduce the public's access to Internet" (Kamal 1997) in countries with a low average income, such as Egypt or Morocco, will fail in the wealthier Gulf countries. Monthly expenses for an E-mail account in Saudi Arabia can reach $200, but direct access barriers and filter systems are more frequently used there. Saudi Arabia, a country confronted with an "electronic opposition"[14] formed a government commission (a so-called Regulation Authority) to decide whether or not individual persons and companies may be allowed access to the Internet. Their neighbors are going their own way. Kuwait, for example, keeps an index of prohibited web pages, and certain web presentations have been banned in the UAE as well. In Qatar and Oman, special software development on the basis of so-called "children's protection software," such as *Netnanny* or *Cyberpatrol*, is used to censor banned material. Such programs are usually sold by online services such as CompuServe in order to allow the home user to childproof his PC. They are easy to bypass and only cover parts of network communication (usually the WWW). They are therefore merely obstacles rather than real barriers.

At the end of March 1997, the Gulf countries held a conference to discuss the common handling of the Internet. The main focus of the conference was the unrestricted communication between Arab Net users and other countries, in particular Israel (Gruhler 1997: 133). Compared to the international standard, the efforts at control and censorship made by the Arab countries can be judged as varying between "selective" and "severely restrictive." In his study on the reactions of different countries, Alexander K. A. Gruhler describes several ways of handling prohibited use of the Internet (Gruhler 1997: 51 f.)

Gruhler discerns five levels of restriction (Table 6.4). Arab countries are only found on levels three to five (Table 6.5). Egypt, Tunisia, and the UAE are on level three (use of indices), which corresponds to

Table 6.4: Levels of Restriction.

Level	Measures
1	Democratic measures such as voluntary self-limitations
2	Direct actions of police and justice departments
3	Indices of web-sites
4	Filter-systems
5	Limitations of Internet-access

Table 6.5: Levels of Restrictions in Arab Countries.

Country	Level
Egypt	3
Iraq	5
Jordan	4
Kuwait	4
Qatar	4
Saudi Arabia	4
Tunisia	3
UAE	3

the level of restriction in Germany. Gruhler places Jordan, Qatar, and Kuwait on level four (censorship through filtering systems), the same as Hong Kong or Indonesia. Saudi Arabia and Iraq are, like China, on level five, which indicates those countries that have access restrictions.

One qualifying remark should be added to these details. Gruhler's differentiation relates only to legal and administrative measures or self-restrictions that result from them. Economic access restrictions are not included in this schema.

Most Arab governments justify measures directed towards the restriction of Net access with the necessity to "protect cultural identity." This is the single common denominator of the Arab governments with regard to the Internet. It is a foregone conclusion that the freedom of speech and information is severely limited even on the Internet: "Free speech can never be absolute. (...) It is illegal to make statements that could result in public disorder or lead to criminal acts."[15]

The Arab countries feel that they are being threatened from the outside. Some of them see this threat in the United States' attempt to spread the neglect of ethics into every household on earth (Anderson 1997a). Others fear the misinformation strategies of the Israelis, "who are masters of the information game, (...) masters at manipulating information for their own ends."[16] Network communication has a potential in terms of information and misinformation that is well-recognized and feared. However, there are also controversial reactions to the issue within the Arab region. The Saudi web magazine *Arab View*,[17] for example, is leading an ongoing discussion about the advantages and drawbacks of using information technology.[18]

Another rarely mentioned restriction whose effects should not be underestimated is not caused by Arab governments but by U.S. export regulations for computers and software. Most of the Internet software is manufactured in the United States and license specifications dictate that it is, according to license specifications, not to be exported into countries under U.S. embargo. The following excerpt from the German Netscape license agreements can serve as a general example for browser software, which is almost exclusively manufactured in the United States:

> Neither the software nor the information and technology it is based upon may be exported or re-exported by way of downloading or other processes to Cuba, Iraq, Libya, the countries of former Yugoslavia, North Korea, Iran, Syria or any other country placed under a US embargo, to citizens or permanent residents of one of these countries or to any persons which are registered on the list of "Specially Designated Nationals" of the US Department of Finance or on the US Department of Economy "Table of Denial Orders." For downloading and any other use of the software you must acknowledge the above-mentioned obligations and assure that you do not live in nor are under the control of nor are a permanent resident or citizen of such a country or are registered on one of the aforementioned lists.

COMMERCIAL USE OF THE ARAB INTERNET

The commercial use of the Internet is less controversial but has far-reaching consequences especially for new developments in the trade and service sectors. Considering that 50 to 70 percent (in the United States up to 80%) of the gross national income in the OECD countries falls under the service industries category, it is not surprising that the Net sometimes seems like a services catalogue. Uwe Afemann argues: "Many services are no longer bound to a certain locality but can be manufactured, stored and consumed in different places. Moreover, the manufacturing process can be split between several subcontractors" (Afemann 1996b: 29). This tendency breaks down distances and is intensified by the possibilities of network communication. Data, information, and services can thus be transmitted immediately, interactively, and across continents.

This and the fact that the OECD is making an effort to speed up the Internet's economic development, has started a trend that the rest of the world will be unable to ignore. The countries of the Arab region recognize the opportunities this tendency opens up with regard to new markets. The sponsors and pioneers of network communication in these countries are, however, not the same user groups as in the industrial world. As Jon Anderson says: "Unlike the case in North America and western Europe, it is not the universities that have led the way online in the Middle East, perhaps out of anxiety over just such a development, but 'public-private partnerships' between official and commercial sectors" (Anderson 1997a). In connection with those partnerships, Anderson also speculates about the renewal of the Middle East's historical role as mediator.

Instead of a common Arab presence on the Internet, several profit-oriented network projects have developed over the past three years that roughly correspond to political borders within the region. Those are ArabNet in the Gulf countries and Arabia.On.Line as a joint venture between Egypt and Jordan. "1001 Sites" by the joint US-Arab Chamber of Commerce is another platform for Arabic companies to present themselves. The development of its economic potential thus propels the "Arab info-revolution" (Anderson 1997a), which again is officially funded. This is the reason why commercial rather than academic users are Internet pioneers in the Arab countries, as Anderson argues: "The recent and rapid emergence in the Middle East of commercially based networks, Internet presences and service providers, to be sure, often depends on official sponsorship in some measure, such as in Egypt, the Gulf and fledgling from within and outside Middle East countries, from arabia.on.line in Jordan to Arab Net and the *Middle East Business Review* from London" (Anderson 1997a). Egypt serves as an example of this general development. Even before the country was connected to the Internet, Egypt was one of the region's trailblazers in information technology: "It has the largest, most capable and most internationally oriented computing community in the Arab world and trained people are among its most internationally high-tech exports" (Goodmann and Green 1992).

In the most recent developments, government funding of the commercial use of the Internet is part of the effort to privatize the communication sector. These funds are an example of the close cooperation between the government and the private sector, as Tarak Kamal, Chairman of the Department for Communication of the Information and Decision Support Center (IDSC), says:

Internet commercialization is a new model for cooperation between the public and private sectors in telecommunication. The government has played a catalytic role in raising awareness as well as deployment of the infrastructure, while the private sector carries value-added services to the end users. (...) The Internet has opened a window for marketing information services in Egypt to the world. (...) This has helped in the creation of linkages for the business community in Egypt with the outside world and provides an opportunity to promote tourism, culture, and trade. (...) The success of the government/private sector partnership in the commercialization of Internet services will push deregulation of other value-added services as well as communication services in the country. The communication infrastructure deployment is a promising area for private-sector participation. (...) Egypt is qualified to play a significant role on the regional level as an Internet gateway to other countries in the region and in Africa. (Kamal 1997)

Government support is not only limited to the provision of financial support but also includes the willingness to expand the necessary infrastructure. The establishment of the Information and Decision Support Center (IDSC) shows the degree of importance associated with the new medium. The IDSC is a central Internet authority directly affiliated to the Cabinet, and it works closely with the experts of the Regional Information Technology and Software Engineering Center (RITSEC). According to the IDSC's Tarak Kamal, this official project is evidence of the government's conviction that only those who are able to master the rapidly developing technology will survive in the age of global communication (Kamal 1997).

Numerous private Internet providers offer Internet access aligned with the "official" access provided by government agencies and universities (whereas in 1997 there were only seven private providers, there were already more than twenty in 1997). The costs are high, averaging ten pounds sterling per hour or a 100 pounds sterling monthly flat rate. This, however, does not limit the enthusiasm of most providers. Nagui Khalil of the private Starnet Internet Services believes: "In three years, nobody in Egypt will be able to do business without the Internet" (Hills 1997).

ARAB MASS MEDIA ON THE INTERNET

The media and their exploitation of the possibilities of network communication are at a point of intersection between public and commercial usage. Access to knowledge and information is the user's central incentive for exploring the new media, and Arab media tycoons are aware of this fact. Electronic editions of newspapers and magazines from almost all Arab countries are available on the Internet. In most cases these are only excerpts from the printed editions, but some publications provide complete issues in HTML or PDF format.

There are several noticeable characteristics of the Arab network media: The further back the media tradition reaches in a country, the more present domestic print media are on the Internet, and the more willing they are to face the challenges that come with it, such as interaction and readers' direct participation. Parallel to this development, these countries also have a larger number of other information providers. The "official" media are not the only ones that make use of the opportunities offered by electronic publication. An increasing number of opposition groups do as well, in particular groups with an Islamist tendency (Rathmell 1997). Further uses include new forms of online media, ranging from news services to satirical magazines.

This combination of "old" and new media, often backed by Islamic banks (Anderson 1997a) and government agencies, allows for a glance towards the future of the Internet in the Arab world. The cooperation of the media and corporations justifies the use of network communication, as Anderson argues:

> [It] is commerce that conveys and justifies the Internet, which is arriving at the time not of its development in research and educational worlds, or in the hands of the denizens of those worlds, but in the time of its "graduation" and going to work in the globalized financial and services economy. (Anderson 1997a)

OUTLOOK

David Lerner's *The Passing of Traditional Society*, one of the standard publications of communication science of the 1950s (Lerner 1958), claims that intensive media contact is the most effective means of transforming traditional societies into modern societies. This theory, the result of research commissioned by the CIA, has since been proven wrong (Samarajiva 1987). The history of the introduction of the Internet to the Arab world has supported this criticism. The possibility of receiving detailed information from all over the globe virtually without delay is an enormous addition to the traditional media spectrum. However, only a small part of the population has the skills (reading and writing, a knowledge of English, computer literacy) and the financial strength necessary to take advantage of this possibility. The Internet thus becomes an exclusive medium for the old and especially the new elite (Anderson 1997a).

ENDNOTES

1. See http://www.liszt.com.
2. E.g., with news.sprynet.com.
3. Host Distribution by Top-Level Domain Name. http://nw.com/zone/WWW-9601/dist-byname.html (September 9, 1998).
4. For example, almost all of the Internet accesses available in Africa in 1995 were registered in South Africa (Afemann 1996a).
5. Using commercial Internet suppliers, Libya has recently been trying to establish an "external Internet presence" in the United States.
6. According to http://nw.com/zone/WWW-9601/dist-byname.html (September 9, 1998).
7. The criteria for the distribution of top-level domains are also becoming less strict.
8. A reason for this is TUNIC's price structure.
9. Internet ante Portas: Syrien Online? *Informationsdienst Naher und Mittlerer Osten* (INAMO) 12, 1997: 29 f.
10. The advantages of this data transmission protocol were evident: Data transport and electronic transmission becomes possible on the basis of a heterogeneous telecommunications structure. No greater investments in the reconstruction of the existing national networks are needed. Different data processing platforms can be linked and continue to be used. The access mechanisms are simple and inexpensive (Kamal 1995).
11. See http://www.arab.net/arabview/welcome.html (September 9, 1989).
12. Among the founders are: Al-Asad National Library, Syria; Al-Fatah University, Libya; Arab Petroleum Investments Corporation (APICORP), Saudi Arabia; Birzeit University, Palestine; Central Statistics Organization, Qatar; Centre de Recherche sur L'Information Scientifique et Technique (CERIST), Algeria; Ecole Mohammadia d'Ingenieur (EMI), Morocco; Emirates Telecommunications Corporation (ETISALAT), United Arab Emirates; Egyptian National Scientific and Technical Information Network (ENSTINET), Egypt; Higher Institute of Applied Science and Technology (HIAST), Syria; Information and Decision Support Center (IDSC), The Cabinet, Egypt; National Information Center, Jordan; Institut Regional de Sciences Informatiques et des Telecommunications (IRSIT), Tunisia; Jeddah Chamber of Commerce and Industry (JCCI), Saudi Arabia; Ministry of Communication, Kuwait; Oman Council of Development, Oman; Regional Information Technology and Software Engineering Center (RITSEC), Egypt; Supreme Council of the Universities, Egypt; Syrian Studies and Research Center (SSRC), Syria.
13. The Arab World and the Information Society—Regional Symposium, 4.-8. May 1997. http://www.irsit.rnrt.tn/symposium/ (September 10, 1998).
14. See for example: http://www.saudhouse.com/ (September 9, 1998).
15.. Do Cybercitizens Have the Right to Corrupt? http://www.arab.net/arab-view/articles/ editorial1.html (September 9, 1998).
16. Are We Meeting the Internet Challenge? http://www.arab.net/arab-view/articles/ maeena7.html (September 9, 1998).

17. http://www.arab.net/arabview/welcome.html.
18. Other "Arab News" features concerning this topic are "Why the quandary over the Internet?" (March 13, 1996) and "What's wrong with information technology?" (May 20, 1997). "Arab View" is the Internet edition of "Arab News." As opposed to the printed edition, "Arab View" gives its readers the opportunity to comment on articles directly.

BIBLIOGRAPHY

Afemann, Uwe. 1996a. Zur Bedeutung der neuen Kommunikationstechnologien in der Dritten Welt am Beispiel des Internet. http://www.rz.uni-osnabrueck.de/rz/special/misc/inet-3w/inet-3w.html (July 2, 1998).

Afemann, Uwe. 1996b. Internet und Dritte Welt. In *Jahrbuch Dritte Welt 1997*, edited by Joachim Betz and Stefan Brüne, 28-34. München: Beck.

Anderson, Jon. 1997a. Is the Internet Islam's "Third Wave" or the "End of Civilisation"? http://www.usip.org/oc/confpapers/polrelander.html (January 1, 1998).

Anderson, Jon. 1997b. Bumpy Ride on Jordan's Info-Highway. http://www.georgetown.edu/sfs/programs/ccas/jordan.html (January 17, 1998).

Bangemann, Martin. 1997. Elektronische Demokratie als Schlüssel für die Zukunftsfähigkeit Europas. In *Internet und Politik. Die Modernisierung der Demokratie durch elektronische Medien*, edited by Akademie für das Dritte Jahrtausend, 2-4 (unpublished).

Boldt, Klaus. 1997. Zweiklassengesellschaft im globalen Dorf. http://www.spd.de/einewelt/nsid/76-2a.html (February 8, 1998).

Coy, Wolfgang. 1996. Next Exit: Global Village. In *Kultur-Informatik-Informationskultur: 25 Jahre Universität Klagenfurt*, edited by W. Dörfler, 87-91. Klagenfurt: University of Klagenfurt.

Coy, Wolfgang. 1997. Media Control—Wer kontrolliert das Internet? http://waste.informatik.hu-berlin.de/i+g/coy/media_control_4:97.html (September 10, 1998).

Fandy, Mamoun. 1997. Electronic Resistance. http://www.georgetown.edu/sfs/programs/ccas/infotech/confer1.html (March 8, 1998).

Gates, Bill. 1996. Internet und Demokratie. *Berliner Zeitung*, July 25.

Goodman, S.E., and J.D. Green. 1992. Computing the Middle East and North Africa. http://www.sas.upenn.edu/African_Studies/Comp_Articles/Computing_10174.html (January 17, 1998).

Gruhler, Alexander. 1997. *Das Ende der "totalen" Freiheit im Internet? Die Auswirkungen inkriminierter Inhalte auf die Informationsgesellschaften.* Marburg: Tectum.

Hills, Alison C. 1997. Lost in Cyberspace. http://www.egypttoday.com/jan97/internet.html (January 17, 1998).

Kamal, Tarek. 1995. The Communication Infrastructure and the Internet Services as a Base for a Regional Information Highway. http://www.

isoc.org/isoc/whatis/conferences/inet97/proceedings/e27/e27.htm (February 8, 1998).

Kamal, Tarek. 1997. Internet Commerzialization in Egypt: A Country Model. http://www.isoc.org/isoc/whatis/conferences/inet/97/proceedings/E6/E6_2.htm (February 8, 1998).

Krafsig, Malika. 1997. Telecoms and Internet Connectivity in the Arab World. http://www.georgetown.edu/sfs/programs/ccas/infotech/confer1.html (March 8, 1998).

Lerner, David. 1958. *The Passing of Traditional Society: Modernizing the Middle East.* New York: Free Press.

Rathmell, Andrew. 1997. Netwar in the Gulf. http://www. infowar.com/class_3/class_3q.html-ssi (September 10, 1998).

Rilling, Rainer. 1996. Auf dem Weg zur Cyberdemokratie? http://staff-www.uni-marburg.de/~rillingr/bdweb/texte/cyberdemokratie-text.htm (September 10, 1998).

Samarajiva, Rohan. 1987. The Murky Beginnings of the Communication and Development Field. In *Rethinking Development Communication*, edited by Neville Jayaweera and Sarah Amunugama, 3-19. Singapore (unpublished).

Torres, Asdrad. 1995. Die große Illusion des demokratischen Internet. *Le Monde diplomatique*, November 1.

Zougbi, Saleem. 1995. Internet's Role in Middle-East Development: Palestinian Perspective. http://info.isoc.org/hmp/paper/009/txt/paper.txt (January 1, 1998).

7

Distribution of Ideas: Book Production and Publishing in Egypt, Lebanon, and the Middle East

Stefan Winkler

Compared with other institutions concerned with the distribution of knowledge such as universities, libraries, and research institutes, the importance of publishing companies is often underestimated. Literary criticism neglects the role of the publisher and has reduced it to a mere mediator between author and reader. Lewis Coser was the first to emphasize the significance of this role and described the publisher as a "gatekeeper of ideas," referring to an expression attributed to the editors of news magazines with which they characterize the flow of information in newspaper offices (Coser 1975; Coser et al. 1982: 362-374). Others stressed a more active role of the editor as a "shaper of culture" (Lane 1975). However, before emphasizing a more active or passive role for the publisher, one should note that the term publisher designates such different fields of activity as the production of monographs, textbooks, or trade books. Due to the advent of specialization in publishing houses, which has led to new departments dealing with, for instance, marketing and foreign rights (Coser et al. 1982: 369), the role of the publisher has become more complex. Not only his personal preferences are decisive but so are the considerations of marketing or public relations departments. Other actors such as talk show hosts and book reviewers additionally function as gatekeepers.

In the Middle East, however, this specialization in editing and other departments has not taken place except in the larger and more modern publishing houses. Even editing departments are almost unknown. Manuscripts are accepted without being edited if the author is well-known, but even in other cases the editor rarely interferes. In most cases the publisher himself is the only "gate" to the acceptance or refusal of manuscripts. Some interference, however, seems to occur due to political restraints in the form of self-censorship or external censorship.

Furthermore, the publisher also functions as a bookseller and sometimes as a printer as well. This type of printer-publisher (or publisher-bookseller), which disappeared in Europe at the end of the eighteenth and beginning of the nineteenth century, is still widespread in the Middle East. Whereas in Europe and North America the decision to produce books is embedded in a set of decisions made in specialized departments, decisions of the publisher in the Middle East seem to be more authoritative in that publishers often need not pay attention to the considerations of marketing and public relations departments.

When deciding to produce a book, the publisher puts it into circulation and exposes it to processes of reception and criticism. His decision will depend on the academic, educational, cultural, and political systems of the particular country as well as cost factors. If costs are high and spending power is low, private publishers will tend to minimize their risks, which will have immediate effects on the number and variety of titles. The existence of highly subsidized public competitors increases the risks of private publishers. These realities, in conjunction with a low rate of literacy, a poor distribution network, the lack of export markets, and heavy censorship, may have devastating effects on the whole book publishing industry of a particular country. This is in fact the situation in some Middle Eastern countries such as Egypt and Syria.

The description of the role of the publisher as a gatekeeper of ideas is not applicable to the complex process of book production in these countries. Here, other agents of the educational, scientific, and cultural systems interfere in this process. The decision to publish one text and not another is made according to the sociocultural environment. However, whereas in industrialized countries the deluge of newly produced books casts doubts on the "efficiency of publishers to act as gatekeepers" (Coser et al. 1982: 365), their role in developing countries seems to be more decisive. Philip Altbach focused on the connection between publishing and development and emphasized the fact that there are interrelations between the mechanisms of publication and education, research, academic, and cultural life. On an international level, especially in developing countries, the question of access to international knowledge networks is a crucial matter (Altbach 1987: 179 f.). In developing countries, for example, the bulk of published books are textbooks and the educational system is the biggest consumer of books (Altbach 1992: 9). Publishing serves as an input into the cultural, academic, and educational systems of a country and, conversely, incorporates the output of these systems and mirrors the intellectual life. In this light, book production is an indicator for development.[1]

BOOK PUBLISHING IN ARAB COUNTRIES

A comparative analysis of book production in developing countries reveals some common deficiencies including, according to Datus Smith, a high rate of illiteracy, low spending power, a lack of distribution outlets and possibilities, poor printing quality, the lack of a reading public, language problems, and competition from Western publishers (Smith 1995). The last two points are not very important for the conditions in Arab countries because Arabic has a long and lively tradition as a cultural and scientific language, and competition from Western books is not as important as in some African and Asian countries where vernacular languages are hardly adapted to modern sciences.

Book publishing in various Arab countries shares some general features: the widespread combination of publishing and printing or bookselling (or even all in one); the lack of special departments for editing, marketing, sales, promotion, and so forth; and a set of obstacles for the development of a flourishing book industry that exists to a varying extent in all Arab countries. Among these obstacles are:

1. High production costs: The most important cost factor in book production is the price of paper. Most Arab countries are totally dependent on foreign imports for paper and consequently have to pay world market prices. Egypt's paper industry is unable to meet its own requirements; imports reached 60 to 72 percent of paper consumption between 1987 and 1992.[2] In Egypt customs duty of around 15 percent is added to the price of imported printing paper. This development has resulted in continuously increasing book prices in Egypt. Lebanon is totally dependent on imported paper and in general it could be said that Lebanese books are more expen-

sive than Egyptian ones. However, many Egyptian publishers continue to print their books on low quality paper to maintain affordable prices.

2. Import and export regulations: Numerous regulations for the export and import of books impede transnational trade. Sometimes books are banned for export or import or even confiscated, and the rules governing this banning are not always clear.[3] Customs duties imposed on imported books add to their high price. However, according to Egyptian publishers, export regulations in Egypt were eased in recent years.

3. Censorship: Censorship is still common in all Arab countries in various degrees. Whereas preprint censorship does not exist in Egypt or Lebanon, it is common in Syria. In Egypt the role of Al-Azhar, the center of Sunni Islamic scholarship, in banning books for export has gained importance in recent years.[4] Self-censorship is another problem that should not be underestimated. In 1995 the falsification of some literary works by Najib Mahfuz, Yusuf Idris, and Ihsan Abd al-Quddus has discovered. "Blasphemous" words and sentences had been changed or deleted to enable the books to be sold in Saudi Arabia (*Al-Ahram Weekly*, August 10-16, 1995).

4. Weak infrastructure: Books have a long way to travel before they reach the interested reader. Due to the lack of distribution systems and catalogues of books currently in print, ordering books is very difficult, especially if the publisher is unknown. In many cases the publisher himself goes to the different bookstores to sell his books. Rural areas and minor cities are poorly covered. Only large companies such as Al-Ahram or the General Egyptian Book Organization (GEBO) in Egypt and Maktabat Lubnan in Beirut own several outlets.

5. Low reader demand: The markets are small due to insufficient readership, a lack of purchasing power in comparison with increasing book prices, and the small budgets of universities and libraries. In addition to export regulations and censorship, the loss of the export markets in Iraq, Algeria, and Libya have further reduced the possibilities of selling books. This development has led to a decrease of print runs. Publishers from Egypt and Lebanon claim that except for *Islamiyat*, books dealing with Islamic guidelines for practical life, dictionaries, university textbooks, and some nonfiction titles, print runs have decreased to 1,000 to 2,000 copies.

6. Copyright and piracy: Book piracy is very common in and between Arab countries. In fact, although most Arab countries

do have copyright laws or have signed international agreements[5] (see Table 7.1), these laws and agreements are either not applied or not sufficiently implemented by the authorities. Ibrahim al-Muallim estimates that piracy in Egypt costs the state at least 70 million Egyptian pounds annually, more than it earns through customs and other duties on books. Piracy is more lucrative than producing a book: the pirated edition is usually 30 to 35 percent cheaper than the original edition (al-Muallim 1998). In 1981 the Arab League Educational, Cultural and Scientific Organization (ALECSO) prepared the "Arab Copyright Convention" which grants literary, artistic and sci-

Table 7.1: Introduction of National and International Copyright Laws in Arab Countries.[*]

	Berne[1]	UCC[3]	WIPO[3]	ACC[4]	National Laws[5]
Algeria	1998	1973	1975	s	1973 (25)
Bahrain	1997	-	-	s	1993 (50)
Djibouti	-	-	-	s	French Law
Egypt	1977	-	1975	-	1954/1992 (50)
Iraq	-	-	1976	r	1971 (25)
Jordan	-	-	1972	r	1992 (30)
Kuwait	-	-	-	r	1999
Lebanon	1947	1959	1986	-	1999 (50)
Libya	1976	-	1976	s	1968 (25)
Mauritania	1973	-	1976	s	1957 (French Law)
Morocco	1917	1972	1971	s	1970 (50)
Oman	-	-	-	s	-
Palestine	-	-	-	s	-
Qatar	-	-	1976	r	-
Saudi Arabia	-	1994	1982	r	1989 (50)
Somalia	-	-	1982	s	1977
Sudan	-	-	1974	s	1974 (25)
Syria	-	-	-	s	in preparation
Tunisia	1887	1969	1975	r	1966/1994 (50)
UAE	-	-	1974	r	1992 (25)
Yemen	-	-	1979	s	1994

[*]Sources: Copyright Bulletin (Paris), Bulletin du Cedej 25, 1989 (Cairo), Amri 1986, *Al-Jadid Fi Alam Al -Kutub Wal-Maktabat 1*, 1994: 22-25, and ALECSO 1996.
[1]Berne (Berne Convention for the Protection of Literary and Artistic Works 1886, last revision Paris 1971)
[2]UCC (Universal Copyright Convention, Geneva 1952)
[3]WIPO (World Intellectual Property Organization) - date signed
[4]ACC (Arabic Copyright Convention, Baghdad 1981), s = signed; r = ratified
[5]Numbers in parentheses refer to the term of protection after the death of the author

entific works a protection period of twenty-five years after the
death of the author.[6] All Arab states signed the convention
with the exception of the most important book producers:
Egypt and Lebanon.[7]

PUBLISHING SYSTEMS IN THE ARAB WORLD:
EGYPT AND LEBANON

Publishing systems in Arab countries vary. Following the classification
suggested by Ben Cheikh there are three kinds of systems, depending on
the degree of influence of the state on the industry: (1) State-controlled
and planned publishing (Libya, Algeria); (2) mixed-economy publishing
(Egypt, Iraq); and (3) commercial and private publishing (Lebanon) (Ben
Cheikh 1982). In this chapter I will focus on the last two types and will
show the differences between them. Egypt and Lebanon are the most
active publishing countries in the region and will be taken as examples
of these two systems respectively.

The first printing in the Arabic script in the Middle East was carried out in the eighteenth century in Aleppo by the pioneer Abdallah
Zakhir, who moved to the monastery of Shuwair in Lebanon in 1734. It
began with religious books produced to meet the needs of the Christian
Oriental churches. Publishing really started with the press of the
American missionaries, which Faris al-Shidiaq brought from Malta to
Beirut in 1834. At the end of the nineteenth century over twenty printing
presses in Lebanon had published more than 1,000 titles (Atiyeh 1995:
240). But political and economic conditions forced many of the writers,
intellectuals, journalists, and publishers to emigrate—which was to
Egypt's benefit. The strengthening of the Ottoman censorship laws in
1885 was a major cause of the emigration of intellectuals.

In the first half of the twentieth century publishers started to
become emancipated from the missionary and clerical presses, and
focused on printing textbooks. In the middle of the century some of the
large Lebanese publishers started as textbook publishers or booksellers;
these included Maktabat Lubnan (1944), Dar Al-Ilm Lil-Malayin (1944),
and Dar Al-Kitab Al-Lubnani (1952) (Istifan-Hashim 1993: 44 ff.).

As a result of the nationalization of the Egyptian publishing
industry in the 1960s Lebanese publishing gained influence. The relatively free atmosphere attracted writers from other countries to publish
in Beirut and many of the leading intellectual magazines of the Arab
world were established in Beirut, among them *Al-Tariq* (1941) and *Al-
Adab* (1953). Magazines like *Al-Fikr Al-Arabi*, *Al-Mustaqbal Al-Arabi*, and
Al-Fikr Al-Arabi Al-Muasir were established at the end of the 1970s and

the beginning of the 1980s. The civil war does not seem to have affected book production (except perhaps in the worst years), but it did encourage the different groups and factions to publish books representing their own interests. The number of publishing houses increased in the 1970s and 1980s to several hundred. More than 600 publishing houses are registered today, but only 150 are considered to be really active.[8]

In Egypt, the first encounter with the art of printing during the French expedition of 1798 did not have lasting consequences. The printing presses brought by Napoleon disappeared after his retreat. But shortly afterwards, as part of his reform program, Mohammed Ali Pasha, Viceroy of Egypt, established a press in Bulaq in 1821 to meet the requirements of his administration. The introduction of newspapers followed, initially in the form of a governmental newsletter—the *Al-Waqai Al-Misriyya*, which still exists as a law gazette (together with the *Al-Jarida Al-Rasmiyya*). Its aim was the instruction of the administrative elite. Private publishers did not appear until the 1860s and it was not until the 1870s that a reading public developed. A new phenomenon became apparent: the private public press and with them "a demand on the part of the governed, articulated by an intellectual leadership, to be involved in matters of the government, to be informed, and to be consulted on questions relating to their future" (Ayalon 1995: 43). Among the Syrian-Lebanese emigrants were many of the later founders of Egyptian magazines and publishing houses: the Taqla brothers founded *Al-Ahram* (1875), Najib Mitri established *Dar Al-Maarif* (1890), and Jurji Zaydan *Dar Al-Hilal* (1892). Ahmad al-Babi al-Halabi, who founded the oldest Egyptian publishing house in 1859, dedicated to *turath* (classical heritage), and Yusuf Tuma al-Bustani, founder of Maktabat Al-Arab (today Dar Al-Arab Lil-Bustani), were also among them. At the end of the nineteenth century publishing was booming in Egypt, and 10,405 titles were produced by the end of the century, two-thirds of them between 1880 and 1899 (Nusair 1994: 53-70). Annual book production grew from between 100 and 300 titles at the end of the nineteenth century to between 300 and 500 titles by the mid-twentieth century (Khalil 1993: 55), with Matbaat Riwayat Al-Jib, Dar Al-Maarif, and Mustafa Al-Babi Al-Halabi among the biggest publishers (Khalil 1993: 271).

The events following the 1952 revolution gave the Egyptian publishing industry its special features: in 1960 the big publishers were nationalized through law no. 156. At first this was aimed at gaining control over the press houses Al-Ahram, Al-Akhbar, Al-Hilal, and Ruz Al-Yusuf. By 1968 eight establishments (the national press houses) were created to be subject to the national press law; as well as the four mentioned above, Dar Al-Maarif, Dar Al-Taawun, Dar Al-Tahrir (Al-Jumhuriya), and Dar Al-Shaab were also included. The construction of this semipublic sector is as subtle as it is effective: all the establishments must observe the press law in its amended form from 1996 (law no. 25/1996). The second chamber of the Egyptian Parliament appoints the majority of members of the different executive bodies. This pattern guarantees the control of the government: "This elaborate arrangement assures that ultimate policy-making responsibility rests with appointees of the state, while day-to-day management is left, as before, in the hands of professionals" (Rizk and Rodenbeck 1985: 101). In the publishing field this strategy seems to have helped to avoid some of the mistakes of the public sector. However, in terms of quality and quantity the book production of the eight establishments differs widely. Whereas Dar Al-Maarif has a backlist of 4,000 titles, less than 100 titles are available in Dar Al-Taawun. Al-Ahram is very eager to produce bestsellers: the average print run is 5,000 copies with titles from Mohammed Hasanain Haikal, a famous Egyptian journalist and friend of former President Gamal Abd al-Nasser, reaching 40,000.[9] In 1998 all eight establishments are engaged in producing both books and newspapers.

Other measures were started in 1961 to concentrate all book-related activities under one organization. Publishing houses and printing presses were incorporated into this new institution, which changed its name several times. After years of experimentation and mismanagement with disastrous effects (more than 3.4 million books went unsold in 1966) (Khalifa 1974: 255 ff.), a reorganization took place. In 1971 different presses, nationalized publishing houses, and government authorities including the National Library (Dar Al-Kutub) merged to form the General Egyptian Book Organization (GEBO), which still exists in this form today—with the exception that in 1993 the National Library and Archive were separated from the GEBO. In this environment, in which public and semipublic institutions had a monopoly on book importation and distribution, private publishers could not thrive. Private publishing was nearly destroyed at the beginning of the 1970s. Or, as Marina Stagh has stated, "the monopoly as such, with all its bureaucratic and political check-points, was probably a more efficient gate-keeper than censorship" (Stagh 1993: 22).

In the 1980s things changed with the open-door policy of the Mubarak government. But private publishers still suffer due to the strong position of the public sector. Only recently (the end of 1980s and beginning of 1990s) an increasing number of publishing houses was founded in an effort to meet the demands of the public, among them literary and secularist publishers such as Dar Al-Sharqiyat and Dar Sina, but also a greater number of publishers of Islamiyat, such as Dar Al-Fadila or Dar Al-Wafa. Nowadays there are around 250 active publishers in Egypt, compared with ninety at the beginning of the 1970s

(Khalifa 1974: 379-382). This gives Egyptian publishing today its special characteristic: the mixture of public and private publishing. Even though private publishing has gained ground in the 1980s and 1990s, GEBO and Dar Al-Maarif are still the biggest publishers, with an annual production of several hundred titles.

GEBO and other public publishers must be given credit for publishing quite a number of cultural books in cheap editions that have provided and continue to provide the population with affordable books in huge quantities. In 1943 Dar Al-Maarif started its series *Iqra* (Read!), a small pocket-size book that has appeared every month since then, and in 1949 Dar Al-Hilal launched its monthly *Riwayat al-Hilal* (Novels of al-Hilal), which today has reached between 10,000 and 20,000 copies. During the last number of years several campaigns were launched to disseminate cheap books under the motto *Al-Muwajaha* (Confrontation) and *Al-Qiraa lil-Jamia* (Reading for everybody) by the GEBO—efforts that the private publishing industry is not able to undertake because it could not produce at such low prices. These booklets were sold for twenty-five or fifty piasters and were very quickly out of print. The series *Al-Muwajaha* was part of the government's fight against fundamentalism. Many secularist or critical texts by Ali Abd al-Raziq, Farah Antun, Salama Musa, Mohammed Abdu, Ghali Shukri, and Jabir Usfur appeared in this series.

Concerning book production, frequent complaints about "a book crisis" appear as a Leitmotiv (Gonzalez-Quijano 1990: 116). According to Farid Zahran, there is no book crisis, but a crisis of the secularistic and leftist books, whereas religious books are sold in millions.[10] However, a set of obstacles does prevent the Egyptian publishing industry from growing: these obstacles include production costs (in particular the cost of paper), quality of raw material, poor access to the book (lack of outlets, unsatisfactory modes of distribution), bureaucracy and censorship, inflexible import/export regulations, and copyright problems.

A useful indicator to evaluate the Egyptian publishing system is the reader-access ratio, as introduced by Shigeo Minowa, which allows a comparison of different publishing systems (Minowa 1995: 336 ff.). It is calculated by dividing the average book price by the per capita national income. A ratio that shows limited access to books in a country suggests poor conditions for the book publishing industry. In this case, books are expensive and not available to the majority of people in a country. In these countries textbooks are subsidized by the state so as to ensure sufficient supply. On the basis of figures for 1994 the calculation of the access ratio resulted in 1.62.[11] In comparison with the figures provided by Minowa for other countries the book accessibility is very low.[12]

ARAB BOOK PRODUCTION IN STATISTICS

An evaluation of the Lebanese publishing industry is even more difficult, as reliable statistical data is not available. No national bibliography exists,[13] and the National Library has yet to recover from war damage. Book production between 1961 and 1972 was estimated at between 2,500 and 3,000 titles annually (Istifan-Hashim 1993: 27). However, statistical data from the war years shows only between 222 and 685 titles annually. Statistical data for the 1980s does not reveal major differences. The only recent attempt to work on a national bibliography was for the year 1995 when the Ministry for Culture charged a private company with the preparation of a national bibliography. Despite the lack of time and cooperation of some publishers, 2,689 entries were included.[14] Unfortunately the ministry did not continue this project. It seems that there was no substantial change in the quantity of title production from the 1960s onward. Furthermore, it is claimed that the active role of the publisher diminished in favor of reprints and reeditions (Donati 1996: 37 ff.).

In Egypt, instead of a national bibliography the *Legal Deposit Bulletin* is published by the National Library, Dar Al-Kutub. In an analysis of African national bibliographies the adequacy of bibliographic data of the Egyptian bibliography before 1987 is valued as "poor" (Gorman 1989: 505). Between 1988 and 1993 the National Library was even unable to prepare the bibliography—only since 1994 have they produced the parts which had been lacking, publishing them in retrospective issues. Taking these figures, which do not cover all book production, one finds an average of 4,317 titles per year for the years 1990 to 1995.

In quantitative terms, Egypt and Lebanon produce about two-thirds of all Arabic titles per year. Other Arab countries barely reach 1,000 titles annually; the most productive of them are Syria, Jordan, and Tunisia. Iraq has lost its former position as producer and consumer: the saying once had it that "Egypt writes, Lebanon prints, and Iraq buys"; nowadays it is the economically powerful states in the Gulf area that buy. However, it is very difficult to evaluate statistical data because the criteria are not always clear. Sometimes theses are included, sometimes children's books are excluded. The same question applies to government publications, books in foreign languages, translations, and unpublished material. Is a new edition counted as a new title, or only if substantial changes in the edition have occurred? Are titles published in more than one volume counted as one or more entries? The unclear application of theses rules makes it quite difficult to compare the statistical data. Even within a country different sources provide different figures for the same year.[15]

INTER-ARAB TRADE

Book production sometimes leads to a boom, that is, a significant increase in book production figures, provided that specific factors are present.[16] None of the Arab countries has reached this level so far. Nevertheless, there is a lively book culture in Arab countries: Egypt, after South Africa, is the most important book producer in Africa and has a remarkable cultural impact on other Arab countries. Lebanon gained its importance due to the relatively high degree of political freedom and lack of censorship. Despite the fairly positive conditions for a publishing boom in Egypt, the influence of the state seems to have prevented such a development.

The low level of inter-Arab book trade is also important. Egyptian production is still suffering from a heavy loss of export markets due to political problems (Iraq, Libya, Algeria). Lebanon is even more dependent on exports: 80 to 90 percent of the production is exported. In fact, this kind of trade is affected by customs regulations and the censorship policy of the Arab countries as well as by piracy. The loss of export markets complicates book pricing in Lebanon and Egypt. It is in the interest of publishers, especially those in Lebanon, to work on building new export markets; today the Gulf region is the most important market for Lebanese publishers.

But it seems that Arab publishers have recognized these problems. New efforts of the Arab publishers have activated both the Egyptian and the Arab Publishers Union who are aiming at facilitating inter-Arab trade and fighting piracy. These have reached the level of joint projects such as coproductions by publishers from Lebanon, Jordan, and Syria. This is remarkable for two reasons: first, a private association is representing the interests of its members in the form of a pressure group, and, second, it is an attempt to coordinate inter-Arab activities by building a new network. The Arab Publishers Union managed to unite almost all national publisher unions in 1996 and since then has begun a range of activities:[17] in February 1998 its first bibliography of all new books published in 1997 by 132 members appeared during the Cairo Book Fair. It seems to be of a high quality, including indices and short annotations for 2,954 new books.[18] Other activities include numerous meetings with the authorities to urge the removal of trade obstacles. The Arab Publishers Union has also established a committee to fight piracy that publishes a monthly newsletter.

CONCLUSION

The evaluation of publishing in Arab countries is very difficult due to the lack of reliable statistical data and information on the book markets in general. Numerous obstacles, which vary from country to country, impede the further development of the publishing industry. But there is a strong basis for a boom: twenty-three countries with a vast readership—despite illiteracy—and a rich cultural heritage and modern intellectual production provide a growing market for transnational publishers. This market is restricted by a low book-access ratio due to high book prices. Publishers interested in transnational business are represented by the Arab Publishers Union, which is attempting to improve export and import facilities. Whether this initiative will contribute to an increase in the number of cultural books or only to a wider dissemination of cooking and computer books is as yet uncertain.

ENDNOTES

1. Various activities by UNESCO focus on the connection between culture and development. Many book-related figures could serve as cultural indicators for development. *The Cultural Dimension of Development. Towards a Practical Approach.* UNESCO. Paris: UNESCO, 1995; *Towards a World Report on Culture and Development. Constructing Cultural Statistics and Indicators.* UNRISD/UNESCO. Geneva: UNRISD, 1997.
2. These figures are calculated according to the statistics in the UNESCO Statistical Yearbook. Some recent news suggests plans to establish new paper factories that should produce more than 60,000 tons of printing paper and 120,000 tons of newsprint beginning in 1999. See Egypt: Four New Projects for the Production of Paper with Investments about 600 Million Dollars (in Arabic). *Al-Hayat*, February 19, 1996.
3. Sometimes one suspicious word in the title can be enough for the work to be banned. According to Ibrahim al-Muallim, president of both the Arab Publishers Union and the Egyptian Publishers Union, a title is sometimes banned due to its title (al-Muallim 1998: 34).
4. There is still little research on these issues other than the reports of human right organizations, e.g., *The Egyptian Predicament.* Article 19. London: Article 19, 1997; *Syria Unmasked.* Human Rights Watch. London: Human Rights Watch, 1991. An exception is the thorough study by Marina Stagh (Stagh 1993).
5. For a brief survey of different approaches to international copyright see Gleason 1995. International copyright is now included in the World Trade Organization (WTO) and monitored by the Council for Trade-Related Aspects of Intellectual Property Rights.

6. Arab Copyright Convention. *Al-Jadid Fi Alam Al-Kutub Wal-Maktabat* 1, 1994: 22-25; Adoption of the Arab Copyright Convention by the Third Conference of Arab Ministers of Cultures, Baghdad, Iraq, November 5, 1981. *Copyright Bulletin* 1/2, 1982: 82-90; Arab Agreement for the Protection of Author's Rights. *Arab Law Quarterly* 4, 1989: 206-215.
7. Arab Copyright Convention. *Al-Jadid Fi Alam Al-Kutub Wal-Maktabat* 1, 1994: 22-25; *Author's Rights in Arab Countries between Legislation and Application* (in Arabic). Tunis: ALESCO, 1996.
8. Personal communication of the author with Bashar Shabaru, General Secretary of the Syndicate of Publishers Union, Beirut, February 23, 1998.
9. Personal communication of the author with Hani Tulba, General Manager of Al-Ahram Distribution Agency, Cairo, July 27, 1998.
10. Personal communication with Farid Zahran, owner of the Al-Mahrusa Publishing House, in 1996. To give an idea of the sales figures of Islamiyat, at the Cairo Book Fair in 1996, Al-Akhbar publishing house claimed that the complete print run of the famous television preacher Shaikh Sharawi reached 17.5 million copies.
11. The basis of my calculation is the *Nashrat Al-Ida* (Legal Deposit Bulletin) 1, 1994, where the average price of one book amounts to 3.91 Egyptian pounds. However, only 16 percent of 1978 registered titles are priced, most of them being the low-priced publications of the public sector. That means that the reader access ratio is even more unfavorable.
12. Minowa gives, for example, for the United States 0.062; Switzerland 0.12; Lebanon 0.45; Indonesia 0.74; Nigeria 1.36 and India 3.69 (Minowa 1990: 42-45). Compared to the high book prices in Lebanon, the figure for this country seems questionable.
13. The National Library issued a national bibliography for the years 1964, 1965, 1971, and 1972 (Istifan-Hashim 1993: 27).
14. For an evaluation of this bibliography see Istifan-Hashim 1996. It was published on CD-ROM and includes 1845 books, 437 theses, 10 new periodicals, 22 maps, 6 microfiches and 360 other entities.
15. For example, vary the statistics for Egypt for the year 1991 in the Cultural Statistics 1373 entries (Central Agency for Mobilization and Statistics, Cairo/CAPMAS), UNESCO *Statistical Yearbook* 2599, and the *Nashrat Al-Ida* (Legal Deposit Bulletin) 6939. For a critical discussion of UNESCO book production statistics see Whitney 1995.
16. For a discussion of these factors see Minowa 1990, especially Chapter 1. Minowa analyzes the relationship between a publishing boom and scientific research, economic development, technological innovation, marketing infrastructure, and reading environment.
17. News about the activities of the Union can be found in the quarterly magazine *Al-Jadid Fi Alam Al-Kutub Wal-Maktabat*, Amman and Beirut, and after its cessation in *Al-Nashirun*, Beirut.
18. *New Publications of Arab Publishers* (in Arabic). Cairo: Al-Ittihad Al-Amm Lil-Nashirin Al-Arab 1997; *General Arab Publishers Union 1995-1998* (in Arabic). Cairo: Al-Ittihad Al-Amm Lil-Nashirin Al-Arab 1998.

BIBLIOGRAPHY

ALECSO (Arab League Educational, Cultural and Scientific Organization). 1996. *Author's Rights in Arab Countries between Legislation and Application* (in Arabic). Tunis: ALECSO.

Altbach, Philip G. 1987. *The Knowledge Context. Comparative Perspectives on the Distribution of Knowledge.* New York: State University of New York Press.

Altbach, Philip G. 1992. Publishing in the Third World: Issues and Trends for the 21st Century. In *Publishing and Development in the Third World*, edited by Philip G. Altbach, 1-27. London: Hans Zell.

Amri, Abderrahmane. 1986. Protection of Literary and Artistic Works in Comparative Arab Law. *Copyright Bulletin*, 4-16.

Atiyeh, George N. 1995. The Book in the Modern Arab World: The Cases of Lebanon and Egypt. In *The Book in the Islamic World: The Written Word and Communication in the Middle East*, edited by George N. Atiyeh, 233-253. Albany: The State University of New York Press.

Ayalon, Ami. 1995. *The Press in the Arab Middle East: A History.* New York: Oxford University Press.

Ben Cheikh, Abdelkader. 1982. *Book Production and Reading in the Arab World.* Paris: UNESCO.

Coser, Lewis A. 1975. Publishers as Gatekeepers of Ideas. *Annals of the American Academy of Political and Social Science* 421: 14-22.

Coser, Lewis A., Charles Kadushin, and Walter W. Powell. 1982. *Books: The Culture and Commerce of Publishing.* New York: Basic Books.

Donati, Caroline. 1996. L´édition: des chiffres et des lettres. *L´Orient-Express* 5: 36-43.

Gleason, Paul. 1995. International Copyright. In *International Book Publishing*, edited by Philip G. Altbach and E. S. Hoshino, 186-199. New York: Garland.

Gonzalez-Quijano, Yves. 1990. Politiques culturelles et industrie du livre en Égypte. *Maghreb Machrek* 127: 104-120.

Gorman, G.E. 1989. African National Bibliographies as Selection Resources. *International Library Bulletin* 21: 495-508.

Istifan-Hashim, Maud. 1993. *Trade of the Printed Word: Publishing of Books in Lebanon and their Distribution in the Arab World* (in Arabic). Beirut: Dar Al-Saqi.

Istifan-Hashim, Maud. 1996. *The Book in Lebanon: Experience of National Bibliographic Control and New Tendencies in Publishing* (in Arabic). Paper presented to the Arab Federation for Library and Information (AFLI) annual meeting, Amman, November 1996.

Khalifa, Shaban. 1974. *Publication Movement in Egypt. A Practical Study* (in Arabic). Cairo: Dar Al-Thaqafa.

Khalil Mohammed Khalil, Samira. 1993. *Publication Movement in Egypt in the First Half of the Twentieth Century* (in Arabic). Ph.D. thesis, Cairo University.

Lane, Michael. 1975. Shapers of Culture: The Editor in Book Publishing. *Annals of the American Academy of Political and Social Science* 421: 34-42.

Minowa, Shigeo. 1990. *Book Publishing in a Societal Context: Japan and the West.* Tokyo: Japan Scientific Societies Press.

Minowa, Shigeo. 1995. The Societal Context of Book Publishing. In *International Book Publishing*, edited by Philip G. Altbach and E. S. Hoshino, 331-341. New York: Garland.

al-Muallim, Ibrahim. 1998. Piracy of Books is More Profitable than Publishing. *Al-Ahram Al-Arabi*, February 14.

Nusair, Aida Ibrahim. 1994. *Publication Movement in Egypt in the Nineteenth Century* (in Arabic). Cairo: Al-Haya Al-Misriyya Al-Amma Lil-Kitab.

Rizk, Nadia A., and John Rodenbeck. 1985. The Book Publishing Industry in Egypt. In *Publishing in the Third World. Knowledge and Development*, edited by Philip G. Altbach, Amadio A. Arboleda and S. Gopinathan, 96-110. Portsmouth: Heinemann.

Smith, Datus C. 1995. The Economics of Book Publishing in Developing Countries. In *International Book Publishing*, edited by Philip G. Altbach and E. S. Hoshino, 71-80. New York: Garland.

Stagh, Marina. 1993. *The Limits of Freedom of Speech: Prose Literature and Prose Writers in Egypt under Nasser and Sadat*. Stockholm: Acta Universitatis Stockholmiensis.

Whitney, Gretchen. 1995. International Book Production Statistics. In *International Book Publishing*, edited by Philip G. Altbach and E. S. Hoshino, 163-185. New York: Garland.

8

Interaction Between Traditional Communication and Modern Media: Implications for Social Change in Iran and Pakistan

Shir Mohammad Rawan

A common misconception regarding countries of the less developed world, according to John Lent, is "that communication networks do not exist if they do not conform to Westernized, more modern information systems" (Lent 1982: 14). This hypothesis is based on the opinion of media experts of the 1950s and 1960s in Western industrial nations as well as Western-oriented academics in the less developed world, who called for an unconditional acceptance of Western media concepts while ignoring the relevance of other, traditional, and oral forms of communication.

According to Michael Kunczik, Daniel Lerner's *The Passing of Traditional Society* of 1958 was considered "the standard work on mass media and its development, and its conclusions have decisively influenced international media politics, like UNESCO" (Kunczik 1985: 76). In his theory, Lerner considered the Western model of modernization a historical fact whose social changes and components bore relevance for the countries of the Middle East and the world as a whole. According to Lerner, as the modernization of a society takes place primarily through communication development, the existing oral communication systems of cultures based on tradition are an obstacle to the modernization of society and its media systems, which has to be overcome on the way to a modern society (Lerner 1958).

The miscalculation of imposing the Western model onto less developed countries in general, and on countries of the Middle East in particular, does not take into consideration sociocultural, political, economic, or religious differences between the industrialized and nonindustrialized countries. Furthermore, Kunczik states that because traditional values do not necessarily oppose the Western, old traditions do not have to be replaced by Western values. Lerner's hypothesis that modern mass media are the sole driver of social change also contradicts surveys on what influences voters and their voting patterns, such as the one conducted by Elihu Katz and Paul F. Lazarsfeld in 1955. The result of these analyses, the model of the "two-step-flow of mass communication," reveal that many people do not acquire their political views from the mass media, but obtain them through conversing with other people in direct and personal dialogue. It is this latter group that predominantly draws its opinions from the media and is thus better informed. They are what Katz and Lazarsfeld refer to as "opinion leaders." Hamid Mowlana generally approves of the two-step-flow communication theory; however, he criticizes its ambiguity when applied to non-Western countries. Although results of the empirical studies demonstrate the indirect influence of the mass media on American recipients, the authors make no mention of the theory when discussing the development of the media in less developed, non-Western countries in the 1950s and 1960s when modern communication systems had not yet taken root. Instead, they emphasized the necessity for modern, centralized communication technology. Mowlana, however, argued: "It was only in the 1970s and as a result of a number of socio-cultural analyses, coupled with the drastic changes in political, economic, and social systems of many developing countries, that the function and role of traditional communication systems (such as religious meeting places and market places) as independent and fully integrated systems of their own were realized" (Mowlana and Wilson 1990: 58).

At the same time the significance of interpersonal communication received an international hearing through the publication of one of the most important documents since the Second World War, which was presented to the twenty-first General Conference of UNESCO in Belgrade in October 1980. The final report of a two-year enquiry headed by former Irish Minister for Foreign Affairs, Sean MacBride, concerned international problems of communication. The report argued:

First, traditional forms of communication, and particularly interpersonal communication, maintain a vital importance in all parts of the world, both developing and developed, and are even expanding. Second, the majority of people in the world, particularly the rural inhabitants of developing countries, comprising as much as 60 to 70 per cent of the world's population, continues to impart, receive and, what is more, accept messages through these channels of communication. Third, it is impossible to comprehend completely the advantages and limitations of modern media if they are treated as factors separate from the interpersonal communication, for clearly communication networks grow cumulatively, with each new form adding to but not eclipsing the older systems. On the contrary, interpersonal communication takes on a whole new significance in the face of the depersonalizing effects of modern technology and it remains an essential feature in the furtherance of democracy within societies.[1]

According to Lent the application of traditional media seemed to push into the background old perceptions of the 1960s that saw traditional forms of communication as an obstacle to the modernization of society. The debate reached its climax with the victory of the Islamic Revolution in Iran, when an appreciation of the extent of the debate's impact and the efficiency of traditional modes of communication were acknowledged.

The main focus of my research on traditional structures of communication and their impact has been on Iran and Pakistan, though reference will be made to other Islamic countries. Using Iran as an example, I want to illustrate the roles of traditional and personal forms of communication, that is, mosque, bazaar, and religious academic institutions both in the city and in the country in the organization and mobilization of people during the Islamic revolution. Furthermore, I would like to show how traditional forms of communication are used today by the ruling class in order to achieve their political and ideological aims. I will then elaborate on a field study that I conducted in autumn 1995 in the North West Frontier Province (NWFP) in Pakistan.

FORMS AND MEANING OF TRADITIONAL PERSONAL COMMUNICATION

The media in Islamic countries and in the less developed world function on two levels. On the one hand, the media operate through the latest technologies, which mainly address those members of the intellectual and urban population. On the other hand, there is a separate complex system of mass communication that operates along traditional lines. In this case, communication occurs through face-to-face relations and is determined by the standard of social life experienced in each individual country (Rawan 1992: 44). In contrast to modern mass communication, which can only flourish in an economically advanced society, the less developed world concentrates on developing journalism, which is a necessary building block for improving the mass media. Whereas the target group of advanced journalism is spread over a comparatively large territory and varies constantly, traditional communication usually addresses smaller groups in more localized areas (Roschani-Moghaddam 1985: 120). In the Islamic countries the popularity and credibility of modern mass media are restricted for the following reasons: (1) the high degree of illiteracy;[2] (2) the numerous differing languages and dialects spoken by the populations; (3) the price of the media tends to limit newspaper circulation and prevent the purchase of televisions and radio by individuals and families; (4) the countries are often geographically extensive with wide stretches of rural land, causing delays in newspaper delivery and great difficulty in the transmission of radio and television signals; (5) the tendency of the media to act as mouthpieces of the governments; and (6) the traditional system of values in place in these countries. As the majority of the populations live in rural areas outside of the main towns and cities, they are particularly affected. According to Wolfgang Slim Freund, modern mass media (press, radio, television) in North Africa and the Middle East have until now retained their status as "instruments of urban communication" (Freund 1986: 94). There, the mass media are the mouthpiece of the ruling elite as they bring their often strongly ideologized messages to the people. Freund argues: "Neither do 'the masses' communicate with each other via the media, nor do 'the masses' use it to influence their respective élites" (Freund 1986: 92). This narrowness of modern media legitimizes the existence of the centuries-old system of traditional communication.

However, the diffusion of personal influence, which takes place through various traditional and religious channels of communication, is more effective than through modern media. Everett M. Rogers and George M. Beal state one of many reasons for the significance of personal influence in decision making:

> In most cases the persons who interact have a similar value system, so a shared common level of discussion is an important means of reference. Not only are pieces of information exchanged, but also a degree and intensity of feeling and conviction. Here mutual communication is possible, and the recipient of the message can ask the informer for clarification or additional information and will receive it. (...) Impersonal sources are evaded much more easily—they can simply be ignored. (Rogers and Beal 1962: 257-258)

For the majority of the population in the Islamic world, especially for those in rural areas, the traditional channels of communication are centers that fulfill the needs of the people: mosques and other educational institutions, religious celebrations, family meetings, markets and bazaars, assemblies of members of a village or a tribe, games. The *MacBride Report* argues: "All these and many others provide occasions to exchange information, elucidate issues, ventilate grievances, resolve conflicts or assist in opinion-forming and decision-making on matters of common interest to individuals, groups or society as a whole."[3]

The fact that interpersonal communication plays a central role in the distribution of new ideas in Islamic countries can be illustrated by the example of the 1979 Islamic Revolution in Iran. Traditional channels of communication played a decisive role, especially *minbar* (pulpit) in the mosque, the shrines, the *madrasseh* (theological school), *khaneghah* (the *Sufi* house of worship), *rowseh khani* (gatherings for religious mournings), *tafsir* Quran (gatherings for the interpretation of the holy book), *hosseinieh* and *fatemieh* (meeting halls for religious sermons and culture activities), and *takyeh* (annual tents put up for large religious mournings) (Tehranian 1981: 50). The role of the mosque and the bazaar will be closely examined as examples.

MOSQUE AND BAZAAR AS CHANNELS OF INFORMATION

The mosque and the bazaar have always been considered the most important pillars of traditional and interpersonal communication throughout traditional Islamic society. Mehdy Naficy puts it as follows: "Here cities have their centers, here contacts are made, transactions are developed or finished. Here people haggle, praise God or exchange news" (Naficy 1993: 13). The function of the mosque as a place of communication goes back to its foundation. Following Mohammed's journey from Mecca to Medina in AD 622, the prophet built a mosque: According to Asghar Fathi, it was not exclusively a place of saints. As well as being a place of worship, the mosque provided education and acted as a forum for the discussion of social problems. During Mohammed's work in Medina as a political and religious envoy, he introduced decrees concerning taxes and jurisdiction. Although the mosque served as a place for the collection of taxes, it was also an overtly political institution where Mohammed received envoys from other lands. In addition, during the Caliph period of AD 632 to 661, the mosque was important as a military headquarters from where Muslim soldiers were dispatched to the various war fronts. It would, therefore, be a mistake to compare the mosque to a Christian church (Fathi 1979:

tor of education and information is symbolized by its intellectual bond with modern institutions of education. Examples of this can be seen in Egypt, Iran, Pakistan, and many other Islamic countries of the Middle East where mosques and universities coexist or exist within each other up to this day (Mowlana 1996a: 38 ff).

However, as well as being the only institution of learning in many Islamic countries up to the end of the nineteenth century, the mosque also formed the intellectual and political center of communication both in independent and in colonized countries. This is clearly reflected in Iranian history where the mosque—the pulpit—was active in political events such as the so-called "Tobacco Movement" of 1890, the "Constitutional Revolution" of 1907, and the opposition of religious dignitaries to the "White Revolution" instigated by the Shah in 1963 (Mowlana 1988: 24-29). The mosque played a special political role during the "Islamic Revolution" of 1979 in Iran through traditional interpersonal forms of communication. The Shah's Western-oriented media policy, which stood in opposition to many cultural and religious traditions in Iran, widened the gulf between two irreconcilable media systems. The media, which "was directed against the interests of the people as it was 'anti-communicative'" (Motamed-Nejad 1990: 19) and "under state control" (Mowlana 1996b: 17) stood against traditional forms of communication, whose roots lay in religion and the political tradition. The most important factors in the organization and mobilization of the Islamic Revolution were mosques and bazaars as well as religious institutions of education (Mowlana 1996b: 17).

The Shah regime was equipped with one of the most developed media systems in Asia. But as its elite was no longer in touch with the traditional system of values, it erred by accepting the mass media as a substitute for an effective general means of communication (Tehranian 1979: 10). Mowlana has argued that in 1979 the Western-oriented urban middle and upper classes of Iran had relied more and more on Western media when asked to assess the political situation in their own country (Mowlana 1979: 110). Although the traditional media system remained intact and was operated by 200,000 *mullahs* in about 90,000 mosques, the official media, and the radio in particular, lost its credibility (Tehranian 1982: 4). Thus, the most effective channels of communication in prerevolutionary Iran were bazaars, mosques, and the institutions of Islamic education in the cities and countryside. This system of information played a crucial logistical role during the Iranian Revolution of 1979 (Ende 1980: 34).

The oriental bazaar (Arabic: *suq*) is usually situated in the center of the Islamic town, marking the traditional business district. Its brick stalls harbor bustling activity all through the week, except for bank holidays. As well as being a market place, the bazaar has an important political, religious, and entertainment function, as it is the main center of public life in Middle Eastern towns (Grötzbach 1979: 153). In addition, there are so-called "market days" in rural areas of Islamic countries which, apart from their economic function, offer a forum for conversation, making acquaintances, and exchanging news. The markets exist in large, open areas, devoid of brick stalls, and they are used by the local population for the buying and selling of goods. Usually regular or periodical markets occur over one or two days in the week. In north and northwest Afghanistan there are two days reserved for the market; in the south and southeast it takes place on just one day. According to my own observations, one market is held per week in northwest Pakistan, which is inhabited by Pashtunes. Whereas the Friday of the Islamic calendar is designated market day in Afghanistan, Saturday is the market day in rural areas of northwest Pakistan. Friday, a holiday in Islamic countries, has been chosen for market day in Afghanistan so that shoppers can attend mosques once the shops have closed. A traditional market would usually open between seven and eight o'clock in the morning and close around noon. After that, shoppers can exchange the latest news in numerous tea houses and at hot food stalls. They can also discuss matters of importance to their villages, arrange marriages, and negotiate contracts (Fischer 1984: 221).

Market days are also used by state officials to announce new resolutions and decisions. In Afghanistan, for example, this happens in the afternoon when people come together at the close of the market. Peter Heine considers rural markets in the countries of the Middle East as political forums where, as in Morocco, policy agendas are publicized by political parties during election campaigns. In addition, governments utilize the meetings of farmers on market days in order to publicize new working techniques and to introduce new farming machinery (Heine 1989: 149). The Iranian bazaar holds a special position as an economic institution as well as a political, religious and communicative center of the Islamic world. The bazaar has always played a key role during political and social change in Iranian history. Naficy describes in detail the working relations between clergy and stall-holders and their importance in connection with social change from 1960 until the revolution of 1979 (Naficy 1993).

However, we are primarily concerned with the communicational role of the bazaar in Tehran during the Islamic Revolution. An example of the bazaar's importance in times of political unrest, when radio and press were strictly censored, and when political protest, demonstrations, and strikes were prohibited by the administration, was the closing of the shops as a sign of protest. This became the signal for demonstrations by the population against the Shah's regime. The early closing of shops was an unusual event that aroused public curiosity. When the clergy rejected the Shah's reforms, the so-called "White Revolution" of 1963, there was no media coverage of the incident. The closing of the shops of the Tehran bazaar, however, was the signal for action against the Shah regime. As a result, political rallies were held in mosques, leaflets were distributed at the bazaar and in the city, and statements from the clergy were read out (Atiqpour 1979: 7 ff.). Thus, the bazaar was an important nerve center for the organization and mobilization of large parts of the population during the Islamic Revolution of 1979. The anti-Shah movement, which recruited from various political factions, kept close contact with the underground movement, or "cells," of the *bazari*. The cells, recently founded, were in possession of printing machines for the production of tracts. Mohammed Shanechi, who belonged to the organizing network of the bazaar, describes the well-organized system for the distribution of leaflets (Naficy 1993: 24). As the bazaar used to be the center of all trade in Iran, news spread like wild-fire throughout the country.

Today, the bazaar is still the traditional center of Iranian communications and it influences the economic and political actions of the government. Carpet sellers, for instance, a rich and influential group, provide financial support for the conservative wing of the clergy and think little of the modernization plans of the Rafsanjani government. In 1996, the government intended to make them contribute more to the development of the country by making them disclose their salaries and pay higher taxes. The *bazari* went on strike and the government dropped its proposals.

OPINION LEADERS AND INTERPERSONAL COMMUNICATION: A FIELD STUDY IN PAKISTAN

The empirical studies that were conducted by Katz and Lazarsfeld in the United States at the end of the 1950s, which included definitions of the general functions of opinion leaders, show a diffusion of specialist knowledge occurring within a two-step communication process rather than directly via the mass media. The surveys concluded by revealing the specializations of the opinion leaders. Every interest group had its own opinion leader, in politics, fashion, sports, and so forth (Katz and Lazarsfeld 1955). The results of these surveys, which are highly interesting for communicational theories of Islamic countries, point at the same time to the difference between opinion leaders in less developed countries and those in industrial countries which, according to Kunczik, lies in the polymorphic nature of the former's opinion leadership (Kunczik 1985: 106). This also holds true for Islamic countries.

The polymorphic nature of opinion leadership in Muslim countries is based on Islam, where there are no borders between religion, politics, and ethics. However, the individual often exists as a member of a clan that is a traditional structure. The clan is responsible for the behavior of every one of its members. A *mullah* or senior clansman might be asked for advice not only on religious or traditional matters but also on social and political issues. Traditional and religious opinion leaders play a crucial role in forming public opinion. There are no clear distinctions in communication between the religious and the traditional opinion leaders in Islamic countries, who bear different titles in different languages, irrespective of the particular functions they perform or offices they hold. In Afghanistan and Pakistan, the senior clansmen are called *khan* and *malek*. In Turkey he is the *agha*, in Arabia there are the *sheikh* and *malek*, and in Persian he is the *rysh-e-safyd* (white-beard), and *imam* (village teacher).

Power is exerted in different ways by the opinion leaders in these various countries, a fact that has been subject to little scientific analysis to date. Whereas, according to Dariusch Mehrdjui the *mullah* holds the leading position in a village (see Ansari-Chahrsoughi 1980: 155), he comes only second in the scheme of the rural clan system in Afghanistan. This also holds true for the rural areas of Pakistan (Weggel 1992: 67 ff.). The leaders with the greatest influence in the Pashtun society are the *khan*, the *malek*, and the *mullah*. The difference between *khan* and *malek*, according to Willi Steul, is that the *khan* possesses more land. However, their political standing and their influence on political decisions are of equal importance (Steul 1981: 70). The *khan* and the *malek* are acknowledged authorities of a group. A *khan*'s power manifests itself through his personal attributes and his financial dominance over his followers (Steul 1981: 70). The *malek* is the elected representative of a village or a clan, chosen by the menfolk at the traditional open village assembly, the *jirga*. He is mainly responsible for the external relations of the village—for contacts with representatives of the state authorities and for relations with other villages. When the *khan* or *malek* meet other representatives in negotiations, their actions are controlled by certain regulations and they can only make concessions to reach an agreement if such concessions were discussed and agreed by the group in advance. They have, however, significant influence at the preliminary stage and, as members of the *jirga*, at the council meetings also. The *mullah*, the religious leader of the village in a Pashtun society, is ranked second in significance to the *khan* and *malek* as opinion leader. He is paid by the council in the same way as the dome-barber, "beadle," and musician (Steul 1981: 70 ff.).

There are numerous examples of how traditional opinion leaders influence the distribution or suppression of new ideas and technologies through the communication process. As there has been little research done in the field of communication in the Islamic world, I shall try to analyze the role of the opinion leaders in daily communication processes with the help of a field study I conducted in the North West Frontier Province of Pakistan in the autumn of 1995.

In order to better understand the political and communicative significance of the field study, some relevant political aspects must be considered. The identity of the multiethnic state of Pakistan, which was created in the twentieth century as the youngest state of the Islamic world, is based on the Islamic religion. The various nationalities and ethnic groups do not share any significant historical, political, or cultural heritage other than through their religion. The particular Pakistani lack of historical roots has made it difficult to find a political identity or even to maintain national unity. Islam has played a crucial role in the foundation of Pakistan as a focal point for the various minority ethnic groups, firstly during their fight for independence against British colonial rule and subsequently in the emergence of a sense of national identity when faced with potential threat from its non-Islamic neighbor, India. However, Islam cannot play this unifying role internally as a state religion to bind the various Islamic nationalities together (Jettmar 1992: 11), as was witnessed when East Pakistan (now Bangladesh) gained its independence from West Pakistan in 1971. As their regional power base lay in their home provinces of Punjab, Sindh, Bengal, North West Frontier Province, and Belutshistan, they always held regional interests above national interests (Berg 1991: 72-73).

Unlike the Indian National Congress, the representation of all Indian interests, Pakistan's intellectual elite has not succeeded in forming an all-Pakistani party because Pakistani society is based on a vertical group structure. Richard Reeves describes this hierarchical group structure, which he considers an obstacle to the formation of a political party on the Western model:

> If an agricultural laborer has got a problem he will solve it according to the traditional pattern by climbing the vertical ladder to consult the land owner. Members of a tribe do the same; they speak before the leader of the clan who in turn appeals to a more senior member of the clan who is a minister or high official in the government. (Reeves 1986: 120)

Thus, the origin of Pakistan's political parties lies with the clans from which they emerged, for example, the People's Party of Pakistan (PPP) with its headquarters in Sindh, the Awami National Party (ANP), which is based in the North West Frontier Province, the Pakistan National Party (PNP), representing the Belutshistani people (Reetz 1992: 26), and the Awami League, representing Bengali in east Pakistan. "The ruling Nawabs and Khans, the landowning Jagidars and Zamindars and the Islamic Pirs and mullahs being representatives of the old feudal system, exert more influence than party members," writes Hans Walter Berg, a senior correspondent of German television (Berg 1991: 73). These are not only the most important political pillars (especially in rural areas) on which every political party and the central government depend, they are also the center of the information network for the villages and their clans.

The field study conducted by the author in the North West Frontier Province corroborates this view. It was carried out in three villages in the form of a questionnaire with thirty-six categories—two of the villages, called villages A and B, lying in the "Tribal Area" about 170 km away from the provincial capital of Peshawar, and village C lying in the "Settled Area" about 25 km away from Peshawar. Both villages A and B are situated in a rural setting whose Pashtu residents, mostly farm laborers, lead traditional lifestyles according to the Pashtunwali[4] codex rather than following the regulations set down by the state. Village C represents a relatively urban lifestyle based on its location and social makeup (artisans, clerks, lower civil servants, few illiterate people) under Pakistani jurisdiction and state executive. In all, 420 persons were questioned. Special surveys of 100 people took place in each village, apart from village A where 120 were questioned, of whom 30 were Taleban religious scholars. It is important to mention that all three villages are connected to the state power supply system. However, in evaluating the resonance of modern mass media and the influence of traditional communication systems, it was crucial to view the entirety of all sociological and geographical criteria mentioned beforehand. Furthermore, the survey hoped to determine what interplay exists between the outdated forms of interpersonal communication and those of modern communication systems.

The communication processes forming public opinion in the survey areas are naturally diverse. Information sources include the family, word-of-mouth within the village, the opinion leaders, contacts with the cultural life of the nearest city, and the mass media. However, though differences between the villages are acknowledged, opinion leaders still play the most important role in matters of political importance. This can be illustrated by the following figures:

On average, 67 percent of those questioned were in possession of a radio, a TV set, or newspaper. Yet, 84.4 percent of the interviewees used interpersonal communication to gain knowledge of events in their town or region. Whereas 29.4 percent quoted the opinion leaders as direct sources of information, only about 15.6 percent cited modern media. In order to discover people's depth of information regarding current national political issues, they were asked whether they knew about the state of civil unrest in Karachi, which had arisen through ethnic conflicts, and what their sources were. About 64.2 percent of those questioned were first informed by modern media; 29.4 percent through interpersonal communication, out of which 14.2 percent named the opinion leader with 11.9 percent citing relatives and neighbors as sources; 6.4 percent had no knowledge of the events.

Not only does the impact of modern media depend upon the scope of its reception, but also upon how the opinion leader views its credibility, and how he interprets and comments upon the news. As modern media are still a privilege of the upper class in a village, the opinion leaders can monopolize the choice and interpretation of radio programs, as the price of a TV set equals a year's wages for people on an average income. The *khan* is always a wealthy man, and many of his followers work for his family as tenants or farm laborers. The *malek* is usually not a poor man either. Both establish their authority through hospitality and generosity. Often the followers of the *khan* and the *malek* visit their guest houses in the evening where they listen to the radio together or watch TV, regardless of whether they own their own sets. The choice of program is made by the *khan/malek* and is commented on by him.

Within the surveyed area, 30.5 percent of the interviewees owned their own TV set. However, as TV viewing is a communal exercise—with relatives, the *khan*, the *malek*, and so forth—45.5 percent of those questioned had frequent access to a TV set. Of them, 32 percent viewed TV in the guest house of the *khan* or *malek*, 28.9 percent watched TV in the guest house of their family, 24.4 percent watched TV in their own house together with their family, 7.2 percent with relatives and neighbors, and 7.2 percent in a restaurant or tea house. The influence of opinion leaders extends also to consumers of modern media individually and directly. The survey reveals that 42.4 percent of the people discuss the news with opinion leaders—the *khan* or the *malek* (22.4%), the *mullah* (7%), and the teacher (12.4%).

In order to find out about the credibility of the information received, the interviewees were asked to state who in their eyes possessed the best ability for objectively evaluating reality. Of those asked, 64.3 percent named the opinion leader who was said to inform them best in the following order (Table 8.1). The dominance of opinion leaders in providing information was increased by the absence of foreign satellite broadcasting during the time of the survey. Its reception had been prohibited by a decision of the jirga because of the "undermining" of reli-

Table 8.1: Credibility of Opinion Leaders and the Mass Media.

Opinion Leaders/Media	Credibility
khan/malek	37.2%
mullah	26.6%
teacher	0.5%
radio	14.2%
TV	13.8%
newspapers	7.8%

gious and traditional values through the spread of Western culture. This prohibition to receive news via satellite was supported by the *khans* and the *maleks* and was particularly welcomed by the clergy. As far as I could observe there was no breach of this decision.

The influence exercised by the opinion leaders is not only confined to the village or tribe but has, as previously mentioned, a cumulative effect on the entire political system of Pakistan. Ch. Muhammad Amjad characterizes the role of the opinion leaders in the feudally structured society of Pakistan as follows: "When in a village (...) Mâlek Sahib suggests the people to vote for a particular person, they go for it. Only, those people don't observe and analyze things by themselves" (Amjad 1992: 39). This also holds true for the surveyed village C. However, in the surveyed villages A and B, only the village elders, the *khan* and the *malek* cast votes as representatives of about two million people in these semiautonomous tribal areas.[5]

Words like democracy and political participation have never been heard of in most rural areas of Pakistan. A farm laborer from Mirpur, in the southern Pakistani province of Sindh, hit the nail on the head when he said in an interview with a local journalist from the BBC, regarding the latest parliamentary election in February 1997:

> We are free to vote if we want to, but we believe our master has got the right to vote for us. We work on his land. It will always be like that, it will be the same for my children because I can't afford a school education for them. That's why they want to work on the land, just like me.[6]

Thus, those who are dependent on the goodwill of the master lend him their vote, even though there is a democratic alternative.

The role of religious and traditional opinion leaders in the past and present, particularly in rural areas of Islamic countries, should not be underestimated when investigating traditional forms of communication. Firstly, opinion leaders have to be taken into consideration when considering the introduction of development measures and the organization of public life because of their political and economic importance within a village or tribe. Secondly, as the majority of the population are unable to fully understand information distributed by the mass media, they will remain dependent on the interpretative skills of their opinion leaders. Therefore, according to Sherdoost, Ali-Asghar, the former chairman of the first national radio station in the Islamic Republic of Iran, opinion leaders will continue to remain in competition with modern media, which depends on their support, especially in developing educational programs (Sherdoost 1991).

THE RELATIONSHIP BETWEEN TRADITIONAL COMMUNICATION AND MODERN MEDIA IN IRAN

According to Mowlana, the lessons of the Iranian revolution illustrate that it is not enough to simply control modern mass media in order to legitimize political power; it is also necessary to control traditional channels of communication. Traditional and religious structures, such as customs and practices, legitimize modern mass media, rather than the other way round. Therefore, the way to political recognition and cultural identity is through the linking of traditional and modern channels of communication (Mowlana 1996b: 17).

There are some journalists who use the interplay between traditional communication and modern mass media to their advantage. Traditional forms of communication are quite open to innovation despite their long-established use. They can link tradition to progress, provided that political, social, and economic innovations accommodate religious and cultural values.

After the victory of the Islamic revolution, Khomeini's followers seized control of the mass media of the Shah regime, converting it into the mouthpiece of their own philosophy. By doing so, they combined modern technologies with traditional teachings to create a partially successful system of communication. Investigating the structure of Iranian TV in 1988 and 1989 Mowlana also found a high degree of interplay between modern and traditional communication systems. Mowlana notes that the technological infrastructure of television remained intact during the years of the revolution and beyond, although the nation's symbolic and cultural institutions had changed (Mowlana 1989: 36).

After the Islamic revolution the Khomeini regime profited from the experience Khomeini had gained during his exile in Paris.

Khomeini's followers, Abolhassan Bani-Sadr and Sadiq Quotbzadeh among them, had established a strictly organized center of information and propaganda in Naeuphle-le-Château, a small village near Paris. From there they sent important messages to Iran via telephone and short-wave radio transmitters. Khomeini's speeches were recorded on tapes, printed on leaflets, and taken to Iran by special messengers, or transmitted directly via telephone or radio to the three regional centers of Iran: Tehran, Qom, and Yazd. Khomeini's contacts were Ayatollah Montazeri and Taleqani in Teheran, Ayatollah Shirazi in Qom, and Ayatollah Saduqi in Yazd (Sreberny-Mohammadi and Mohammadi 1994: 119-124). These men copied Khomeini's messages on tapes and distributed them through religious and traditional gatherings throughout the country—in mosques, shrines, the *madrasseh* (theological schools), *hosseinieh* and *fatemieh* (meeting halls for religious sermons and cultural activities), *takyeh* (annual events where tents are put up for large religious mournings), *jaleseh* (meetings for women), and *heyat* (meetings for men) in the country. The Shah regime and its media were ineffective in the face of traditional methods of communication; the government failed to prevent the distribution of information.

Today, religious and traditional life takes place in the public places mentioned above. State control of religious and social life is only possible to a certain degree. Yet the religious leaders of Iran who control traditional communication—unlike those of the Shah regime—have often used channels of the mass media during the last eighteen years. These media have been combined with traditional forms of communication. These processes take place on various public and interpersonal levels of communication around which daily life revolves, both in the country and in the city. The Iranian academic Fariba Adelkhan describes very vividly the traditional social and religious intercourse in Iran's urban areas with a particular emphasis on the role of communications (Adelkhan 1996).

The most important religious and social festivities in Iranian cities are the celebrations of Shiite feast days. These include Passion plays (*tazyia*), religious meeting of men (*heyat*) or women (*jaleseh*), visits to the mosque celebration of the sacrifice, as well as personal religious/social festivities, such as mournings. These events are significant in facilitating the establishment of public life and civilized society. *Jalesehs* are called by the women of a district at regular intervals, bringing together women of the neighborhood. They develop friendships and are events for the creation of new acquaintances and for the exchange of information. A woman who joins a new society introduces herself to the community through attending the *jaleseh*. The political and religious impact of the *mullah* regime in a *jaleseh* is exercised through the "dame" who acts as religious authority, and who is also referred to as "spokes-woman" on a par with TV and radio commentators. She receives her education at a theological school or has a privileged status in clerical circles. On the one hand, the *jaleseh*'s role as a charitable institution meets the economic demands of the state and clergy, particularly through the levying of religious taxes. On the other hand, the dame must fulfill the expectations of her audience, which despite the *jaleseh*'s increasing orientation towards a religious discourse, maintains rational lines of argumentation and remains a superior institution (Adelkhan 1996: 56 ff.).

The *heyat* functions similarly to the *jaleseh*. However, the men who meet there are qualified in a profession, allowing them to maintain relations beyond their immediate district, especially through their connection with trade organizations. The social gatherings are based, like the women's, on a degree of confidentiality and comradeship. These are closed meetings where the information discussed is only disclosed within one's own circle of friends.

These so-called religious gatherings, *jaleseh* and *heyat*, are not necessarily exclusively religious. Adelkhan argues:

> They talk about many other things apart from God, and they are an opportunity for the exchange of important information about the day-to-day life, like matters of housing and marriage. People can display their social status through their clothes, their alms and their food. They can re-sell goods which were purchased in Free Trade Areas of their country, from Dubai, or from a place of pilgrimage. (Adelkhan 1996: 56)

Jalesehs and *heyats* usually take place without the presence of the media, as do religious festivities, such as the "feast of sacrifice" (in Farsi: *aid al-qurban*) and "small celebration" (*aid al said-e fater*), or the "festival of mercy and good deeds" on the first day of spring, and the "festival of affection" on the first day of school, as well as the religious celebrations of major Shiite feast days. Celebrations highlighting urban public life, such as *hosseinieh* and *fatemieh*, have taken place since the Islamic Revolution in the presence of the media.

During the festivities the media records interchanges between the various districts of the cities. A kind of story evolves from heated debates about social commitment and help for the needy (Adelkhan 1996: 57). The highest clergy also take part in the festivities, which establish the link between the national and the local and mediate between control by the government above and participation by the people below: the unity of politics and religion. As well as demonstrating the religious and historical significance of the rituals, the festivities proclaim the "conspiracy of world imperialism, especially that of the United States," often holding it responsible for current political and social problems in Iran. The religious ceremonies attract the media, which is used by religious leaders in Iran to legitimize their political and religious position among the people. During the religious festivities special programs are broadcasted that report the occurrence of various events. In live programs the organizers and participants also get the chance to speak. The clergy and their speeches are also given broad coverage in the media.

Another important facet of the correlation between modern media and traditional forms of communication is the Friday prayer—a periodic forum for millions of people everywhere in Iran that is transmitted nationally by radio and television and is reported in great detail by the press. The Friday prayer is, in the words of Khomeini "an entirely political prayer."[7] Its sermons have become the medium of revolutionary Islamic discourse and have been the source of religious legitimization since the Islamic Revolution. Adelkhan describes the course of Friday prayers: "Its first prayer is strictly religious, the second one contains political or social content. It is (...) normal to hear a minister or technocrat talking before the first prayer, who, sometimes in technical language, explains the progress of his 'measures for reconstruction'" (Adelkhan 1996: 56). The political representative announces new initiatives of the government in domestic and foreign policy. Examples of important events in domestic and foreign policy illustrate this. In 1996, Iran's president Rafsanjani defended his political course of liberalism towards Western countries before supporters of the radical Islamic wing during several Friday prayers (Massoud 1991). On another occasion Rafsanjani delivered a report on the political and economic situation of the country of the previous year.[8]

The Mykonos case, of Autumn 1996 in Berlin, triggered a political crisis between Bonn and Tehran. As a result, German Chancellor Helmut Kohl attempted to defuse the situation by writing a letter to Iranian president Rafsanjani in early November. Rafsanjani replied, not via radio, television, or press, but at a Friday prayer on November 22, 1996 in Teheran. His opening remarks were:

> You know last week has been hard. The German chancellor wrote to me, and he wants me to help him save our relations. There are clear signs that the larger part of the German government is not interested in a deterioration of relations between Iran and Germany because of the procedure of the court in Berlin. (Lüders 1996)

An analysis of the content of Friday prayers in Tehran and Qom dealt with in the national newspapers *Kayhan* and *Jumhuri Islami* for February, April, and May 1995 shows a great diversity of topics.

Table 8.2: Contents of Friday Prayers in Newspapers.

Topic	Kayhan	Rank	Jumhuri Islami	Rank
economy	22.2%	1	6.4%	5
religion	22.2%	1	13.3%	2
politics	18.5%	2	23.3%	1
political argument with USA	11.1%	3	13.3%	2
crime	7.4%	4	-	-
education/science	3.7%	5	13.3%	3
other	-	-	10.0%	4

Although the main focus of topics dealt with in the Friday prayers differs between the two dailies, the prayers according to all papers contain 80 percent nonreligious topics. The main focus lay with domestic and foreign political topics in both newspapers. The political discussion of the effects of America's policy on Iran played an important role.

In Mohsen Khandan's opinion, the role of the *minbar* will remain a medium of communication in the future. Modern mass media cannot replace traditional media, mosque, and *minbar*. Khandan concludes from a survey conducted in 1989 that the minbar as a mode of communication throughout Iran has more influence than modern mass media, with the exception of some large cities. The impact of the *minbar* in large cities is much greater than that of modern mass media during particular religious phases, for example during the month of Ramadan (Khandan 1989: 226 ff.).

The impact of the link between traditional and religious institutions and the modern media as centers of communication has not yet been empirically analyzed. It is clear, however, that traditional systems of communication in modern Iran are the most important distributors of information, ahead of the mass media, especially at local and regional level. Illiteracy was successfully tackled after the Islamic revolution, as the *imams* of the mosques saw it as a religious duty to invite the illiterate to participate in reading and writing programs (Gottfried 1983). The success of such quasi-religious campaigns was considerable. The proportion of illiterate people aged over seven years in Iran fell from 59.9 percent in 1975 (Tehranian 1981: 28) to 25.9 percent in 1992.[9] When the socialistic Democratic people's party of Afghanistan came to power in 1978, the opposite occurred. The *mullahs* called for a boycott of the campaign against illiteracy that had been initiated by the government, arguing that a communist ideology would be taught. Such action illustrates clearly the political role of the clergy.

In the opinion of the Iranian journalist Ahmad Jafari-Chamazkoti, traditional channels of communication organized and mobilized the country's youth during the eight-year war between Iran and Iraq. They triggered a fighting spirit for the defense of the country. Religious institutions also played a major part in rebuilding the country after the war. Local opinion leaders, notably the *imams*, informed the population of short-term and long-term plans for rebuilding in their respective regions. They discussed the necessity and usefulness of the plans with the people during Friday prayers and called on the population to participate in the work (Jafari-Chamazkoti 1995).

CONCLUSION

The pivotal problem of the development of communicational structures in Islamic countries, Iran and Pakistan among them, lies in the formation of modern media structures that acknowledge traditional, economic, ideological, and existing communicative structures. Current media structures in Islamic countries are concentrated mainly in capitals where their political and ideological resonance is restricted to a small group of urban intellectuals. The development from a seemingly static tradition towards a dynamic modern age should not only lie in the hands of a small elite but must be considered the collective national responsibility of a large part of the population. As long as the people are not conscious of the necessity of socioeconomic development, modernization will always remain only "partial." In the final analysis, it depends upon the willingness of a broad cross-section of the population to participate as active members in cultural change.

There is only a small chance for lasting cultural change if it does not accommodate traditional values. The participation of the population in this process is therefore a necessary factor. This can only become possible if the various communication cultures interact. Achieving this would require a consideration of technical structures and methods of broadcasting on the part of the media of the Islamic world. Given the fact that the economies have a regional structure and that the societies are multiethnic and multiregional, the media should exert its influence at a more regional level. This would address the problem of understanding in the respective regions and create a direct link between traditional forms of communication and modern media. In the course of this process the respective media should be gradually extended throughout the regions according to local demand. This would initially mean the establishment of radio, with television and the press following. In delivering their three main services (information, entertainment, and education), the regional media must constantly reflect the ethnic and cultural diversity of the existing languages and dialects. Thus, the information and content of educational programs should relate directly to issues concerning the local population. In the long term it is the task of the local media to establish a link between local political discussion and the national debate.

Local media should use traditional channels of communication for its purposes, discuss questions of education at home and in school, expose social and economic mismanagement, and inform the population of their rights and responsibilities. It is of great importance for the local media to win the support of opinion leaders for their work. Friedrich Karl Rothe writes: "A change is achieved more easily if usual patterns of behavior and long-established ways of thinking, if traditional customs and inherited knowledge is respected and existing structures of leadership are considered" (Rothe 1972: 37). The establishment of an effective system of communication in an Islamic country, irrespective of the government that holds power, can only be brought about by combining modern, often imported ideas, with traditional, national views and forms of communication, in order to develop a modern media culture of its own.

ENDNOTES

1. *Many Voices, One World*, International Commission for the Study of Communication Problems. London: Kogan Page, 1980.
2. According to a report of the Islamic Organization for Education, Science and Culture (ISESCO), the average illiteracy rate in Islamic countries in 1991 amounted to almost 51 percent of all Moslems aged fifteen years and older (Deutsche Welle, Monitor-Dienst, December 3, 1991).
3. *Many Voices, One World* (see note 1).
4. See in detail about unwritten traditional norms of the Pashtunwalis: Spain 1990; Rawan 1992.
5. MDR-Informationsdienst: Islamabad (Reuters), December 12, 1996.
6. Quote taken from a German TV program (ARD, Weltspiegel, February 2, 1997).
7. These words said by Khomeini about the political meaning of the Friday prayer are inscribed in a plaque at the Tehran University, in which the Friday prayer also takes place.
8. President Rafsanjani Reports on the Economic and Political Situation in Iran (in Farsi). *Kayhan*, March 15, 1997.
9. *Iran Yearbook*. Bonn: MB Medien und Bücher, 1995: 247.

BIBLIOGRAPHY

Adelkhan, Fariba. 1996. Iran: Islam des Regimes oder Islam des Volkes? *Der Überblick* 4: 56.

Amjad, Ch. Muhammad. 1992. *Towards Journalism.* Lahore: Emporium.

Ansari-Chahrsoughi, Mahmoud. 1980. *Produktionsbedingungen für Film und Fernsehen im Iran unter der Schahherrschaft,* Ph.D. thesis, University of Cologne.

Atiqpour, Muhammad. 1979. *The Role of the Bazaar in the Islamic Revolution* (in Farsi). Tehran: Kayhan.

Berg, Hans Walter. 1991. *Das Erbe der Großmoguln,Völkerschicksale zwischen Hindukusch und Golf von Bengalen.* München: Heyne.

Ende, Werner. 1980. Der schiitische Islam als politische Kraft. *In Iran in der Krise—Weichenstellung für die Zukunft,* edited by Günter Esters and Jochen Langkau, 19-36. Bonn: Neue Gesellschaft.

Fathi, Asghar. 1979. Communication and Tradition in Revolution. The Role of the Islamic Pulpit. *Journal of Communication* 2: 102-106.

Fischer, Wolfram. 1984. *Periodische Märkte im Vorderen Orient, dargestellt am Beispiel aus Nordostanatolien (Türkei) und Nordafghanistan.* Hamburg: Deutsches Orient-Institut.

Freund, Wolfgang S. 1986. Presse, Rundfunk und Fernsehen in Nordafrika und Nahost. *The European Journal of Communication Research* 1: 91-104.

Gottfried, Herrmann. 1983. Bericht über eine Informationsreise in die "Islamische Republik Iran," 19-31. Mai. *Orient* 3: 413-419.

Grötzbach, Erwin. 1979. *Städte und Bazare in Afghanistan.* Wiesbaden: Ludwig.

Heine, Peter. 1989. *Ethnologie des Nahen und Mittleren Ostens: Eine Einführung.* Berlin: Reimer.

Jafari-Chamazkoti, Ahmad. 1995. The Role of the Friday-Imam and Mosque for National Development (in Farsi). *Ettelaat,* October 21.

Jettmar, Karl. 1992. Die pakistanische Nation. In *Pakistan—Zweite Heidelberger Südasiengespräche,* edited by Dieter Conrad and Wolfgang Zingel, 1-13. Stuttgart: Steiner.

Katz, Elihu, and Paul F. Lazarsfeld. 1955. *Personal Influence.* Glencoe: Free Press.

Khandan, Mohsen. 1989. *Culture and Islamic Communication* (in Farsi). Tehran: Imam Sadiq University.

Kunczik, Michael. 1985. *Massenmedien und Entwicklungsländer.* Köln: Böhlau.

Lent, John. 1982. Grassroots Renaissance: Folk Media in the Third World. *Media Asia* 9: 9-15.

Lerner, Daniel. 1958. *The Passing of Traditional Society: Modernizing the Middle East.* Glencoe: Free Press.

Lüders, Michael. 1996. Die Fatwa als Theaterdonner. *Die Zeit,* November 29.

Massoud, Mari. 1991. Der Iran im Spagat zwischen Satan und Mullahs. *Die Tageszeitung,* June 14.

Motamed-Nejad, Kazem. 1990. Communication and Information (in Farsi). *Rasaneh* 2: 14-21.

Mowlana, Hamid. 1979. Technology versus Tradition: Communication in the Iranian Revolution. *Journal of Communication* 2: 107-113.

Mowlana, Hamid. 1988. *Communication, Legitimacy, and Revolution: A Study of Opposition Media Outside National Boundaries.* Paper Read at the XVI World

Congress and General Assembly of the International Association for Mass Communication Research, Barcelona, Spain.

Mowlana, Hamid. 1989. The Islamization of Iranian Television. *Intermedia* 5: 35-39.

Mowlana, Hamid. 1996a. Communication, Ethics and the Islamic Tradition (in Farsi). *Pazhuhesh Wa Sanjesh* 8: 38-45.

Mowlana, Hamid. 1996b. Image and Political Legitimacy (in Faryi). *Rasaneh* 2: 10-17.

Mowlana, Hamid, and Laurie J. Wilson. 1990. *The Passing of Modernity: Communication and the Transformation of Society*. London: Longman.

Naficy, Mehdy. 1993. *Klerus, Basar und die iranische Revolution*. Hamburg: Deutsches Orient-Institut.

Rawan, Shir Mohammad. 1992. *Grundlegende Aspekte der Entstehung und Entwicklung des Journalismus in Afghanistan—Ein Beitrag zur Erforschung des nationalen Kommunikationssystems dieses Landes von 1873 bis 1973*. Ph.D. thesis, University of Leipzig.

Reetz, Dietrich. 1992. Strukturelle Konstanten der pakistanischen Innenpolitik. In *Pakistan—Zweite Heidelberger Südasiengespräche*, edited by Dieter Conrad and Wolfgang Zingel, 21-32. Stuttgart: Steiner.

Reeves, Richard. 1986. *Reise nach Peshawar: Pakistan zwischen gestern und morgen*. Braunschweig: Westermann.

Rogers, Everett M., and George M. Beal. 1962. Die Bedeutung des persönlichen Einflusses bei der Übernahme technischer Neuerungen. In *Soziologie der Entwicklungsländer*, edited by Peter Heintz, 257-267. Berlin: Kieperhauer & Witsch.

Roschani-Moghaddam, Nematollah. 1985. *Kommunikationsplanung und Entwicklungsprozesse, Modell eines Kommunikationsservices als Hilfsfaktor bei der Vollziehung von sozialer Planung in Entwicklungsländern*. Frankfurt: Lang.

Rothe, Friedrich Karl. 1972. *Erziehung und Ausbildung in den Entwicklungsländern*. Essen: Neue Deutsche Schule.

Sherdoost, Ali-Asghar. 1991. The Role of Radio in the Development (in Farsi). *Rasaneh* 4: 74-75.

Spain, James W. 1990. *The Way of the Pathan*, 6th ed. Oxford: Oxford University Press.

Steul, Willi. 1981. *Paschtunwali. Ein Ehrenkodex und seine rechtliche Relevanz*. Wiesbaden: F. Steiner-Verlag.

Sreberny-Mohammadi, Annabelle, and Ali Mohammadi. 1994. *Small Media, Big Revolution. Communication, Culture and the Iranian Revolution*. Minneapolis: University of Minnesota Press.

Tehranian, Majid. 1979. Iran: Communication, Alienation, Revolution. *Intermedia* 2: 6-12.

Tehranian, Majid. 1981. *Communication and Society, Socio-economic and Communication Indicators in Development Planning. A Case Study of Iran*. Paris: UNESCO.

Tehranian, Majid. 1982. Communications Dependency and Dualism in Iran. *Intermedia* 3: 40-45.

Weggel, Oskar. 1992. Dorfislam in Pakistan. In *Der Islam—Ein Lesebuch*, edited by Maria Haarmann, 67 f. München: Beck.

MEDIA AND CULTURE

9

"Coming Close to God" Through the Media: A Phenomenology of the Media Practices of Islamist Women in Egypt

Karin Werner

The following article explores the socioreligious practices of the female members of an Islamist group in Cairo. Its main focus is on these women's use of the media in everyday life. A basic assumption is that religious practices and the media are strongly interwoven. This is evident in the creation and conservation of religious knowledge, which is mediated as a text or a narrative as well as in sacral or sanctual spaces, which are composed using various media such as architecture, interior design, figural and nonfigural visual art, sound, light, and so forth. From the perspective of this article, religion is regarded as a complex symbolic system that shapes and is shaped by social practice, its particular time-space orders, and the set of experiences related to these.[1]

One of the central arguments articulated here is that religion and the topography of experiences related to it are subject to shifts and changes due to political, economic, and technological developments. Stanley Aronowitz' statement that "we live in technology" (Aronowitz

1994) and his appeal for the close connection of culture and technology in people's everyday lives to be highlighted guide this article. Specific evidence is given in an empirical case study about female members of Islamist groups in Egypt. They have developed their own mode of intertwining modern mass media and religion by creating sacral spheres on a regular basis as niches of individual contemplation, catharsis, and purification. These practices, which the women regularly perform in their domestic sphere, offer the particular individuals increasing possibilities of intensive self-affection and introspection as micropractices of self-improvement.

As these observations suggest, modern mass media not only work as powerful mediators and production forces of a "disenchanted, rational modernity" in the Weberian sense, but also as mediators of a modernity of "enchantment" and "aesthetics" in the Benjaminian sense.[2] It is one of the purposes of this article to show that these two readings of modernity and the related theoretical concepts of the subject as a detached controller of his environment in the Weberian sense and as seduced by his environment in the Benjaminian, are not necessarily contradictory concepts. Instead one can argue that both theorize different forms of communication or media practices in modern societies. From this perspective, the observation of the local practices of Egyptian Islamists directs the analysis towards a complex, multilevel notion of an information society, the topography of which not only connects different regions of the world to the "global village" of media networks but on a deeper level works as a system of symbolic differentiation that relates to different mental states of the individual (Kerckhove 1995). On this level, media consumers can use the media to detach from the "profane" activities of their everyday lives and to slip into the hyperreality space[3] of the media, which invites the user to go on mental journeys. In the case study presented here the media are used among other things to "come closer to God." In the practice of the group explored one can observe fascinating new patterns of the intertwining of media and religion. The subject of description and discussion is the phenomenon of mostly young women building their sacral sphere in their homes, going on their mental journeys by turning themselves to the strands of media hyperrealities.

CONDITIONS AND CHARACTERISTICS OF THE FIELD STUDY

For several reasons, I seem to be an enticing catch for Hint, who is about to make a brilliant career within her group context. As I realize during my communication with her, she perceives me as a "divine challenge to test the depth of her belief" on the one hand, and, on the other, as a verbal sparring partner with whom she can put her methods of conversion into practice. Correspondingly, Hint structures our discourse by stressing the difference between "Islamic" and the "Western culture" in moral terms as good and bad or in hierarchical terms as superior and inferior, twisting discourses of Western cultural hegemony. (fieldnote)

The material presented here was collected between September 1992 and July 1993 in Cairo.[4] During this time I studied an Islamist women's group whose members are living in the Cairene quarters Dokki, Muhandesin, and Imbaba. The group of about fifty women gathers around two well-respected religious authorities, one of whom frequently writes articles in the Islamist paper *Al-Muslimin*. In their large flats the two well-respected women in their late forties host religious lectures and Koran recitations, which take place two nights a week. These events are usually attended by an audience of twenty to thirty women. The members of the group, which is part of a loose network of religious groups in Cairo, have certain social characteristics in common: their high level of education; their youth (the majority is between eighteen and thirty years old), as well as the fact that most of them belong to various factions of the middle class. Whereas the initiators and hostesses of the group belong to the upper-middle class, which is expressed by various aspects of their material culture, most of the members are less well-off. The group also includes a few poor members who would sell handmade head garments and gloves to the more well-to-do members of the group after the lectures.

In public most group members wear a head garment covering head, shoulders, and a large part of their torso, a face veil, gloves and a wide, long dress reaching to the ankles. The women who are most advanced in their religious careers express this status by wearing black clothes and covering their eyes with gauze, whereas the less advanced, mostly younger women wear clothes in pastel tones. The hierarchical order of the group is related to factors such as age, duration of membership, and intensity of the individual effort to lead a devout life. According to my findings the group plays an important role in the social life of the women, who recruit friends and older consultants from it. The solidarity between them is also expressed by the habit of the group's members of referring to each other as "sisters" and the cultivation of a social climate during the group's meetings that is warm and respectful at the same time. All women with whom I interacted emphasized the importance of the individual effort in leading a religious life and they strongly distanced themselves from violent groups who were said to be "on the wrong track." At the same time the women expressed their mistrust of the government's accounts of the series of terrorist attacks that took place in spring 1993.

During my stay I joined various social activities of the group and its members as a participant observer. I did structured and narrative interviews with six members of the group on a long-term basis; with another twelve members I had occasional conversations during the meetings. I used to spend time with group members at their homes, at the university campus, and at the group meetings, where I was accepted as a Christian who wanted to convert to Islam. As the women became increasingly afraid of "governmental spies" I was not allowed to record interviews and talks on tape, yet I got permission to write notes while we were talking. The following descriptions and quotations are based on these communications and observations, and should be understood as a phenomenology of the media practices of the members of the Islamist milieu I studied.

THE ISLAMIST SUBJECT POSITION[5] AS RELIGIOUS AVANTGARDE: FROM A "NORMAL TEENAGER" TO A "DEVOUT WOMAN"

I begin the presentation of my empirical case study with the conversion narrative of a eighteen-year-old student living in Aguza, a quarter in Cairo. Hint's case is presented here to show some of the typical characteristics of young Egyptian college students in Cairo who adopt an Islamist lifestyle. As her conversion narrative illustrates, the members of the group I explored perceive themselves in explicit opposition to "the West" on the one hand, which is considered an omnipresent enemy of Islam, and to "the majority of lazy Muslims" on the other. Distinguishing themselves from these two "imagined communities" the Islamists described themselves as a religious vanguard. The trajectory of the individual move from a "normal" to a "devout" lifestyle is expressed in the following narrative, which illustrates several layers of the subject position of the young members of the Islamist group I explored in Cairo. As this fascinating narrative illustrates, "becoming devout" involves the particular individual in specific forms of media use.

> I am lucky, as mother did not forbid us to don the *hijab* as other parents do. After I donned the *hijab*, my religiosity rapidly increased. I recognized that previous doubts and insecurities had faded away. In this respect my contacts with other religious girls played a crucial role; in particular, my friends at school were very important to me during this time as we had the same aim, and we had clear ideas of how to realize it. We knew that we had to go step by step, and that we would profit most if we took the steps together and helped each

other. It was remarkable that our strong will somehow infected others. For instance, in my class the girls were split into good and bad. After the religious group became stronger, we had the capacity to convince others of the justness of our path. In the course of the following year, the year before the final exams, many of the bad girls changed sides and decided to improve their low moral standards. Only a few of my classmates remained in the state of superficiality. It was a marvelous time we had together. We felt like sisters and encouraged each other to improve our standards. We said: "Come on!" to each other. During this time I became strong enough to don the *khimar* [veil covering head and shoulders/K.W.], which I had perceived as the proper Islamic dress from the beginning. Yet I had to start with the *hijab* [veil covering only the head/K.W.] and then take the next step, which happened after about half a year. In our opinion, wearing the *khimar* is not just a question of dress. It is the outer manifestation of an inner development which implies a growing devotion to God. The three components of body, mind and soul have to undergo a change in this process. For me this meant among other things completely giving up watching TV and listening to music, and instead concentrating on the taste of Koran. This was not easy at all for me, and the first months I shifted between a high state of mind while I was praying, and an extremely low state of mind when I watched TV. Although I knew that God's way was the best, I was not able to progress lineally. I still made many mistakes as I let myself be seduced so often. But my struggle paid off. After a while I became stronger and won the fight against Satan and was able to control the TV button and do without the bad things like TV, radio, and music. This was parallel to changing my dress. Burkan, Niran, and I were in the same situation, we exchanged Koranic tapes and booklets, and we focused on our common thoughts and words about God who became more and more the center of our life. It became more and more important for us to please Him, and after several months He gave us the strength to take the next step by donning the *khimar*. During this time I joined Heba, who attended Islamic lectures held at private places not far from here and in a mosque. Here I realized that by way of further improvement I could profit from mixing with more experienced women. As mother did not allow me to go there alone, I asked Dina to accompany me, which was a good thing, as we could continue memorizing the lectures at home, pray together and help each other to improve our standards. This was particularly important when I started my studies at the Alsun faculty, which is a bad environment for us religious girls. The choice of the Alsun faculty was problematic for two reasons: First of all I had to get my family to accept my wish to study at this faculty which was not easy, as they wanted me to become a medical doctor. As I was able to persuade my older brother to support me, I eventually succeeded in my aim of studying languages. For me languages are important, as I intend to translate Islamic texts into different languages to spread Islam throughout the globe. After I had convinced my mother and my uncle, I had to get used to the faculty, which is a horrible environment and quite different from our school. At the Alsun faculty there are only a few religious girls, most of the girls are very bad and hypnotized by the superficial things of life. They look down on us religious girls and give us a hard time. Their minds and souls are closed, they remain stubborn in their false ideas. Also the majority of the professors are against us and make malicious remarks intending to humiliate us, but as we have God on our side, and we also have a little group of friends here, I think things are getting better even in this horrible faculty. The faculty surroundings did not foster my religious development, and as I had to get used to it in the first year, I could not improve very much in the religious field. I also had a lot to do for my studies. But in the last summer holidays I spoiled myself with a wonderful religious program which included much reading, attending lectures, listening to Koranic tapes, and spending much time with my religious girlfriends, whom I only met at the religious lectures during the first year at the faculty. After this magnificent time I felt prepared to take another step, or to reach another level. My thoughts had revolved around the *niqab* [face veil/K.W.] before, but I had lacked the strength during the first year. In the summer break I met Heba and the twins several times. All of them had become *munaqqabat* [women wearing the face veil/K.W.] in the meantime and gave me a good example. So I prayed a lot and became capable of also taking this step before I returned to the faculty after the summer holidays. When I returned to the faculty I recognized that God had given me a beautiful surprise, as a fellow student of mine had also decided to don the *niqab* during the holidays. So I had a companion during the first difficult weeks, and, as in the previous decisions, I am hundred per cent sure that I am on the right path which leads me to God.

ISLAMIST MEDIA CONCEPTS: MEDIA BETWEEN GOOD AND EVIL

As Hint's conversion narrative indicates, "becoming religious" (*tadayun*) is described as an individual decision to question the common sense knowledge of Egyptian society, and replaces many facets with alternative patterns that all together form a distinct Islamist subject position. One of the realms that is highly questioned and subject to regrouping concerns the media, regarded as powerful instruments for controlling the mind. As such, they are feared and highly valued at the same time, depending on whether they are used to "deflect people from the important things in life" as is said to be the case with the Egyptian mass media, or to "bring the believers closer to God" as the Islamists say about their own media. As interviews and observations illustrate, media use plays an important role in the conversion to a "devout" life.

The Islamist discourse about the media revolves around the topic of Western imperialism, which in the Islamist view combines economical exploitation with political suppression. The women I talked to named the cultural imperialism of the West, which consists in "filling the minds of Muslim people" with consumer goods and media products as the most severe component of Western imperialism. During my stay I noticed a strong sympathy of the women with the Bosnians, which was caused by the media representations of the civil war in Bosnia. Besides anti-Western accounts on Egyptian TV, the group's members had access to informational material sponsored by Saudi Arabia such as photographs of the tortured bodies of Bosnian Muslims. The gruesome images, which were framed with texts accusing the West of pursuing the genocide of the European Muslim population, circulated among the members of the group and beyond. They were brought to the university campus and home to the families. Wherever the material appeared, it unleashed strong emotions among the observers, who sighed and cried about the martyrdom of their Muslim brothers and sisters.

In this context physical violence was described to me as only one, but not necessarily the most effective weapon of the Western aggressors against Muslims. The Islamists identified the "soft" Western strategies of "seduction," which is used as the key concept of the Islamists' media discourse, as much more effective than killing and torture. As Hint's conversion narrative illustrates, the young women describe their former relationship to the media as a serious addiction that was difficult to overcome. Others described it as a "drug," as a "superficial," "lulling" experience that the West gave the Muslims to "deflect our attention from the important things in life." Watching TV, in particular, was compared to a trancelike state which completely occupied the spectators' flow of consciousness. In their new state of devoutness the women completely avoided watching TV, which they believe has a polluting effect even "if we only watch a few seconds of this brainwash." As Randa's sister Dina expresses, full of anger: "It gives me the shivers when I remember how I watched TV before I became devout. If I had died while I was watching TV, I certainly would have gone to hell!"

The members of the Islamist subculture of Cairo also accused TV of encouraging idolatry. Raving about the glamorous film and TV stars is considered by them as a severe sin, "as the attention of devout Muslims should rather be directed towards Muslim martyrs who deserve the admiration and loving thoughts of their brothers and sisters." In this context one woman made the point that she considered it a "shame" that millions of Egyptians cried when the famous Egyptian singer Umm Kulthum died, whereas hardly anybody cried for our Muslim victims in the Bosnian war. Other women stressed the point that the Muhammadiya should be the subject of idolatry, which was not considered a bad mental state as such, yet terribly misdirected towards Western pop stars. In other words: They found it very important to make the prophet Mohammed their only idol and did this very consciously. The most disturbing thing for Hint and her friends was the presentation of scantily dressed dancers on TV during the holy month of Ramadan, which was condemned as a "major sin hurting the feelings of each believing Muslim." As a "clean" counter example to the Western-infiltrated Egyptian television, Hint and others pointed to the Saudi Arabian television stations, which were said to broadcast "many instructive films about the beauty of the creation and religious TV programs."

In interpreting these statements one gets the impression that television as well as other modern media are not rejected in principle by the Islamists; they are rather considered powerful weapons in an ideological struggle that targets the flow of individual consciousness. In analogy to the politics of competing media or television stations the Islamists' approach is concerned with an economy of attention, and, similar to their competitors, it is the Islamists' goal to strongly intervene in the flow of consciousness and to canalize individual thoughts. In their reflections and practical orientations the Islamists relate positively to the power of the media; they have understood the potential uses of media technology and try to exploit them for their own purposes. The Islamists do not mind the fact that television is a medium of idolatry (it is a comparatively weak medium for idolatry however, according to recent media theory in the tradition of Marshall McLuhan),[6] yet they want to use these possibilities against the "threat of Western imperialism" and in the service of their own beliefs and needs.

Accordingly, the young women discussed the role of the media in their religious practice in quite pragmatic ways. The Islamists with whom I talked were in general positive about the use of the media; the power of a TV set or a tape recorder in stimulating a mental state was not fundamentally criticized, for example, as an overwhelming or manipulating technology. On the contrary, media technology was seen as a "gift from God to mankind" that can be used for good and for bad purposes. From this perspective Islamists appear as "media tacticians"[7] who entangle themselves in the dialectics of the media: They use the media and they let themselves be used by the media in the sense that they give the media space within themselves.

ISLAMIST MEDIA PRACTICE: ELEMENTS OF A MASS-MEDIATED SACRAL SPHERE

The following descriptions focus on the Islamists' particular media practices, their struggle to "overcome the seduction" of the Egyptian popular media and replace them by alternative programs. In the following passages, emphasis is placed on the use of diverse media and their contribution to a lifestyle of socioreligious careerists who use a repertoire of books, booklets, photographs, audio-tapes, and video cassettes to form their own landscape of realities, deliberately countering popular cultural influences by sensually experiencing the Islamic alternative in their everyday life.

The media practices of the women discussed here seem to be very regular and uniform. They are embedded in a thick maze of discourses that articulate the high degree of reflection on the use of the media. During my numerous visits to the women's homes I noticed that the way they use the media is subject to thorough consideration, as media are an important element of their methodological lifestyles. This means that similar to many other activities individual media consumption is made compatible with the general postulate of "profitable use of time." The individual time-economy that sharply distinguishes between "profitable use of time" and "wasting time" is shaped here to a large degree as an economy of consciousness. This is to control which outer events are permitted to enter the inner stage of individual consciousness.

The Use of the Sound Media Tape Recorder and Radio

> The tape recorder and the radio are used very often. Most of the time when Hint does housework like preparing food or washing, cleaning and ironing, she listens to recitations and sermons from her voluminous tape collection. Hint presents herself as a connoisseur of Koran recitations, and she names as her favorites some Saudi Arabian shaikhs whose sound she prefers to her Egyptian favorite Shaikh Gibril. She also likes to listen to Koran recitations broadcast by the National Islamic radio station. (fieldnote)

Tape recorder and radio play an important role in the Islamist milieu, and the young women emphasized that these media can help the individual believer "to come closer to God." As I found out during my visits to their homes, the women were well-equipped with a collection of audio cassettes containing Koran recitations, sermons, religious lectures, and various contributions (poems, songs, etc.) to current political topics (during my stay the war in Bosnia was one major topic in Islamist circles). Other tapes contained practical information on topics such as marriage, family, motherhood, and polite behavior in public. Whereas the latter are used to gain practical information, the Koran tapes and sermons are used by the women to acoustically witness God's revelation. The tonal enrichment of the individual domestic space with the divine revelation is a form of media consumption practiced daily in the Islamist milieu. Koran recitations of their favorite *shaikhs* were absorbed by the women while they were cooking, cleaning the flat, or chatting with other family members. The sound of the recitations created a solemn atmosphere and helped to build a contrast to the noise of the crowded streets of Cairo. When I asked Hint about her habit of turning on the cassette recorder as soon as she entered the flat she explained that she needed "to get clean from the dirt and the noise of the streets and the market."

Besides using the Koran tapes as calming background sound these tapes are put to a second use in the Islamist milieu. Listening to Koran tapes can also be an activity to which the recipients devote their full attention. The women indulging in it described the sentiments stimulated by the recitations as "peaceful," "inspiring," and giving them "exaltations." As one woman described: "When I listen to the Koran I feel sheltered and safe. I feel a strong harmony and all feelings of discomfort vanish immediately." Other women also described themselves as being deeply touched by the sound of the Koran recitations and commented positively on this kind of sentiment, which is part of their conscious project of becoming devout. These feelings of devotion and "growing weak when listening to the *shaikh*" cause the women to withdraw from other activities in their everyday lives and to enter a sacral sphere of transcendental experience where one "gets closer to God." The importance attached to "growing weak" in this milieu is illustrated by accounts in which female Islamists express their admiration of men who "are usually very strong but faint when listening to a harsh *sura* predicting torments of hell." That the intensive bewilderment is considered desirable in the Islamist milieu is also illustrated by some younger women who consciously practice at "becoming more sensitive and receptive for God's word." As Hint's close friend Afaf (twenty-one) described: "Two years ago I was quite dull. When I listen to the Koran these days some sura have a much stronger effect, and for the future I hope that I will taste the Koran even more strongly than I am able to now."

Listening to the Koran is valued by the women as an immediate experience of divine revelation and highly stylized as the aesthetics of listening and being sensually and emotionally touched. As the women emphasized in conversations with me, the reproductive aspect of this media experience of revelation is not seen in a critical light; on the contrary, the women stressed the positive effects of the frequent closeness to

God that is made possible through electronic media. Radio and cassette recorder are used as technical vehicles that make it possible to participate in this deep, cathartic space of sensation regardless of external time-space and community structures. Their use of sound media enables the women to cultivate individual sacral spaces that are independent of external human and institutional resources such as preachers and mosques.

Simultaneously, the Islamists whom I spent time with distanced themselves from nonreligious radio programs and cassettes of pop music and other popular forms of entertainment, which they felt should not be given the slightest chance to further occupy their consciousness.

The Use of Books

> When studying, Hint withdraws to her room where the furniture consists of a bed, a big closet, a desk, a chair and a shelf which is filled with books for her studies and Islamic books, which Hint tenderly calls her library. Expanding the library (representing religious knowledge) is described by her as an important goal for the future, and, among other things, Hint mentions the volume of his library as a criterion for evaluating the quality of a suitor. Hint's place of work consists of a small desk on which a few books, a pencil, a few exercise books and an alarm-clock are symmetrically arranged. To prevent people from looking into her room from outside, the shutters of the balcony door are kept closed as long as Hint stays in it. (field-note)

Whereas sound media enable the consumers to deeply experience the single moment,[8] books are not only used by readers to emphatically and intensely experience the moment but also to build up a sequential, linear horizon of time that corresponds to the methodological lifestyle of the members of the Islamist group. In the past few years the number of texts that address the members of the Islamist subculture in Egypt has markedly increased. A large number of these texts that deal with questions concerning individual life orientation and planning are read by Egyptian university students, many of whom face the threat of unemployment and poverty after graduation. When I accompanied Hint to a small Islamic bookshop on a few occasions, she showed me the books that interested her the most. These books, the majority of which were published in Saudi Arabia, dealt with the following topics: how to give up alcohol and cigarettes; how to build and maintain a contented Islamic family; how Muslims should behave towards Christians; how to read the Koran; how the pious Muslim can use the life of Prophet Mohammed as an example; the meaning of the Sunna for a Muslim today; how to speak successfully in front of a large audience; how to cope with the threat of Western and Zionist imperialism; how to raise children in the spirit of Islam. As became obvious by leafing through the books, the diverse texts give readers practical information on how to become more religious and more successful, which are discussed in the publications as one and the same thing.

The equation of piety and socioeconomic success that is explicated in the Islamist texts indicates the close connection between Islamist norms and those that are valid in competitive arenas such as the capitalist market economy, sports, and the education sector. The cultivation of a notion of success that aims at the practical control of the outer world by the individual corresponds with these norms. This instrumentalist disposition is also articulated by the women in their resolutions "to do the best in every situation," emphasizing that this motivation also includes the educational and professional sphere. This motivation also became observable in the daily routine of the women, which was structured by thorough time management. The main concern of the practice of "using time optimally" was to integrate the individual's professional and religious careers.

Whereas the highly popular practical guides were used by the women to find meaningful arrangements for their everyday life, one can observe a second style of using texts in this social milieu. This second style is mainly practiced with the Islamic written sources such as the Koran and the Sunna, which are regularly read silently and aloud by the young members of the group that I studied. Especially, reading them aloud is considered both an art and a rewarding activity that was practiced by all the women I talked to. When they described what the loud Koran recitations meant for them, the young women emphasized that they regarded the vibrations and the resonances caused by God's revelation in their own bodies as an outstanding experience. Devoted recitation stimulates a strong affection in both the reciter and the audience. The skilled use of the pitch and timbre of one's own voice phonetically modulating passage for passage creates a close connection between the reciting subject and the text, which is transformed into an aesthetic unity in the course of this process. In this experience of salvation, which is incorporated in the vibrating body, the experience of the reader, the reciter, and the listener of the divine revelation can overlap in one person. The description of the sensations felt by the young women during their daily reading ritual resemble the ones they experienced when listening to Koran tapes, yet they are described in even stronger terms. They indicate a strong affective involvement that can be expressed by the voice, mimicry, and gestures of the reciter. The women described their experience as reciters as calming, safe, and trancelike, "which makes you forget your here and now for strongly tasting God." Hint also emphasized the importance of reciting the Koran daily for "strengthening one's belief." Another aspect of the reciting practice is concerned with the high prestige that is attached to the skill of recitation. I observed that women who have advanced recitation skills are highly respected in their group context and are asked to perform on various occasions. The close relationship that the young women maintained to the written Islamic sources struck me as a remarkable feminization of religious authority; Hint and others told me that they even read in the Koran while menstruating, although this was only possible when they wore gloves in order not to pollute the holy book.

The more intensively the young women engaged in reading the Islamic written sources, the less important other texts became, and they described many of them as harmful. Romances, comics, and detective novels in particular, which the young women loved to read before their turn to an Islamist life, are strongly rejected now as "superficial," "stupid," and "immature" reading. These books were put out of sight and instead the women started to build up their own Islamic library of "important, profitable books," which they treated like a treasure.

The Use of Language

The set of media practices of the Islamist group described here also included spoken language. The sphere of the spoken word is perforated by a repertoire of pious phrases and exclamations that are used frequently. For a lot of different practical situations, such as leaving the house, getting on the bus, and going to the restroom, to mention only a few, a catalogue of phrases exists that remind the speaker and the listener of God's presence. The phrases *al-hamdullilah* and *subhan Allah*, which praise God, are particularly popular. Although the women assured me that the utterance of each of these phrases was rewarded by God, they conceded that this was only the case when they were meant sincerely and not just repeated as "empty phrases as most people do." Hint and her friends described "having an awareness of God's mercy in all situations of everyday life" and drawing the attention to the partner of communication towards it too as the aim of their micropolitics of speech.

The more the women implanted the new phrases into their language practice the more they began to "clean" their language of popular teenage slang in English and colloquial Arabic. As Hint and some of her "sisters" confirmed, these had been very important in their former lives as members of teenage groups who used to pick up the latest phrases from TV and the movies. The young women now adopted a new habitus of speech that they described as "speaking moderately" or "speaking

politely." The new speaking habits form an element of a comprehensive
retraining of the social body. This program implied that the repertoire of
the "sexy teenager" that had dominated their habitual performances
before was replaced with the moderate body of the "young mature
woman who knows her boundaries." As I observed, this repertoire combines a slow and moderate voice modulation with small, inconspicuous
body movements.

The Use of Television and Video

Although the Egyptian Islamists managed to develop alternative media
platforms of radio, audio cassette, book, and spoken language, this was
not entirely successful for television and video. Egyptian TV, which is
controlled by the government, broadcasts a program that is strongly criticized by the Islamists. The main points of critique are the low moral
standards (presentation of sex and violence) and the superficiality of the
most contributions. This critique goes hand in hand with a strong aver-
sion to Egyptian television, which is demonized by the young Islamists.
As Hint's conversion narrative also illustrates, the women describe their
former pattern of watching TV as an addiction that was hard to overcome, as the pleasant and easily consumable TV realities lull the mind
into a state of agreeable laziness. Hint stated with conviction that "the
infidels and the lazy Muslims who have a nice, agreeable time in this life
will go to hell whereas the pious Muslims have to struggle and suffer in
this life in order to please God and to enter the paradise." In this context
she formulated a harsh criticism of the "lazy people" who do not care
about the state of the society they live in. She said: "They do not care if
everything falls apart and decays, but our generation has understood
that we have to devote our lives to save the Muslim world from Western
decadence." The women described satellite dishes, which are becoming
more and more widespread in Egyptian upper- and middle-class contexts, as the most powerful instrument of Western cultural imperialism.
When we strolled through Cairo the women frequently pointed at the
dishes and predicted that their owners would "all go to hell for sure."

　　　The members of the Islamist subculture regard Islamist videos
that circulate between the group members as a "clean" alternative to the
polluted messages entering Egyptian living rooms by satellite dishes.
The range of videos, many of them are financed by Saudi Arabia,
includes sermons, religious discussions and features, films about nature
that praise the beauty of the genesis, and the history of the Islamic civilization. Other films treat topics from the (natural) sciences and languages. Mere entertainment is replaced in these films by learning about
and enjoying the divine revelation and creation. The fact that they were

not allowed to set up and maintain their own TV station was regretted by many of the Islamists, who improvise with videos to compensate for this lack.

Social Contextualization of the Islamic Media Practice

This contribution works on the assumption that in modern consumer societies media-based forms of communication play a crucial role in forming individual practices, including religious practice. It was the purpose of the empirical case study to show how the reality formats offered by different media are used to generate specific socioreligious everyday practices in the context of an Islamist women's group in Cairo. As the descriptions illustrate, the newly developing socioreligious style of the Islamists is to a strong degree individualist, competitive, and strongly influenced by the capitalist rhetoric of "success." The religious practice of the observed individuals, which takes the shape of continuous micro-practices of self-observation and self-correction, is realized by intensive and extensive use of modern media. The fact that these communication devices are exploited by young Islamists to form individual sacral spaces, which are to a certain extent independent of collective resources and influence, can be interpreted as an autonomization process of educated young women or as a "feminization of religious authority," which is achieved for the price of an increased level of self-control.

The need articulated by the young women to involve themselves in intensive therapeutical processes of self-purification cannot be adequately understood without considering the changes that have taken place in Egyptian society during the last twenty years: the Infitah, the economic open-door and liberalization policy of Presidents Sadat and Mubarak. In other words, the dwindling of the state's importance as a macroeconomic agency taking care of large portions of the population on the one hand, and the new prominence of individualistic patterns of social actors "taking care of themselves" by adopting individualist strategies to gain private and professional success on the other should be seen as interrelated phenomena. The collapse of "Arab Socialism" as the predominant regional identity and the rise of an Islamist identity of success, which is strongly evident in the rich Arab gulf countries, is another crucial factor influencing the development of new socioreligious forms in Egypt.

The fact that the current situation in Egyptian society is characterized by competing Westernizing, nationalist, and diverse neo-Islamic identities is particularly precarious for young women in urban contexts, as the competing identities also include highly different concepts of femininity and related gender contracts. As interviews with young Islamists indicate, the contradictions between the different models are not always easily reconcilable. Autobiographical narratives of members of the Islamist milieu illustrate that individual engagement in Islamist subcultures is often preceded by biographical disorientation and crisis. Another important factor in this context is the gloomy professional and financial prospects of university graduates that fuel individual disorientation and anxieties.

Under these conditions Islamist lifestyles offer individuals the possibility of joining a horizon of meaning, where powerful narratives of success hold out the prospect of a career combining private and professional aspects and even reach out into the hereafter. Islamist lifestyles combine life economy and aesthetics by integrating offensive forms of intervention into the outer world and introspective, meditative forms of relationships with the self. Regarding their strong engagement in these various areas of experience one can assert that the Islamists in Egypt make themselves at home in the world through the media. They use the media to get practical and normative knowledge as well as to go on cathartic inner journeys.

ENDNOTES

1. This definition resembles the one developed by Thomas Luckmann in his study *The Invisible Religion* (Luckmann 1976).
2. Most of the current media theory emphasizes this notion of modernity. Marshall McLuhan (McLuhan 1968) and Raymond Williams (Williams 1980) are the most important contributors.
3. The notion of hyperreality was elaborated by Jean Baudrillard in 1990. The changes of time-space perception through the media is discussed in detail by Götz Großklaus (Großklaus 1995) and Friedrich Kittler (Kittler 1986).
4. The following descriptions are part of the dissertation *Between Westernization and the Veil: Gendering in Egyptian Youth Cultures* (Werner 1997).
5. The term "subject position" is derived from my reading of Michel Foucault and a number of postmodern feminist theories. Their understanding of the subject contrasts with classical modern views of this category, which separate and oppose subject and object in an essentialist manner. In the postmodern view, the subject is seen as an entity of differences and not as a holistic entity. In the context of this article the term subject position is valid, as it helps to counter essentializing views of "Islamic fundamentalists" in order to understand Islamist womens' social practice. I am aware that my position is also opposed to the Islamists' own essentializing views of themselves.
6. For a more detailed reading of the strong opportunities and seductions that the media offer social actors to restructure their everyday life see:

Dienst 1994; Foster 1983; Großklaus 1995; Hammel 1994; Hauser 1980; Kerckhove 1995; Kittler 1986; Lau 1993; Meyrowitz 1990; Rushkoff 1994; Thomä 1994; Williams 1980.

7. I employ the term "tactitian" in opposition to the hitherto very strong dichotomy between media producers and media consumers. Contrary to this I lay emphasis on media use that includes specific local possibilities of using media according to one's own needs and pleasure. The concept of the tactician underscores the work that has to be done by the autopoietic— thus aesthetically and cognitively active—media-using subject as well as the integration of media in social actors' life regimes, i.e., forming discourses and rules around the use of media. See Werner 1998.

8. Wolfgang Hagen argues that the radio presents itself as "the absolute performative, as a pure event apparatus" that creates a specific way of listening. This aesthetic experience of listening to the radio stretches the present. Hagen compares this with a "one dimensional room" or a "tomb." Thus, it is not remembered in the same way as, for example, books and other media (Hagen 1993).

BIBLIOGRAPHY

Aronowitz, Stanley. 1994. Technology and the Future of Work. In *Culture on the Brink. Ideologies of Technology*, edited by Gretchen Bender and Timothy Druckrey, 15-31. Seattle: Bay.

Baudrillard, Jean. 1990. *Revenge of the Crystal*. London: Pluto.

Dienst, Richard. 1994. *Still Life in Real Time. Theory after Television*. Durham, NC: Duke University Press.

Foster, Hal. 1983. *TV in Two Parts*. New York: Kuklapolitan.

Großklaus, Götz. 1995. *Medien-Zeit Medien-Raum. Zum Wandel der raumzeitlichen Wahrnehmung in der Moderne*. Frankfurt: Suhrkamp.

Hagen, Wolfgang. 1989. Hören und Vergessen. In *Arsenale der Seele*, edited by Friedrich Kittler and Georg Christoph Tholen, 139-150. München: Fink.

Hammel, Eckhard. 1994. Medien, Technik, Zeit. Zur Geschichte menschlicher Selbstwahrnehmung. In *Zeit-Medien-Wahrnehmung*, edited by Mike Sandbote and Walther Ch. Zimmerli, 60-78. Darmstadt: Wissenschaftliche Buchgesellschaft.

Hauser, Arnold. 1980. Im Zeichen des Films. In *Film und Fernsehen*, edited by Manfred Brauneck, 67-80. Bamberg: Buchers

Kerckhove, Derrick de. 1995. *Schriftgeburten. Vom Alphabet zum Computer*. München: Fink.

Kittler, Friedrich. 1986. *Grammophon, Film, Typewriter*. Berlin: Brinkmann und Bose.

Lau, Jörg. 1993. Medien verstehen. Drei Abschweifungen. *Merkur* 9/10: 829-853.

Luckmann, Thomas. 1976. *The Invisible Religion. The Problem of Religion in Modern Society*. New York: Macmillan.

McLuhan, Marshall. 1968. *Die magischen Kanäle*. Understanding Media. Düsseldorf: Econ.

Meyrowitz, Joshua. 1990. *Überall und nirgends dabei. Die Fernsehgesellschaft I*. Weinheim: Beltz.

Rushkoff, Douglas. 1994. *Media Virus. Die geheimen Verführungen in der Multi-Media-Welt*. Frankfurt: Eichborn.

Thomä, Dieter. 1994. Zeit, Erzählung, neue Medien. Philosophische Aspekte eines Streits der Medien um das Leben. In *Zeit-Medien-Wahrnehmung*, edited by Mike Sandbote and Walther Ch. Zimmerli, 89-110. Darmstadt: Wissenschaftliche Buchgesellschaft.

Werner, Karin. 1997. *Between Westernization and Islam. Contemporary Lifestyles of Women in Cairo*. Bielefeld: Transcript.

Werner, Karin. 1998. Neue Medien und Neue Religionen: Islamistinnen in Ägypten als Medientaktiker. *asien, afrika, lateinamerika* 1: 29-52.

Williams, Raymond. 1980. *Problems in Materialism and Culture*. London: Verso.

10

The Global Flow of Information: A Critical Appraisal from the Perspective of Arab-Islamic Information Sciences[1]

Dagmar Glass

And pursue not that thou hast no knowledge of.[2]

Circulate knowledge and teach the ignorant, for knowledge does not vanish except when it is kept secretly.[3]

Arab-Muslim information specialists have been trying since the late 1950s and early 1960s to develop concepts for domestic as well as global practices of the information flow (Arabic *iʿlam*, i.e., the act of transmitting information to someone). As the academic debate shows, perceived difficulties such as an unbalanced global media flow (McQuail 1994: 113-116) have been looked at from a theoretical angle over the past few years. Likewise, academics have outlined the potential dangers to receptive cultures such as the Arab-Islamic one, which find themselves in situations of varying dependence.

Arab-Islamic information concepts have long been neglected by
Western scholarship. The aim of the following contribution is, firstly, to
shed light on some of the major issues in the Arab-Islamic academic
debate on information. Secondly, Islamic definitions of information and
criticism of information in the Arab world will be examined. For the
paper, some forty Arabic publications have been consulted. At the time
their works were published, the authors were mostly staff members or
academic lecturers at Arab-Islamic universities, working, for example, in
faculties of information or education and departments of journalism.
Some also held leading positions in publishing houses, newspapers,
radio stations, and TV stations as well as governmental offices; others
worked as religious propagandists.

THE HISTORICAL PERSPECTIVE

The history of Arab-Islamic civilization can be read as the history of the
acquisition of religious and secular knowledge or information as well as
the history of scientific development. Politicians are also guided by this
view. Prior to the first Islamic Information Ministers' Conference within
the framework of the Organization of Islamic Conference (OIC),
Abdelhadi Boutaleb, Director General of the Islamic Educational,
Scientific and Cultural Organization (ISESCO), commented: "Islam realized the religious, political and economic importance of information
fourteen centuries ago and organized its means, stated its goals and
exhorted Muslims to make good use of it for the sake of their religion
and their commonweal" (Boutaleb 1986: 7).

The basic notion of Arab-Islamic information is ᶜilm, a derivation
of the root ᶜ-l-m "to know." ᶜIlm means first "knowledge (of God),"
knowledge of anything that concerns religion. The opposite is jahl (ignorance). Furthermore, ᶜilm (pl. ᶜulum) also means "science." Whereas in
pre-Islamic times the root ᶜ-l-m is said to have played only a marginal
role, ᶜilm was literally born in the first breath of Islam.[4] For the Muslims
of the classical period, however, information was not merely a commod-
ity, as it is today, but "a moral and ethical imperative" (Mowlana 1993:
11). According to Ziauddin Sardar, "Islam was synonymous with ᶜilm;
without it, an Islamic civilization was unimaginable. For a Muslim civilization of the future, it is even more so" (Sardar 1993: 43).

The significance of knowledge in Islam is highlighted by the two
quotations at the beginning of this text. The first one comes from the
Koran, the second one is a Hadith, a prophetic tradition. Also of relevance here are the Koranic words Rabb zidni ᶜilm ("O my Lord, increase
me in knowledge"),[5] the saying Niᶜma al-sharaf al-ᶜilm ("Knowledge is the

greatest honour" or: "Knowledge ennobles") and the words *Al-ʿilm ra'id al-ʿaql* ("Knowledge is the guide of the intellect"),[6] as is the prominent feature of Muslim intellectual life in medieval times, which in Arabic is called *talab al-ʿilm* ("search for knowledge").

Besides *ʿilm*, other Arabic notions of knowledge and information became basic tenets; for example, *maʿrifa* (knowledge, cognition),[7] *ʿirfan* (esoteric knowledge),[8] *ʿaql* (intellect, intelligence),[9] *ra'y* (opinion, view),[10] *hikma* (wisdom, also science and philosophy),[11] *haqiqa* (reality, fact, truth, the content of *khabar*),[12] *khabar* (pl. *akhbar*), and *daʿwa* (see below). Such notions embraced both the religious and secular fields, labeling not only a particular but a universal claim of Muslim society to knowledge, information, and communication, that is, the "act of transmitting information, ideas and attitudes from one person to another" (Agee et al. 1982: 4).

With the development of the "software of information," that is, with new spheres of knowledge and scientific disciplines, a diversification of its "hardware" took place. The media (*wasa'il al-iʿlam*) or the means of knowledge and information transfer changed. Besides such pre-Islamic media as markets, councils, poems, public speeches and narratives, Islamic media such as sermons, the Koran and Hadith emerged (Hamza n.d.), later followed by the Islamic college (*madrasa*) (Makdisi 1981) or epistles and (handwritten) books (Atiyeh 1995). In the early seventeenth century, the first Arabic books were printed *in* the Arab world. They were followed in the nineteenth century by the first mass media, that is, Arabic newspapers and magazines. In the twentieth century, audio-visual mass media entered the region, such as radio, film, and television; these were later followed by electronic means of information distribution such as the compact disk, the computer, and the Internet.

All of these media, whether they are traditional and of pre-Islamic and Islamic origin or modern and of Western origin, have one thing in common: They are all agents of social and intellectual change and have far-reaching effects on society and communication. The mass media have called traditional hierarchies, as well as monopolies of knowledge into question, and individual as well as societal behavior. They all put the restructuring of the conditions of communication on the agenda.

In today's era of Arab mass media, indigenous practices of information exchange are facing new challenges. In principle, they are the result of the encounter between East and West since the last century. Contrary to medieval times, the East has found itself in a situation of dependence from the nineteenth century. Since that time, the West has dictated the global flow of information, especially in the field of the mass media, by setting its patterns and norms, thus imposing on the

East "the widespread adoption of, or adaption to, foreign cultural models" (McQuail 1994: 113).

      Likewise, Arabic authors now refer to a "debate between North
and South" instead of the former "debate between East and West." A
particular problem today is the difference in the type of dependence.
The East—or the South—faces a type of dependence, according to Sardar
and non-Western authors, that may be more subversive and devastating
than any in the past. More than ever questions such as the following
have become relevant for Arab-Muslim information theorists: Should
"Muslim countries embrace a compulsive, totalitarian technology and
risk inducing a new, more subversive and devastating type of dependency; or should they preserve their meagre and valuable resources,
ignore the developments in information technology and leave their destiny in Western hands?" (Sardar 1988: 3) and "Is the emerging global
information communication community a moral and ethical community
or just another stage in the transformation in which the West is the centre and the Islamic world the periphery?" (Mowlana 1993: 11).

ARAB-ISLAMIC INFORMATION SPECIALISTS: FIVE GROUPS

The development of Arab-Islamic information sciences (ᶜulum al-iᶜlam)
and the theoretical foundation of information through the mass media
and communication began in Egypt in the late 1950s and early 1960s.[13]
Arab-Islamic information sciences are, in principle, an academic
response to authoritarian Arab information policies (al-Jammal 1991:
211), especially since the first ministry of information was founded in
Egypt in November 1952 (Hatim 1989, II: 37). The numerous publications on this matter are neither uniform, nor are they a generally recognized body of literature (Tehranian 1988: 191). On the contrary, they
reflect a diversity of tenets, concepts, and strategies. In order to deal
with the academic debate and with Arab-Islamic media and communication theories, it is necessary first to become familiar with this diverse
body of literature. Information scientists from some forty Arabic publications can be divided into five groups, whereby some authors may be
classified as belonging to two groups.

  • The first group includes authors who since the late 1950s have
    been examining the structure and functions of the Arab infor-
    mation process. These authors are attempting to draw up a
    model of the information process and to describe the social
    functions of information and the phenomenon of public opin-
    ion. Their theories are strongly, sometimes even exclusively

based on Western information and communication models, mainly American ones.[14] Ibrahim al-Imam (al-Iman 1967, 1969), Mohammed ʿAbd al-Qadir Hatim (Hatim 1978, 1989), Jihan Ahmad Rashti (Rashti 1978), ʿAli ʿAjwa (ʿAjwa 1985), ʿAbd al-Hamid Hijazi (Hijazi 1987), and Basyumi Ibrahim Hamada (Hamada 1996) belong to this group. As a rule, these authors do not refer to indigenous sources and classical Islamic traditions. They will be excluded here, but are likely to be of special interest for anyone dealing with the Arab-Islamic reception of Western information sciences from a purely theoretical point of view.

- The second group established itself at the same time as the first one. It has been trying ever since to give practical journalistic activities such as news editing and program making an academic foundation. Authors such as Jalal al-Din al-Hamamisi (al-Hamamisi 1965), ʿAbd al-ʿAziz Sharaf (Sharaf 1979, 1987), or Mahmud Adham (Adham 1987, 1989) belong to this group, which advocates academic training for journalists and information experts. Apart from criticizing what is known as "media Arabic" (Sharaf 1979), the representatives of this group tend not to look critically at established information practices and policies in the Arab world. This second group will not be discussed here either, but the following three groups are of interest.

- The third group comprises authors who, since the 1960s, have been concerned with (pre-) Islamic media history. They deal with the subject of the media in Islamic history and in pre-Islamic times, or with classical Islamic theories of information. Representatives of this group include ʿAbd al-Latif Hamza (Hamza n.d., 1967, 1978), Fuad Said Haddad (Haddad 1984), Mohammed ʿAbd al-Qadir Hatim (Hatim 1985), Ibrahim al-Imam (al-Imam 1985), Sayyid Mohammed Sadati al-Shinqiti (al-Shinqiti 1986a, 1986b), and Mahmud Adham (Adham 1990). Like the first two groups, representatives of the third group hardly ever criticize official Arab information policies. But we may well assume that some of these authors, who like Hamza, Hatim, or al-Shinqiti worked on Islamic media history or the Koranic concept of information, contributed to preparing and encouraging the formation of the next two groups.[15]

- The fourth group began to establish itself in the late 1970s. The number of its publications has increased enormously in the intervening period. The group's representatives try to develop theories in two main ways: by deriving them from

classical Arabic sources (mostly from the Koran and Hadith),
or by following traditionally oriented authors, but going
beyond them by harmonizing classical references with
Western ones (see below). Representatives of this fourth
group include Muhyi al-Din cAbd al-Halim (cAbd al-Halim
1982, 1984), Yusuf al-cAzm (al-cAzm 1980), cAmara Najib
(Najib 1980), Mohammed Sayyid Mohammed (Mohammed
1983), Marci Madkur (Madkur 1988), Mohammed Khair
Ramadan Yusuf (Yusuf 1986, 1989), Mohammed al-cUlaiwat
and cAbd al-Latif al-Shabib (al-cUlaiwat and al-Shahib 1993),
Mohammed Sacd Abu cAmud (Abu cAmud 1994), or Ghazi
Zain cAudallah (cAudallah 1995). Authors in this fourth category advocate the (re-)Islamization of Arab information. They
call for an Islamic conceptualization of information (iclam islami). This includes a sharp criticism of official information
practices in the Arab world. This group seems to be more heterogenous than the others. One can distinguish, for instance,
between purely academic authors, such as Muhyi al-Din cAbd
al-Halim, the Director of the Department of Information at
Azhar University—the center of Sunni Islamic scholarship in
Cairo—and academic propagandists such as Yusuf al-cAzm,
who started his career around 1976 by giving lecturers to different groups of Muslim students in Riyadh, Mecca, and
Alexandria.

• Last but not least, a fifth group of information theorists must be
mentioned. This group appears to be a product of the 1980s. Its
representatives advocate an Arab conceptualization of information. They call for a sovereign, independent Arab concept of
information (iclam carabi), but not explicitly for an alternative
Islamic one. For this reason they can be called protagonists of a
(re-)Arabization of information. Authors such as cAwatif cAbd
al-Rahman (cAbd al-Rahman 1984), cAbd al-Wahhab Kahil
(Kahil 1987), cUlaiwa Hasan (Hasan 1990), Rasim Mohammed
al-Jammal (al-Jammal 1985, 1990, 1991), cAli Watfa (Watfa
1994), and Ahmad Faris cAbd al-Muncim (cAbd al-Muncim
1994) are typical representatives of this group. Some of the
authors have joined the call for a "New World Information
Order." In this way, they support a demand made by Mustafa
al-Masmudi on behalf of UNESCO in the late 1970s; since that
time it has continued to be on the agenda.

There are some similarities between the authors of the fourth and fifth
groups. Above all, they view established Arab information practices crit-

ically. Both groups regard them as deficient, unbalanced, and in need of reform. Despite holding these common views, however, there are important differences. Both groups not only differ in their concepts and terms, but also in their strategies. In what follows the main positions held by representatives of the latter two groups are outlined.

PLEAS FOR THE ISLAMIZATION OF ARAB INFORMATION

Generally speaking, the communication of knowledge that is determined by the "Islamic community's paradigm of revelation" correlates with what is known as persuasion in the framework of the "Information society's paradigm of information" (Mowlana 1993: 13). Islamic information more than Western information—or possibly in contrast to it—is enlightenment and mental instruction, and therefore persuasive communication. As far as the concept of persuasion is concerned, Gerald R. Miller argues that it is one of the most extensively described concepts of communication: "The term 'persuasion' refers to situations where attempts are made to modify behavior by symbolic transactions (messages), which are sometimes, but not always, linked with coercive force (indirectly coercive) and which appeal to the reason and emotions of the intended persuadee(s)" (Miller 1987: 451). It is worth noting that the first Arab ministry of information (founded in Egypt in November 1952) was not initially called *wizarat al-iᶜlam* (ministry of information), as it is common today, but *wizarat al-irshad al-qaumi* (ministry of national instruction) (Hatim 1989, II: 37).

It must be said that although they encourage the same four functions of communication as Westerners[16]—that is, to inform, to teach, to propose or persuade, and to please—Muslim thinkers appraise these functions differently. Compared to Western concepts of information, Islamic interpretations often put more emphasis on the religious-instructional qualifications of the communicator. Objectivity, also essential in Western concepts, is sometimes interpreted in a specific way; some Muslim thinkers define it as divine wisdom (*hikma*). In addition to this, some Muslim thinkers include notions, such as *daᶜwa*, that are excluded by others. Unlike pleas for the Arabization of information, pleas for its Islamization usually begin with definitions of key notions concerning information, such as *iᶜlam*, *daᶜwa*, and *khabar*.

- *Iᶜlam* (information): A remarkable definition still used today derives from ᶜAbd al-Latif Hamza:

[Information is/D.G.] providing the people with proper news
(*akhbar sahiha*), correct pieces of information (*maᶜlumat salima*)
and firm truths (*haqa'iq thabita*), which help people to form a
correct opinion (*ra'y sa'ib*) of an event or problem.
Furthermore, information is an objective expression (*taᶜbir
mauduᶜi*) of the mentality of the people (*ᶜaqliyyat al-jamahir*),
their inclinations and ambitions (Hamza 1978: 75).

The connection between correctness and reliability of information, on the one hand, and the mentality of the masses, on the
other, took on a normative character and was adopted by a
number of Arab-Muslim thinkers, among them the leading
Azhar information theoretician Muhyi al-Din ᶜAbd al-Halim.
As for Hamza's understanding of mass mentality, it should be
pointed out that this is not an ordinary reference to Western
media because his primary role models are not American:
they include the German news specialist Otto Groth, an outstanding representative in this field in his time.[17] ᶜAbd al-
Halim, however, tried to islamize the concept of information
in the following way at the beginning of the 1980s.
Information, he says, "provides the people (...) with the truths
of the Islamic religion (*haqa'iq al-din al-islami*) on the basis of
the book of God and the Sunna of his messenger." These
truths, he continues, are provided directly or indirectly, either
through specific religious media or through general mass
media. The process requires specialists, that is, Muslim communicators who must possess special qualifications, including
a comprehensive knowledge of the religious message. ᶜAbd al-
Halim, like Hamza, believes in shaping a correct opinion (*ra'y
sa'ib*) with the people as the addressee of information, but he
holds that information should also enable the people to recognize religious truths. Only in this way does it enable the masses to be guided by truths in faith, worship, and life (ᶜAbd al-
Halim 1984: 147). By advocating a religious approach, ᶜAbd al-
Halim's definition exemplifies how the Islamization of information concepts occur.
- *Daᶜwa* (Muslim call to believe in God): *Daᶜwa* literally means
  "call" or "invitation." In the religious sense, *daᶜwa* is the invitation, addressed to men by God and the prophets, to believe
  in the true religion. In the Middle Ages this word stood for
  religious propaganda, which above all manifested itself in
  Fatimid Egypt. At that time *daᶜi* was a propagandist, who with
  the slogan "sword and gold" propagated the teachings of the
  Ismaᶜili sect. Such a propagandist had to have special political

and religious capabilities. *Da^{c}wa* has to be distinguished from *di^{c}aya*, which mostly refers to nonreligious propaganda. Furthermore, it is worth noting that departments of information sciences in modern Islamic universities of the Arab world are usually called *kulliyat al-da^{c}wa wal-i^{c}lam* and a Muslim professor of information is called *ustadh al-da^{c}wa.*[18] In the given Islamic context of information, *da^{c}wa* is theorized as the call to participate and gather in order to follow the path of divine truth, the straight path to God. Today, especially Islamist authors stress this idea. It is by subordinating the notion *i^{c}lam* to *da^{c}wa*, that Muslim authors such as ^{c}Amara Najib or Mohammed Khair Ramadan Yusuf try to distinguish their concepts from other Islamic ones. Najib, for example, rejects Hamza's statement that information is an "objective expression of mass mentality" by arguing that whereas this can be a correct definition of information, it is not necessarily so (Najib 1980: 16 f.). According to Najib, information can also be an expression of the mentality of an authority or a regime with no connection to the people. Also, the statement that information is "providing people with correct information and firm truths" is theoretical in nature, and hence not conclusive. Whereas information can aim to provide correct messages, it can also be interpreted as disseminating lies and false reports, thus misleading people. It then amounts to negative propaganda. In order to avoid misunderstandings like these, a new conception of information is necessary. This is why Najib suggests that information should be regarded as a manifestation of the entire process of delivering the message of the Lord and should be subordinated to *da^{c}wa*, the call to participate and gather together in order to follow the path of the divine truth, the straight path to God (Najib 1980: 11). *Da^{c}wa*, the message (*balagh*) and information (*i^{c}lam*) must merge into one process. This, however, requires that religion and the state amalgamate (Najib 1980: 35). Furthermore, Najib says—as others do, too— that one cannot inform people without carrying out *da^{c}wa*, or without religious teaching and instructing (*ta^{c}lim*) (Najib 1980: 11-16). He adds that Islamic information also means clearly expressing the truth (*haqq*)[19] in a way that attracts people (Najib 1980: 17-18). This truth, he continues, has to be transmitted by using all means and methods. In order to win the people for the truth, that is, for Islam, they must not only be provided with positive information, but they also have to discover vanity (*batil*) in order to learn to avoid it. In this way, the

Islamization of information means making *da^cwa* the notion at
the top, whereas information and instruction become less
important.

The Muslim (Islamist) author Yusuf sees *da^cwa* as the new
call to believe in the unity of God (*tauhid*), as the call to
Muslims to find their way back to Islam, and to non-Muslims
to join Islam as well as the call for Islamic unity (Yusuf 1989:
14-20). *Da^cwa* is then an objective of information, but cannot be
achieved without searching for knowledge. For "knowledge
(*^cilm*) is the path to belief (*iman*)" (Yusuf 1989: 16). Yusuf's comments on objectivity (*maudu^ciyya*) are striking. Yusuf deviates
from ^cAbd al-Halim and other predecessors by identifying
objectivity as wisdom (*hikma*), that is, a divine principle. The
proof, he says, is given in the Koran 16: 125: "Call thou to the
way of thy Lord with wisdom and good admonition, and dispute with them in the better way. Surely thy Lord knows very
well those who have gone astray from His way, and He knows
very well those who are guided" (Arberry 1983: 273).[20]

The subordination of *i^clam* to *da^cwa* also allows some
Muslim authors such as al-^cUlaiwat and al-Shabib to distinguish between functions, purposes, and features of Islamic
information. According to them, the functions of Islamic information are (1) to circulate tidings or news; (2) to provide
knowledge and thus instruct the intellect; (3) to guide and to
influence one's opinion (*ra'y*), that is, to persuade; (4) to educate and train, and, finally; (5) to please and entertain (al-
^cUlaiwat and al-Shabib 1993: 21-24). But the main purposes of
information (*maqasid al-i^clam al-islami*) are (1) the delivery of the
religious message as well as the religious guidance of the people; (2) the formation of a human being who feels religious
responsibility; (3) the creation of a faithful *umma* and (4) the
creation of an Islamic civilization (al-^cUlaiwat and al-Shabib
1993: 26-40). As special features the authors mention the message (*risala*), wisdom (*hikma*), morality (*akhlaq*), and comprehen-
siveness (*shumuliyya*)[21] (al-^cUlaiwat and al-Shabib 1993: 46-54).

• *Khabar* and *akhbar* (tidings and news): Whereas *i^clam* and *da^cwa*
are notions at the top in the Islamic view of information, *khabar*
(pl. *akhbar*) is usually regarded as the basis of knowledge. That
is why Muslim thinkers pay as much attention to this term as
to the highest ranking.[22] *Khabar*[23] literally means "tidings,"
"piece of information," or "report" of a historical, biographical, or even anecdotal nature; the plural *akhbar* means "news."
But one must also take into consideration the fact that *akhbar* is

also a term that refers to classical Arabic prose literature. In this context *akhbar* are short narrative texts that have "two features in common: they are closed narrative units and they make no mention of the wider historical or textual context" (Leder and Kilpatrick 1992: 10-14; Leder 1991: 141-196). These narratives are ascribed to eye-witnesses or reporters close to the events in question. Thus the term *akhbar* —like news—suggests factuality and reality, although *akhbar* can also contain fictitious or fictional elements. Adham has collected no less than ninety-nine different definitions of *khabar* (Adham 1987: 14-26). A further definition was added by Madkur, a Muslim information expert who specializes in the theoretical basis of Islamic journalism. The definition suggested by Madkur reads: Items of news which are delivered by the Islamic press should have several features. News should (1) be useful and relevant to the recipient; (2) create knowledge; (3) contain objective images of events, thoughts, and phenomena; (4) be free of opinions (*ara'*) and assessments; and(5) should harmonize with Islamic faith. Madkur's references range from the Koran and other classical sources[24] to Western (mostly American) works (Madkur 1988: 23-36). This is what sets his approach apart from the ones used by Najib, Yusuf, and others.

ISLAMIC REPORTING OF NEWS

All news reporting has two underlying features: techniques and rules (norms, values). Regarding techniques, that is, news editing or layout, Madkur postulates no essential differences between Muslim and Western journalism (Madkur 1988: 37-177). However, with regard to the rules of journalism he rejects the Western pattern. Like news anywhere in the world, he argues, Islamic news or items of information (*maclumat*) must answer questions like who, what, when, where, why, and how (Madkur 1988: 40). But these general functions should correspond with Islamic norms or values of truth (*haqq*) and correctness (*sihha*) (Madkur 1988: 28, 182-183). What is more, Muslim thinkers suggest that the Muslim journalist has a special responsibility (*mas'uliyya islamiyya*). With reference to the Koran they argue that the Muslim journalist needs knowledge (*cilm*) and authority (*sultan*) as special forms of legitimation. Verse 17:36 of the Koran prescribes: "And pursue not that thou hast no knowledge of" (Arberry 1983: 278), and verse 40:56 says: "Those who dispute concerning the signs of God, without an authority come to them, in their breasts is only pride, that they shall never attain. So seek thou refuge in God" (Arberry 1983: 487).

Generally, the Muslim journalist—according to Madkur—has to act in the following way: He has to (1) evaluate persons critically; (2) learn continuously; (3) teach and persuade; (4) verify facts and news (by using techniques such as documentation, testimony, witnesses, and reasoning); (5) know the circumstances; and (6) be sensitive to bias and lack of objectivity (Madkur 1988: 185-199).[25] Of course, these principles of Islamic journalism do not seem to differ greatly from the generally accepted journalism code of honor, as even Madkur admits (Madkur 1988: 202). A comparison with the information requirements postulated by Western communication theoreticians shows that correctness or reliability are also demanded of Western reporting. Western sources argue, for example, that "information should be objective in the sense of being accurate, honest, sufficiently complete, true to reality, reliable, and separating fact from opinion" (McQuail 1994: 148). The question arises as to the differences between Western and Islamic reporting. Muslim thinkers assume a special responsibility for news reporting by stressing the norms and values of Islam as a religion. Mostly by referring to the Koran, they suggest a number of modifications for the Islamic reporting of news. Thus, the eyewitness report is given preference over "secondhand information" or archival research (Madkur 1988: 71). Furthermore, the privacy of individuals and families is to be more respected in Muslim journalism (al-cUlaiwat and al-Shabib 1993: 105-113, 143-154). In addition, Muslim thinkers have always warned against false news. This is shown by Ibn Khaldun's *Muqaddima* as well as by the Koran, where verse 49:6 reads: "O believers, if an ungodly man comes to you with a tiding, make clear, lest you afflict a people unwittingly, and then repent of what you have done" (Arberry 1983: 536). Verse 49:6 is of central relevance to Islamic concepts of news (Al Seini 1986: 281; Boutaleb 1986: 8).

ISLAMIC CRITICISM OF ARAB INFORMATION

Muslim critics are afraid of the religious damage caused by established Arab information networks due to their "Western design." Such warnings are not only uttered by Islamist activists but also by scholars. However, the ideas differ as much as the ideological credos. A sharply critical voice is Yusuf al-cAzm, who is clearly inspired by the Muslim Brethren leader Sayyid Qutb (1906-1966). According to al-cAzm, who is an ideologist and religious propagandist rather than a theoretician, information has to consider relevant problems, putting them into words, texts, and pictures so that they actually get to the addressee (al-cAzm 1980: 9 f.). From this point of view, he sees Arab information as being unbalanced and unfair. He attributes this fact to indigenous and exogenous reasons. In his opinion, official information practice has no identity (*huwiyya*), and has been misleading Muslims for generations. Muslims can only read and listen to what "the enemy" provides. Modern media, such as they are, do not serve Muslim matters, they have no relationship with the Muslim legacy, and do not give any orientation or perspective to Muslim society (*umma*). In a nutshell, they have no relevance for Muslims, not to mention that they have divided the Muslim community in ideological and political thinking (al-ᶜAzm 1980: 10 f.).

According to al-ᶜAzm, the history of the Arab press exemplifies this decline and loss of prestige. The famous Egyptian newspaper *Al-Ahram* from its first issue—of August 5, 1876—misled its readers. The no less famous magazine *Al-Hilal*[26] under Juji Zaidan (1861-1914)—al-ᶜAzm calls him a "forger" (*muzawwir*)—and his publishing house *Dar al-Hilal* have had the same effect. Authors like Michel Aflaq, Qunstantin Zuraiq, Antun Saᶜada, Salama Musa, Luwis ᶜAwwad, Philip Hitti, Yaᶜqub Sarruf, or Faris Nimr[27] are said to have seduced the "young Arab spirit" and "Muslim youth" instead of providing a good example. Even the political party press of Egypt (e.g., Mustafa Kamil's *Al-Liwa* and the press of the *Wafd*-movement) have offered no alternative. In any case, this could not be expected of Egyptian, Lebanese, and Kuwaiti journalists who—particularly the latter—are slaves to the West. Hence, according to al-ᶜAzm, what Sayyid Qutb said of the Arab press is still true: it has no influence on public opinion, nor does public opinion influence it (al-ᶜAzm 1980: 14-43).

Madkur expresses further criticism. In his opinion, the members of the Arab-Muslim community only have access to Western-oriented information (Madkur 1988: 201 f.). News about Islam in the Western media is devoid of objectivity (*mauduᶜiyya*). This is why an alternative needs to be established, an information practice that is based on Islamic beliefs and whose main pillar is the Islamic journalistic model.

Another critical assessment of Arab information was undertaken by Ziauddin Sardar, a respected scholar, writer, and cultural critic, whose comments, in comparison to those of al-ᶜAzm, have hardly any ideological connotations (Sardar 1988: 15-20). Even though no *Arab* Muslim author, it is useful to look at some of Sardar's statements. It is striking that he rarely quotes from the Koran and Hadith, but prefers classical works by al-Kindi (died ca. 870), al-Razi (d. 925), al-Farabi (d. 950), al-Ghazali (d. 1111), Ibn Sina (d. 1037), Jalal al-Din al-Rumi (d. 1273), and Ibn Khaldun (d. 1406). Sardar, like others, regards the unbalanced relationship between the Western origins of information and its Muslim recipients as the main problem of communication (Sardar 1988: 105-108). He argues that there is a wide gap between the two sides, because they both differ in their "societal knowledge." Sardar theorizes this term as "a guide" that "provides a mapping of human life and environment" (Sardar 1988: 9 f.). It is influenced by "four types of information systems:" (1) "world view"; (2) national identity (*shakhsiyya qaumiyya*); (3) the social setting (family, job, social status, etc.); and (4) "personal philosophy," which includes self-conscious aspects of an individual's personality. Because of this difference in "societal knowledge," he then concludes, information and perception will be undermined. Muslims might not really understand Western information. By consequence, there is a lack of communication. To illustrate this problem, Sardar refers to an old Sufi aphorism that asks: "'Is there a sound in the forest if a tree crashes down and no one is around to hear it?' The right answer to this question is, of course, 'No'." (Sardar 1988: 106). It is true that the falling tree generates no noise unless it is perceived by someone. Thus, Sardar concludes, developing a communication system that meets the needs of the *umma* cannot be an external affair, but must be undertaken by the *umma*, the Muslim society. The communications system of the *umma* has to provide harmonization between information and Muslim "societal knowledge." Such harmony, however, "can evolve only when Muslim states generate their own information with the relevant apparatus geared to meeting the needs of their decision-makers and communities" (Sardar 1988: 15).

INFORMATION STRATEGIES OF MUSLIM THINKERS

Muslim thinkers, whether they are religious propagandists or scholars, mostly agree that there should be new media that would serve Muslim needs. They are also unanimous in their call for a self-sustaining Islamic network of information. They vary, however, in the scope of their strategical considerations. The new media should deal with problems relevant to the Muslim recipients of information (al-ʿAzm 1980: 44-47). They should be used as instruments of an "educational and cultural enlightenment which is inspired by the right guidance and the divine truth" (al-ʿAzm 1980: 52). The media should then transmit the messages of *daʿwa*. This requires the shaping of a special "information elite," the Muslim propagandists (al-ʿAzm 1980: 89-91). All in all, al-ʿAzm pleads for nine great tasks to be tackled: (1) the reconstruction of the identity of the media on the basis of *umma* and the Koran; (2) the adaptation of media contents to education at school and in the mosque; (3) control of the media through committees; (4) the drawing up of specific Islamic programs for radio and television; (5) the establishment of an Arab-Islamic news agency in an Arab-Islamic country; (6) the creation of an Islamic press;[28] (7) the organization of Islamic book fairs; (8) the creation of a body of Muslim journalists; and (9) the establishment of Islamic radio stations (al-ᶜAzm 1980: 91-97).

Sardar deals with the question of how to create an indigenous infrastructure of information in terms of economic, geopolitical, and cultural structures, not primarily religious ones. He pleads for the "generation of appropriate information in the Muslim world itself" (Sardar 1988: 105) in order to counter Western information dominance. There ought to be an increase in expenditure by Muslim countries on research and development, and the coordination of information resources in Arab countries. He also calls for the development of professional manpower (information scientists, librarians, etc.) and the establishment of regional information networks designed to promote the exchange of ideas between Muslim scientists and intellectuals. He does not actually reject the flow of information from Western countries or the interaction with international information services as provided, for example, by United Nations' agencies—as long as Islamic culture is not damaged by such a transfer of information (Sardar 1988: 104-117).

PLEAS FOR THE ARABIZATION OF INFORMATION

Representatives of the fifth group of theoreticists agree with others that the flow of information in the Arab world is unbalanced, deficient, and lacking in identity. This is due to two factors: state control and foreign information dominance. Authors such as Rasim Mohammed al-Jammal, ᶜAwatif ᶜAbd al-Rahman, or ᶜAli Watfa speak of Arab information dependence. This dependence is said to be of a double nature. The first kind of dependence, according to ᶜAbd al-Rahman, is that of the state, which wields too much power over the media (ᶜAbd al-Rahman 1984: 109-138). He admits that state control over the media means reestablishing national sovereignty. However, over the course of time Arab regimes have abused the media in order to maintain their power and to propagate their ideology, which in turn has entailed a loss of confidence in the media.

Even more decisive than the first dependence, according to several authors, is the dependence on the West. In the view of al-Jammal, Assistant Professor for International Information at Cairo University, this dependence has resulted from differences in political, economic, cultural, and technological development. These disproportions lead to what al-Jammal calls the "disturbance of the practice of information." The result is unbalanced or disordered information. States differ in the media production capacity and the wealth of their national media systems. According to al-Jammal, the Arab countries—like other developing countries—are in a weak position. Nevertheless, Saudi Arabia recently gained informational influence over other Arab states, due to pan-Arab media such as *Al-Sharq Al-Ausat*, ARABSAT, and computer-aided data processing. Developing countries are in general unable to provide information to the extent Western countries can (al-Jammal 1991: 165-188). In the long run, al-Jammal argues, this will hurt both sides. On the one hand, the Arab world might sell less "self-produced information" on both the home and foreign markets. On the other hand, the question will arise whether Arab-Muslim society can provide itself with the relevant information (al-Jammal 1991: 171-175).

The dominance of foreign information has many forms; from the impact of big Western news agencies to fictional products like Dallas or Mickey-Mouse.[29] In the mid-1980s, al-Jammal studied twelve major Arab newspapers (for six days) to ascertain the sources of Arab news on non-Arab countries. It turned out that the four major Western news agencies AP, UPI, Reuter, and AFP are the major sources of information from abroad in the Arab press despite the existence of Arab news agencies. Domestic news agencies only played a minor role and, at times, no role at all (al-Jammal 1990: 118-121). The papers *Al-Ahram* and *Al-Nahar* exclusively use Western news agencies, incidentally above all Reuters and not AFP, as was previously the case. The dependence on Western news agencies has an impact on the contents and modes of presentation in the Arab press. Al-Jammal concludes that the Arab press reports more on the First World than on the Third World of which the Arab countries consider themselves to be a part; news from Western Europe is given priority. These reports are primarily of a positive nature, whereas Third World reports are often negative (al-Jammal 1990: 128 f.).

Arab authors differ, however, in their assessment of the impact of Western information dominance. Al-Sayyid ᶜUlaiwa Hasan sees a danger for Arab national identity (Hasan 1990: 121-140), whereas Watfa, like numerous other authors, goes further when he identifies Western media influence as an "info-cultural invasion" or an "imperialist info-cultural penetration" (Watfa 1994: 63). He thus shares the extreme views of Ilyas Murqus, who went so far as to say:

> Those, however, who attack/invade us (i.e. the Arab world) today are not Descartes, Aristotle (...) Bacon or Hegel. The modern Western conquerors are whisky, cars and pornographic videos. What invades us is the spirit of consumption, decadence (*inhilal*) and Western foreign infiltration (*tagharrub*). (cited in Watfa 1994: 63)

One must be careful in assessing Murqus' opinions. At the time, Murqus found many adherents, but also many critics.[30] It should be added that such arguments are, in principle, not new. In an article on audio-visual mass media in Arab countries, Regina Karachouli shows that the same argument was heard ten years ago. In the 1980s, she states, American TV productions such as Dallas were shown on Arab TV stations to an increasing extent. Critics at the time warned of an "attack on cultural identity" (Karachouli 1987: 851). Al-Jammal points to several major difficulties regarding the dominance of foreign information: (1) Western information practice is unsuitable for developing Arab countries, but there is no alternative as yet, because (2) Arab official development programs do not include the sector of information, and (3) communications systems for the needs of developing Arab countries cannot successfully operate without cooperation at various levels including the national and inter-Arab levels (al-Jammal 1991: 191-206). Like many other authors (including advocates of Islamic information), al-Jammal underestimates or even omits to mention the potential benefits of information transfer from West to East (or North to South) provided there is a *balanced* cooperation between the two worlds

SOME STRATEGIC SUGGESTIONS OF ARAB THEORISTS

Advocates of the Arabization of Arab information tend to look for solutions in socioeconomic, political, and cultural structures, rather than religious ones. Authors such as al-Jammal or cAbd al-Muncim call for restructuring the information sector, and for Arab cooperation and coordination (al-Jammal 1985; cAbd al-Muncim 1994), whereas Hasan emphasizes the importance of political values such as "Arab solidarity" and democracy (Hasan 1990). Al-Jammal, who put forward the most comprehensive strategy study, advocates a "common Arab information practice," for which the League of Arab States should be responsible (al-Jammal 1985). It should organize information on two levels, that is, on an internal national level and an external international one (al-Jammal 1985: 17-19). This collective information practice should neither replace nor duplicate the activities of the individual Arab countries, but coordinate them by means of specific instruments such as Arab summit meetings, the Council of Arab Information Ministers, or the Permanent Information Committee of the Arab League (al-Jammal 1985: 24-41).

In his second work (of 1991) al-Jammal also stresses the need to diminish Western information dominance. Information and communication are part of society and must not endanger values or patterns of behavior or the way of life. But which values or patterns of behavior should be safe-guarded? What responsibility do political, social, and educational systems have in dealing with their own culture? How can the coordination be carried out? Which experts can help with this process (al-Jammal 1991: 202-206)?

Ideally, information strategies, no matter whether they favor Islamic/Islamist religious principles or Arab cultural ones, ought to guarantee equal rights to information for all participants in the global media flow. Information should establish links, but not at the price of domination, and it should not cause trees to crash down without making noise, as the Sufi aphorism says.

ENDNOTES

1.   In the following text the Arabic letters ʿain (transcription: ᶜ) and hamza (transcription: ') will be used.
2.   Koran 17:36 (Arberry 1983: 278).
3.   *Hadith Khan* (n.d.): 79. I am indebted to S. Guenther for this information.
4.   Sura 96, the oldest part of the Koran dating from about 610 where it appears: "Recite: And thy Lord is the Most Generous who taught by the Pen, taught Man that he knew not." For more details on ᶜilm, see Hamadeh 1996: 7-17; Rosenthal 1970; Bellmann 1994: 6-12; Lewis et al. 1971.
5.   Koran 20:114 (Arberry 1983: 319).
6.   This statement is ascribed to Sahl ibn Harun (d. 830), the private secretary of the Abbasid Caliph Harun al-Rashid (reg. 786-809) and al-Mamun (reg. 813-33) (Bellmann 1994: 15).
7.   *Maᶜrifa* is connected with ᶜilm. In comparison to ᶜilm (knowledge of God) *maᶜrifa* means profane knowledge, acquired through reflection or experience, which presupposes ignorance. *Maᶜrifa* enables a person to recognize or identify a thing. For more details see Arnaldez 1991, Lewis et al. 1971; Glassé 1989b, 1989d.
8.   The word is preferred by Shiᶜi thinkers. For more details see Glassé 1989c.
9.   There are various concepts of ᶜaql; the neoplatonic, the theological, and the philosophical (Greco-Christian and Muslim). For more details see Rahman 1960; Chittick 1987; Glassé 1989a; Davidson 1992; al-Qardawi 1996.
10.   In Islamic law a subjective opinion, a decision based on the jurist's individual judgement, not on Koran or Sunna. Note also al-ra'y al-ᶜamm (public opinion) in modern Arabic usage. For more details see Glassé 1989e.
11.   The term is considered as a generic term in the concept of information. Subnotions are ᶜilm, maᶜrifa, khabar, etc. The Koran uses hikma in the sense of "a wisdom (...) which implies knowledge of high spiritual truths." For more details see Goichont 1971.
12.   *Haqiqa* is not Koranic. For more details see Gardet 1971.
13.   Here, we neglect the numerous works on the history of the Arabic press, which were already available at that time, as well as the foundation of the Department of Journalism at the American University in Cairo in 1935 and the foundation of an Institute of Journalism and Translation at Cairo University in 1939.

14. Authors in this group refer to Wilbur Schramm's structural model of the face-to-face communication, Raymond Bauer's views on the relation between communicator and audience, Maxwell E. McCombs' and Donald L. Shaw's theory of the "agenda-setting function" of the media, W. Phillips Davison's and Hadley Cantril's views on public opinion, Carl I. Hovland's theory of persuasive communication and to the theory of uses and gratifications by Herbert Blumer, Jay Blumler et al.

15. In a broader sense we may also include all those authors who deal with the history of the Arab press and other new media (radio, TV, film, etc.). In this context, too, ᶜAbd al-Latif Hamza has played a pioneering role as the author of a standard work on the history of the Arabic press consisting of eight volumes—first published in the early 1950s—that are, however, not discussed here.

16. Wilbur Schramm, for example, is considered to be the spiritus rector of the concept of mass communication (Schramm 1948a, 1948b).

17. Groth, who worked in Munich, was heavily influenced by the sociological school of Max Weber. With his work he essentially contributed to the academic foundation of journalism ("science of newspapers") (Groth 1928-30, 1948, 1960-72).

18. For more details on daᶜwa see Canard 1965.

19. The author *expressly* refers to the Koran 2:42 ("And do not confound the truth with vanity, and do not conceal the truth wittingly") and 2:283 ("And do not conceal the testimony; whoso conceals it, his heart is sinful"), and to 33:34 ("And remember that which is recited in your houses of the signs of god and the wisdom") (Arberry 1983: 6, 43, resp. 430 f.).

20. Opinions on objectivity vary, however. Objectivity is not always defined as wisdom. Al Seini, for example, like Madkur a staff member of the Islamic University of Imam Mohammed Ibn Saud, writes: "(Objectivity is/D.G.) construed to mean: (1) reporting only observable phenomena, (2) reporting without personal emotions, (3) reporting without personal opinion, (4) reporting without personal values, and (5) presenting all sides equally" (Al Seini 1986: 288). Knowing the difficulties of the practical implementation of this concept of objectivity, the author advocates a "relative objectivity" instead of a "pure objectivity." This is based on the "ultimate objectivity of Allah."

21. This means, according to the authors themselves, that Islamic information is not exclusively confined to the content of sermons but must comprehensively inform people (al-ᶜUlaiwat and al-Shabib 1993: 54 f.).

22. It seems that the Koran, however, prefers synonyms such as *balagh* (pl. *balaghat*) and *naba'* (pl. *anba'*) which also often occur in modern Muslim publications.

23. For details see Wensinck 1978.

24. For example Ibn Khaldun's famous *Introduction to History* (Al-Muqaddima) (Rosenthal 1958).

25. For more details see also Al Seini 1986, who derives duties much more strictly than Madkur from the Koran and Hadith.

26. This was founded in Cairo in 1892. In general, Zaidan's *Al-Hilal* is considered an outstanding and influential literary-cultural Arabic magazine.

27.   They are all authors of Christian origin who gained special merits during
      the *Nahda*, the Arab-Islamic cultural-intellectual revival in the late nine-
      teenth/early twentieth century.
28.   Periodicals to be issued are the following: an Islamic educational periodi-
      cal on propagating science and religion, a newspaper, and a weekly,
      whose contents conform to the heritage of Islam and the Muslim code of
      values and behavior.
29.   For the adaption of Mickey Mouse to an Arab-Islamic public since the
      1970s, see Douglas and Malti-Douglas 1994: 9-15.
30.   I am indebted for this information to Professor Dieter Bellmann (d. 1997),
      Leipzig, Germany.

BIBLIOGRAPHY

ᶜAbd al-Halim, Muhyi al-Din. 1982. *Public Opinion in Islam* (in Arabic). Cairo:
      Maktabat Al-Khanji.
ᶜAbd al-Halim, Muhyi al-Din. 1984. *Islamic Information and its Scientific
      Implications* (in Arabic), 2nd ed. Cairo: Maktabat Al-Khanji.
ᶜAbd al-Munᶜim, Ahmad Faris. 1994. Cooperation in Arab Information between
      Accomplishment and Deficiency (in Arabic). *Al-Mustaqbal Al-ᶜArabi* 182:
      102-116.
ᶜAbd al-Rahman, ᶜAwatif. 1984. *Problems of Dependency in Information and Culture
      in the Third World* (in Arabic). Kuwait: Al-Majlis Al-Watani Lil-Thaqafa
      Wal-Funun Wal-Adab.
Abu ᶜAmud, Mohammed Saᶜd. 1994. Arab Information and Arab Foreign Policy
      (in Arabic). *Al-Mustaqbal Al-ᶜArabi* 182: 87-101.
Adham, Mahmud. 1987. *The Art of Reporting News* (in Arabic), 2nd ed. Cairo: Dar
      Al-Shaᶜb.
Adham, Mahmud. 1989. *The Issue of Information* (in Arabic). Cairo (no publisher
      listed).
Adham, Mahmud. 1990. *Information in Ancient Egypt* (in Arabic). Cairo: Maktabat
      Al-Nahda Al-Misriyya.
[Agee, Warren K., et al.]. 1982. *Introduction to Mass Communications*, edited by
      Warren K. Agee, Phillip H. Ault, and Edwin Emery, 7th ed. New York:
      Harper and Row.
ᶜAjwa, ᶜAli. 1985. *Studies on Public Relations and Information* (in Arabic). Cairo:
      ᶜAlam Al-Kutub.
Arberry, Arthur J. 1983. *The Koran Interpreted*. Translated with an Introduction by
      Arthur J. Arberry. Oxford: Oxford University Press.
Arnaldez, Roger. 1991. Maᶜrifa. In *The Encyclopaedia of Islam*, new ed., vol. VI,
      568-571. Leiden: Brill.
Atiyeh, George N. 1995. *The Book in the Islamic World. The Written Word and
      Communication in the Middle East*, edited by George N. Atiyeh. Albany:
      State University of New York Press.

Hamza, ᶜAbd al-Latif. 1967. *Information: Its History and its Doctrines* (in Arabic). Cairo: Dar Al-Maᶜarif.

Hamza, ᶜAbd al-Latif. 1978. *Information and Propaganda* (in Arabic), 2nd ed. Cairo: Dar Al-Fikr Al-ᶜArabi.

Hamza, ᶜAbd al-Latif. n.d. *Information during the Rise of Islam* (in Arabic). Cairo: Dar Al-Fikr Al-ᶜArabi.

Hasan, Al-Sayyid ᶜUlaiwa. 1990. *Arab Information Strategies* (in Arabic). Cairo: Al-Hai'a Al-Misriyya Al-ᶜAmma Lil-Kitab.

Hatim, Mohammed ᶜAbd al-Qadir. 1978. *Information and Propaganda* (in Arabic). Cairo: Maktabat Al-Anjilu.

Hatim, Mohammed ᶜAbd al-Qadir. 1985. Information in the Holy Koran (in Arabic). Cairo: Maktabat Al-Khanji.

Hatim, Mohammed ᶜAbd al-Qadir. 1989. *Public Opinion under the Influence of Information and Propaganda* (in Arabic), *Part I: The Public Opinion, Part II: Information and Propaganda*, 2nd ed. Beirut: Maktabat Lubnan.

Hijazi, ᶜAbd al-Hamid. 1987. *Public Opinion, Information and Psychological Warfare* (in Arabic). Cairo: Dar Al-Ra'y Al-ᶜAmm.

al-Imam, Ibrahim. 1967. *The Art of Public Relations and Information* (in Arabic). Cairo: Al-Hai'a Al-Misriyya Al-ᶜAmma Lil-Kitab.

al-Imam, Ibrahim. 1969. *Information and Mass Communication* (in Arabic). Cairo: Al-Hai'a Al-Misriyya Al-Amma Lil-Kitab.

al-Imam, Ibrahim. 1985. *The Principles of Islamic Information* (in Arabic). Cairo: Dar Al-Fikr Al-ᶜArabi.

al-Jammal, Rasim Mohammed. 1985. *Common Arab Information. Studies on Arab Inter-National Information* (in Arabic). Beirut: Markaz Dirasat Al-Wahda Al-ᶜArabiyya.

al-Jammal, Rasim Mohammed. 1990. Reporting of Foreign News in Arab Newspapers (in Arabic). *Al-Mustaqbal Al-ᶜArabi* 135: 103-129.

al-Jammal, Rasim Mohammed. 1991. *Communication and Information in the Arab World* (in Arabic). Beirut: Markaz Dirasat Al-Wahda Al-ᶜArabiyya.

Kahil, ᶜAbd al-Wahhab. 1987. *Public Opinion and Information Policy* (in Arabic). Cairo: Maktabat Al-Madina.

Karachouli, Regina. 1987. Aktuelle Entwicklungsaspekte der audiovisuellen Massenmedien in arabischen Ländern. *asien, afrika, lateinamerika* 5: 847-858.

Khan, Muhammad Muhsin n.d. *Sahih al-Bukhari. The Translation of the Meanings of Sahih al-Bukhari, Arabic-English*, vol. I, Medina: Dar Al-Fikr.

Leder, Stefan. 1991. *Das Korpus al-Haitam ibn ᶜAdi (st. 207/822): Herkunft, Überlieferung, Gestalt früher Texte der ahbar-Literatur.* Frankfurt: Klostermann.

Leder, Stefan, and Hilary Kilpatrick. 1992. Classical Arabic Prose Literature: A Researchers' Sketch Map. *Journal of Arabic Literature* 1: 2-25.

Lewis, Bernard et al. 1971. ᶜIlm. In *The Encyclopaedia of Islam*, new ed., vol. III, 1133-1134, Leiden: Brill/Luzac.

Madkur, Marᶜi. 1988. *The Islamic Responsibility of the Journalist in Reporting News through the Press* (in Arabic). Cairo: Dar Al-Sahwa Lil-Nashr.

Makdisi, George. 1981. *The Rise of Colleges. Institutions of Learning in Islam and the West.* Edinburgh: Edinburgh University Press.

ᶜAudallah Ghazi Zain. 1995. *Information and Society* (in Arabic). Cairo: Al-Al-Misriyya Al-ᶜAmma Lil-Kitab.

al-ᶜAzm, Yusuf. 1980. *Loss: the Destination of Arab Information* (in Arabic). Jiᶜ Al-Dar Al-Saᶜudiyya Lil-Nashr Wal-Tauziᶜ.

Bellmann, Dieter. 1994. *ᶜIlm* und *ᶜAql* bei Ibn ᶜAbdrabbihi (246/860-328/940) ᶜ Komponenten schöpferischer Lebenstätigkeit des Menschen. ᶜ *Gedenkschrift Wolfgang Reuschel. Akten des III. Arabistischen Kolloquiums Leipzig, 21-22. November 1991*, edited by Dieter Bellmann, 9-18. Stuttgart. Steiner.

Boutaleb, Abdelhadi. 1986. Information Policy in Islam. *Islam Today* 4: 7-11.

Canard, Marius. 1965. Daᶜwa. In *The Encyclopaedia of Islam*, new ed., vol. II, 168-170. Leiden: Brill.

Chittick, William C. 1987. ᶜAql. In *Encyclopaedia Iranica*, vol. II, 194-198. London: Routledge & Kogan.

Davidson, Herbert A. 1992. *Alfarabi, Avicenna, and Averroes, on Intellect. Their Cosmologies, Theories of the Active Intellect, and Theories of Human Intellect.* New York: Oxford University Press.

Douglas, Allen, and Fedwa Malti-Douglas. 1994. *Arab Comic Strips. Politics of an Emerging Mass Culture.* Bloomington: Indiana University Press.

Gardet, Louis. 1971: Haqiqa. In *The Encyclopaedia of Islam*, new ed., vol. III, 75-76. Leiden: Brill.

Glassé, Cyril. 1989a. ᶜAql. In *The Concise Encyclopedia of Islam*, 45. London: Stacey International.

Glassé, Cyril. 1989b. ᶜIlm. In *The Concise Encyclopedia of Islam*, 184-185. London: Stacey International.

Glassé, Cyril. 1989c. ᶜIrfan. In *The Concise Encyclopedia of Islam*, 258-259. London: Stacey International.

Glassé, Cyril. 1989d. Maᶜrifa. In *The Concise Encyclopedia of Islam*, 258-259. London: Stacey International.

Glassé, Cyril. 1989e. Ra'y. In *The Concise Encyclopedia of Islam*, 331 London: Stacey International.

Goichont, Amélie M. 1971. Hikma. In *The Encyclopaedia of Islam*, new ed., vol. III, 377-378. Leiden: Brill/Luzac.

Groth, Otto. 1928-30. *Die Zeitung: ein System der Zeitungskunde (Journalistik)*, 4 vols. Mannheim: Bensheimer.

Groth, Otto. 1948. *Die Geschichte der deutschen Zeitungswissenschaft*. München: Weinmayer.

Groth, Otto. 1960-72. *Die unerkannte Kulturmacht. Grundlegung der Zeitungswissenschaft (Periodik)*, 7 vols. Berlin: de Gruyter.

Haddad, Fuad Said. 1984. *Alfarabi's Theory of Communication*. Beirut: American University of Beirut.

Hamadeh, Basyumi I. 1996. *Media and Policy. Studies on the Formation of the Essentials* (in Arabic). Cairo: Maktabat Nahdat Al-Sharq.

Hamadeh, Anis. 1996. Ilm as a Witness to Islamic Culture and its Development. *Periodica Islamica* 1: 7-14.

al-Hamamisi, Jalal al-Din. 1965. *From News to Themes* (in Arabic). Cairo: Dar Al-Maᶜarif.

McQuail, Dennis. 1994. *Mass Communication Theory. An Introduction*, 3rd ed. London: Sage.

Miller, Gerald R. 1987. Persuasion. In *Handbook of Communication Science*, edited by Charles R. Berger and Steven H. Chaffee. Newbury Park, CA: Sage.

Mohammed, Mohammed Sayyid. 1983. *The Responsibility for Information in Islam* (in Arabic). Cairo: Maktabat Al-Khanji.

Mowlana, Hamid. 1993. The New Global Order and Cultural Ecology. *Media Culture and Society* 1: 9-27.

Najib, ᶜAmara. 1980. *Information in the Islamic Perspective* (in Arabic). Riyadh: Maktabat Al-Maᶜarif.

al-Qardawi, Yusuf. 1996. *Intellect and Knowledge in the Holy Koran* (in Arabic). Cairo: Maktabat Wahba.

Rahman, Fazlur. 1960. ᶜAql. In *The Encyclopaedia of Islam*, new ed., vol. I, 341-342. Leiden: Brill/Luzac.

Rashti, Jihan Ahmad. 1978. *The Scientific Foundations of Information Theories* (in Arabic). Giza: Dar Al-Fikr.

[Rosenthal, Franz]. 1958. *The Muqaddimah. An Introduction to History*, translated from the Arabic by Franz Rosenthal, 3 vols., New York: Pantheon.

Rosenthal, Franz. 1970. *Knowledge Triumphant. The Concept of Knowledge in Medieval Islam*. Leiden: Brill.

Sardar, Ziauddin. 1988. *Information and the Muslim World. A Strategy for the Twenty-First Century*. London: Mansell.

Sardar, Ziauddin. 1993. Paper, Printing and Compact Disks: The Making and Unmaking of Islamic Culture. *Media Culture and Society* 1: 43-58.

[Schramm, Wilbur]. 1948a. *Mass Communications*, edited by Wilbur Schramm. Urbana: University of Illinois Press.

[Schramm, Wilbur]. 1948b. *Communications in Modern Society*, edited by Wilbur Schramm. Urbana: University of Illinois Press.

Al Seini, Sayeed. 1986. The Islamic Concept of News. *The American Journal of Islamic Social Sciences* 2: 277-289.

Sharaf, ᶜAbd al-ᶜAziz. 1979. *Media: The Language of Civilization* (in Arabic). Cairo: Mu'assat Mukhtar Lil-Nashr Wal-Tauziᶜ.

Sharaf, ᶜAbd al-ᶜAziz. 1987. *The Art of Editing News* (in Arabic). Cairo: Al-Hai'a Al-Misriyya Al-ᶜAmma Lil-Kitab.

al-Shinqiti, Sayyid. 1986a. *Concepts of Information in the Holy Koran. An Analysis of the Texts from the Book of God* (in Arabic). Riyadh: Dar ᶜAlam Al-Kutub.

al-Shinqiti, Sayyid. 1986b. *The Principles of Islamic Information and its Fundament* (in Arabic). Riyadh: Dar ᶜAlam Al-Kutub Lil-Nashr Wal-Tauziᶜ.

Tehranian, Majid. 1988. Communication Theory and Islamic Perspectives. In *Communication Theory. The Asian Perspective*, edited by Wimal Dissanayake, 190-203. Singapore: Asian Mass Communication Research and Information Centre.

al-ᶜUlaiwat, Mohammed, and ᶜAbd al-Latif al-Shabib. 1993. *Information in Islam* (in Arabic). Beirut: Dar Al-Safwa.

Watfa, ᶜAli. 1994. The Challenges of Information in the Arab World. A Study of the Contents of Persuasive Information transmitted by Al-Sharq Al-Ausat TV. *Al-Mustaqbal Al-ᶜArabi* 187: 62-73.

Wensinck, Arendt J. 1978. Khabar. In *The Encyclopaedia of Islam*, new ed., vol. IV, 895-896. Leiden: Brill.

Yusuf, Mohammed Khair Ramadan. 1986. *The Islamic Call to Believe in God and the Need of Societies* (in Arabic). Riyadh: Al-Mu'allif.

Yusuf, Mohammed Khair Ramadan. 1989. *Special Features of Islamic Information* (in Arabic). Mecca: Rabitat Al-cAlam Al-Islami.

Author Index

Subject Index